S0-BWC-271

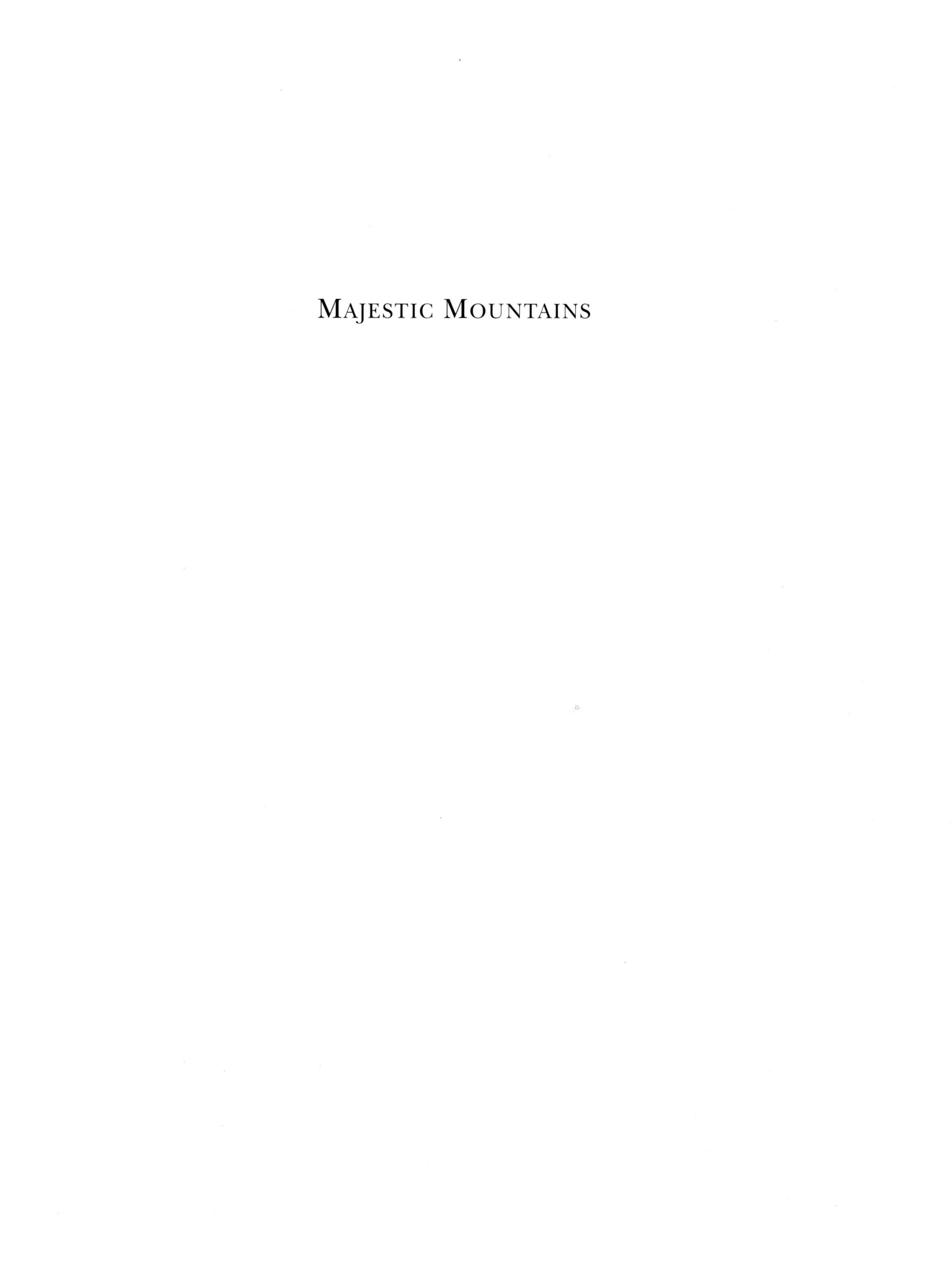

Majestic Mountains

The Earth, Its Wonders, Its Secrets

Majestic Mountains

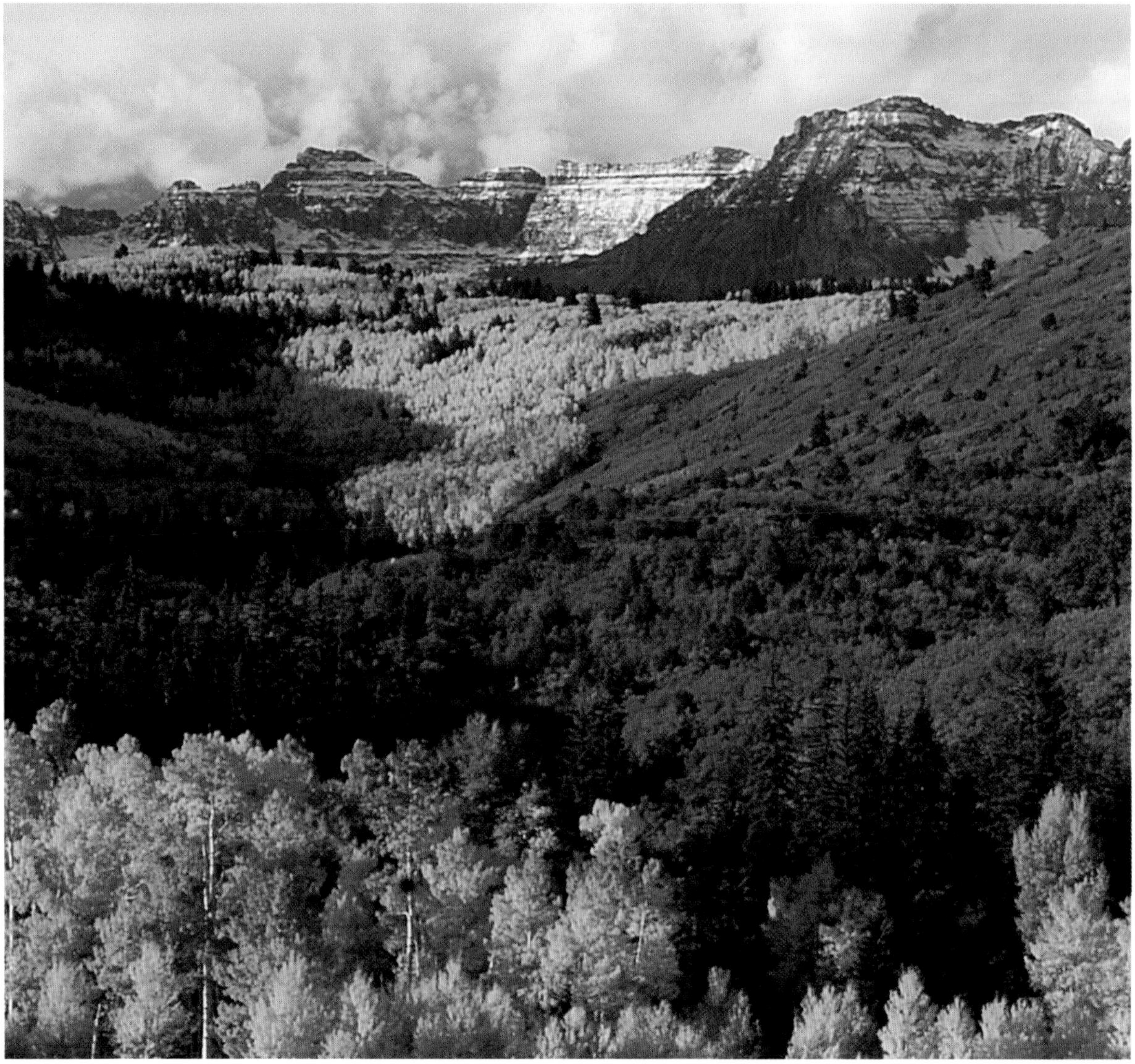

Published by

The Reader's Digest Association Limited

London New York Montreal Sydney Cape Town

MAJESTIC MOUNTAINS
Edited and designed by Toucan Books Limited
Written by Linda Gamlin
Edited by Robert Sackville West, Helen Douglas-Cooper and Andrew Kerr-Jarrett
Designed by Bradbury and Williams
Picture research by Marian Pullen

FOR THE READER'S DIGEST UK
Series Editor Christine Noble
Editorial Assistant Alison Candlin
Editorial Director Cortina Butler
Art Director Nicholas Clark

READER'S DIGEST, US
Group Editorial Director, Nature: Wayne Kalyn
Senior Designer: Judith Carmel
READER'S DIGEST ILLUSTRATED REFERENCE BOOKS
Vice President, Editor-in-Chief: Christopher Cavanaugh
Art Director: Joan Mazzeo

Reprinted with amendments 1999

Separations: David Bruce Graphics Limited, London

Printed in the United States of America, 1999

Library of Congress Cataloging in Publication Data

Majestic mountains.
p. cm. -- (The earth, its wonders, its secrets)
ISBN 0-7621-0136-9
1. Mountains. 2. Mountain ecology. 3. Mountain life.
I. Reader's Digest Association. II. Series.
GB511.M35 1999
551.43'2 — dc21

99-22010

FRONT COVER *Sunlight catches a snow-capped peak in the Italian Dolomites (inset). Background: A purple-tinged mist clings to mountain ridges in the Chinese sector of the Pamir range, an offshoot of the great Himalayan massif.*

PAGE 3 *Quaking aspens and scrub oaks splash the San Juan Mountains in Colorado, part of the southern Rockies, with autumnal golds and browns.*

Contents

HABITATS ON HIGH

From well-trodden foothills to the most inaccessible peaks, mountains frame the surface of the Earth. They shape the lives of plants and animals, and are shaped themselves by immense forces that work on and within our planet.

Climb Mont Blanc, the Matterhorn, or any other peak in the European Alps and, as you ascend above the tree line, there – nestling among the wind-scoured rocks – will be a small plant. It creates hummocks of tiny pale green leaves, each of the hummocks perfectly rounded, its surface studded with star-like pink flowers. This is moss campion whose delicacy conceals a robust tap root plunging deep into the mountain's skin. The root anchors it against the winds that rage about the high peaks, as the journeying air masses of the planet pass by and are forced to negotiate a difficult passage. The long sturdy root of the moss campion also secures it against the turmoils of avalanches and minor rockfalls, and holds it in place as chamois and ibex thunder past, dislodging the surface stones. When the sun torches through the thin mountain air in summer to bake the surface dry, the root – plunging as deep as 12 in (30 cm) to serve a hummock only 9 in (23 cm) in diameter – draws up moisture to sustain the plant.

Walk the mountain trails up Mount Roosevelt, Mount Washburn or any of the other high peaks of the Rocky Mountains, and you will discover the same green hummocks with their starry pink flowers. Botanists have discovered that the larger ones here may be a century old. Climb Ben Nevis in Scotland, and there is moss campion again, thriving on bare expanses of gravel and between loosely piled boulders at heights of 3000 to 4000 ft (900 to 1200 m). Moss campion provides a steady supply of food for the red deer that roam all these North American and European mountains, and yet manages to survive, despite their cropping of the hummocks. Only at about 4000 ft (1200 m) does the moss campion escape this depredation, for few deer ascend this far – except for the more ravenous young ones when there is little to be eaten on the lower slopes.

Moss campion grows on many mountain ranges across North America, Europe and parts of Asia. Like several mountain plants and animals, it lodges on the widely separated peaks as if they were islands set in an inhospitable sea of lowland plains. Each mountain community is separated from other communities of the same species by lands that are too hostile to cross. Many are impassable because

CUSHION OF FLOWERS *In the French Alps, moss campion plants hug a dome of eroding rock. For one of them, the annual rush to flower and seed is well under way.*

they are too hot, too dry, too thickly populated by competing species or, in modern times, too urbanised, road-dissected and intensively cultivated.

When Ice Covered Earth

At the time of the ice ages – cyclical periods of intense cold that recurred between 1.8 million and 10 000 years ago – these intervening lowlands were passable, and the mountain communities connected. At the peak of each ice age, the whole Northern and Southern Hemispheres were sunk into a Siberian climate for thousands of years, while the tropics were cool and temperate. It was then, when the whole Earth was a fundamentally different place, that plants like moss campion spread so widely through the Northern Hemisphere, and established communities across the lowlands and on the lower slopes of many mountain ranges. At that time, neither moss campion nor any other plant could establish itself on the peaks, which were covered by glaciers and inhospitable to almost every form of life.

As each ice age came to an end, and the summit glaciers receded or vanished entirely, the plants of the foothills expanded their range, very gradually, up the slopes. Simultaneously, the foothills and lowlands behind this advancing frontier began to become warmer, and plants such as moss campion eventually died out there, either because they were poorly adapted to the new climate, or because they could not compete with vigorous incoming plants for whom the hotter, drier conditions were more congenial. In this way, moss campion and other species which we think of today as 'mountain plants' became distributed over a huge geographic area, in many small communities living on widely separated peaks.

The same phenomenon, the same legacy of the ice ages, can be seen on the mountains of Africa, which stretch out along the continent's eastern flank, running southwards from the Sahara like a string of beads, or an archipelago of oceanic islands. These volcanic cones and huge massifs rise above the golden-brown sea of the savannah grasslands, soaring up out of the heat haze to create a habitat that is almost always cooler and more moist than that of the scorched plains. Here, at elevations of between 11 500 and 13 000 ft (roughly 3500 and 4000 m) bizarre plant forms loom out of the chill mountain mists. These curiously shaped giants are descended from small and insignificant plants of the lobelia family and the groundsel family, and were once widespread across Africa: they were its typical vegetation during the ice ages. In adapting to the cooler conditions that swept across the continent at this time of change, those small ancestral plants evolved large leaves and thick stems, which were able to conserve both warmth and moisture. At the same time, they developed a pattern of leaf growth which produced dense clusters of leaves hugging the stems and buds; each leaf overlapped the next, like the feathers on a bird's body, to hold an insulating layer of air around the most vulnerable parts of the plant.

Exiles in the Snow *Red deer were originally forest animals. Where forests have been felled, mountains provide them with a safe if cold retreat.*

At Home in a Flower

Hidden deep within these leaves are many small creatures, including a number of wingless flies that have evolved on the mountain peaks of Africa and are found nowhere else. In abandoning their powers of flight, they have escaped the vagaries of the wild mountain winds and confined themselves to the world within the giant lobelias, showing that this confined habitat can satisfy all their needs. Some of these wingless flies are unique to a particular mountain, suggesting that they have evolved in isolation since the ice ages ended 10 000 years ago. Like the giant tortoises of the Galápagos Islands, or the honeycreepers of Hawaii, these mountain flies have gone their own evolutionary way, uninfluenced by others of their kind.

Many other unique plants and animals have evolved in the isolated and rigorous conditions of mountain islands, or have clung to life here while being exterminated by competition or human harassment elsewhere in their former range. High up in the jagged highlands of Ethiopia, large shaggy-coated creatures sit hunched up on the alpine meadows, plucking mouthfuls of grass and chewing them slowly as they look out over the black fractured crags of their high-altitude home. These are baboons known as geladas, which survive in a bleak and cold environment, clambering over the

SIGNALS IN SKIN *A male gelada baboon shows off the vivid bare patches on his chest.*

harsh pinnacles of rock and scaling cliff faces to reach remote mountain pastures where they feed on grasses and other plants. They are insulated from the cold by dense coats of waterproof fur, and the males have great manes of fur that drape their heads and shoulders like a hooded cape. Living in large troops is another help in fighting the cold, as the geladas huddle together amicably at night, getting what shelter they can from an overhanging cliff, but relying mainly on each other for warmth.

Eating nothing but green plants, the geladas do not derive much energy from their food, and to conserve both energy and heat, they feed in a sitting position, shuffling from one clump of grass to another on their haunches without changing their posture. This habit, forced on the geladas by the necessities of their habitat, has a strange social consequence: their hindquarters remain hidden from other members of the troop.

Among most baboons, the hindquarters have a vital role in social signalling, indicating when a female is *in oestrus* ('on heat') by delicate pink swellings. The hindquarters are commonly 'presented' by both males and females to other members of the troop, particularly those higher in the social hierarchy, as a way of defusing tensions, appeasing an aggressor or confirming social ties. Deprived of this avenue of communication, the geladas have evolved a bare pink area on the chest instead. In the females, this area becomes swollen and more vivid when they are *in oestrus*, responding to the same hormonal signals that produce the colourful swelling of the hindquarters in other baboons.

Watching the geladas striving to keep warm in the early morning chill, and surveying the frost-fractured rocks and sparse meadows that are their homeland, it is hard to imagine that these Ethiopian highlands were once an inferno – a seething mass of red-hot liquid stone, surging from deep within the Earth. Fractured by a process of stretching that affected much of East Africa, the Earth's crust had cracked open at this point, and the molten heart of the planet was flowing out, wave after wave of fiery lava, each wave separated by thousands of years from the next, each solidifying into a mound of black basalt only to be overlaid by the next upsurge. In this way the Ethiopian highlands were built up to a massif, reaching heights of over 15 100 ft (4600 m). The original massif has in turn been worn down by the power of ice, rain and wind.

MAKING MOUNTAINS

All mountains have been formed in this way, by the interplay of titanic forces within the Earth which have piled them up, and the equally irresistible forces of erosion that have sculpted them into their present forms. The details vary, but the chief processes of mountain-building are driven either by movements of the Earth's crustal plates, which are driven in turn by the hot currents of the planet's volcanic core, or by violent upwellings of that fiery liquid – or by a combination of the two. Formidable ranges such as the European Alps, Himalayas, New Guinea highlands, Andes and Rockies, are primarily a result of the first of these processes, where two crustal plates are forced together until the rocks at the edge of one plate crumple like sheets of paper, folding up to form peaks and valleys; it is upon this template that the forces of erosion then etch their own chosen pattern.

Both processes continue in young ranges like these – the Alps, for example, were pushed up a comparatively recent 25 to 30 million years ago. Such ranges are both growing and being worn away at every moment of every day. The growth occurs at imperceptible speeds; the erosion happens in more obvious spurts such as rockfalls and mud slides, the tumbling of boulders racing down mountain streams when snowmelt swells the flow in spring, and the downhill scattering of scree slopes under the passing hooves of a mountain goat.

The fossil shells and corals found deep within the rocks of mountain summits speak eloquently of the long journey that these rocks have undertaken in the building of the mountain ranges, and of the massive forces that have raised them from their places of origin. When such fossils were first found in the European Alps and the Italian Apennines, few could accept the obvious conclusion that mountain rocks were originally laid down, aeons earlier, beneath the waves of the sea: this seemed to contravene the Biblical account of Creation in which the mountains and hills were set in place by God and were unchanging. To explain away such fossils, many early commentators invoked the Flood, and proposed that this had washed the shellfish and other marine life upwards as the waters rose, to deposit

WEARING AWAY *Sharp ridges and jagged peaks show that the European Alps are geologically young. In time, erosion will smooth their contours.*

POWER OF EROSION *A cap of vegetation is all that stops this pillar of rubble from being washed away. The rubble was dumped by a retreating glacier.*

them on the summits. Over the centuries, only a few isolated voices spoke up against this doctrine, among them the Renaissance artistic and scientific genius Leonardo da Vinci: 'In the mountains of Parma and Piacenza multitudes of rotten shells and corals are to be seen, still attached to the rocks, and when I was making the great horse in Milan, some peasants brought a large sack full from that region to my workshop, and some of them were preserved in their original condition. . . . And if you wish to say that it was the deluge which carried these shells hundreds of miles from the sea, that cannot have happened, since the deluge was caused by rain, and rain naturally urges rivers on towards the sea, together with everything carried by them, and does not bear dead objects from the sea shores towards the mountains. And if you would say that the waters of the deluge afterwards rose above the mountains, the movement of the sea against the course of the rivers must have been so slow that it could not have floated up anything heavier than itself. And even if it had supported them, it would have scattered them in various places when it subsided. But how can we account for the decayed corals, which may be found any day in the neighbourhood of Monte Ferrato in Lombardy, attached to the boulders uncovered by the river currents? These rocks are all covered with colonies of oysters which, as we know, do not move about, but are always attached by one valve to the rock. . . .'

It took several centuries for Leonardo's commonsense insights to become widely accepted, and even now, with the facts firmly established by geological science, it remains difficult to imagine that the jagged peak of the Matterhorn or of Everest was once a smooth layer of rock lying on an ancient ocean floor – and yet more difficult to imagine a force capable of lifting a vast seabed and compressing it into the great mass of the Alps or the Himalayas. That force, as we now know, comes from the Earth's molten core, and the restless fires of the planet's heart still break through the mountains in places. In the Himalayas there are caves where vents in the rock give forth a steady stream of methane gas, night and day. This gas is considered holy by the Hindus of Nepal, and the vents are kept burning, their flames tended by priests and sought out by pilgrims trekking up the narrow mountain paths.

POWERS OF DESTRUCTION

Volcanoes are another indication of the furnace that burns continuously just below the surface of the Earth and of the forces which built the mountains. Purely volcanic peaks can occur within mountain ranges, such as Cotopaxi in the Andes; this is an outcome of the same subterranean turbulence that produced the folding of the Andes by forcing the Pacific crustal plate against the plate that carries South America. Volcanic peaks can also rise directly out of the sea – such as the mountains of Hawaii or the black mountain island of Stromboli to the west of Italy in the Mediterranean. Or they may stand alone on a plain, a magnificent statement of the mysterious powers and unstoppable forces within the Earth. These

ENTOMBED IN STONE *Fossils like this, found at about 13 000 ft (4000 m), provide evidence for massive uplifting of the Earth's crust.*

BORN OF FIRE *Mount Etna is one of Europe's largest volcanoes. Like many volcanoes, its fertile lower slopes are densely settled.*

isolated volcanic cones include Mount Etna in Sicily, Mount Fuji in Japan, and Kilimanjaro and Mount Kenya in East Africa. Such exquisitely symmetrical peaks, placid and beautiful for decades or centuries and surrounded by richly fertile volcanic soil, may erupt in terrifyingly destructive and murderous falls of ash and lava.

In 1902, an eruption of Mont Pelée on the island of Martinique in the Caribbean killed nearly 30 000 people. The eruption followed weeks of ominous signs from the mountain, including spurts of steam as if from a pressure cooker, and plumes of fine ash. Finally, on the morning of May 8, a mighty explosion pulverised the top of the mountain and sent it thousands of feet into the air, along with steam and ash and bubbling volcanic glass from deep within the volcano. The incandescent mixture swept down the mountainside like a wall of death, a dry burning mass buoyed up by a pillow of hot gases, which enabled it to move with the speed and power of an avalanche. It covered 6 miles (10 km) in two minutes and, reaching the port of St Pierre, set fire to everything on contact. Plunging into the harbour, the hot ash created such a massive wave that moored ships were capsized.

Every inhabitant of St Pierre was killed, except for one man, a convict held in the town's jail whose thick stone walls sheltered him. He emerged the next day, blinking in the daylight, to discover that everyone else and every building had been destroyed, a 'miracle' which perplexed religious moralists of the time: if it was an act of God, it was certainly one with a curious logic. In the months that followed, Mont Pelée continued to spew up ash, and then to produce a viscous lava which congealed within the volcano's vent and the hollow top of the mountain. Further pressure from below then pushed this spire of rock upwards at an average rate of 82 ft (25 m) per day, so that sightseers who came to view the ruined town could watch it grow, high above them, like a mysterious plant made of rock. Its base glowed red like a beacon at night, and the top frequently crumbled away only to be replaced by more rock as the base pushed upwards again.

FROZEN IN TIME

Almost 2000 years earlier, in AD 79, cooler ash from another volcano had inundated two Roman towns, Pompeii and Herculaneum, entombing the population but not burning them. The figures of the dying people were preserved in outline as the volcanic ash set hard around them. Later, the flesh and bones decomposed, but the impressions of the bodies were preserved within the ash. Modern excavators can fill these cavities with plaster, then chip away the volcanic debris, to reveal the figures, caught for ever in their last moments, their bodies expressing the horror of the eruption that destroyed their lives.

Mountains can kill in many ways, and as haunting as the figures of Herculaneum are the herds of kiang, or wild asses, found frozen on their feet in springtime on the stark highlands of Tibet. A Swedish explorer, Sven Hedin, described such scenes at the turn of the century: 'The kiang . . . cannot run when the snow is deep, and after trying in vain to reach bare ground, they die of starvation and are frozen in the snowdrifts. Our three guides . . . assured me that the wild asses are frozen in an upright position, and often stand on all fours when summer sun has thawed the snow. They had seen dead wild asses standing in herds as though they were alive.' Such a sight is far rarer today, for the kiang themselves no longer gallop and wheel across the Tibetan plateau in 1000-strong herds.

Against their natural predators, the mountain wolves, the kiang deploy speed and manoeuvrability, thundering away at speeds of up to 40 mph (64 km/h) and churning up the dust of summer or the snow of winter to create an effective screen. Kiangs are able to sustain a steady speed of 30 mph (48 km/h) for as far as 15 miles (24 km), which leaves wolves panting and weary, so that only the sick or aged kiangs, and sometimes the very young, fall prey. Such tactics, while effective against wolves, cannot protect them from predators with guns and driving motor vehicles: they are fast enough to be a challenge for sportsmen, thereby exciting their interest, but they are too conspicuous to have any real chance of surviving such hunting. The herds are now far smaller and more widely scattered, and extinction seems inevitable unless hunting is curbed. Much the same fate has befallen the large mountain sheep and goats, such as the ibex and markhor. In many mountain ranges, they are in steep decline as a result of hunting, while in others, such as the European Alps, the ibex along with the chamois became extinct long ago, although both have been successfully reintroduced.

The hunting of these large grazing animals is just one of the threats to the ecosystems of the world's mountains. Another is the disappearance of the forests, whether through cutting or pollution. This has lead to the loss of soil from the mountainsides on a huge scale, and so to the silting up of rivers. Sometimes this, in turn, has damaged fish stocks, as with the salmon runs of the Cascade Mountains in western Canada, where commercial logging has generated so much silt that the salmon can no longer swim upstream to spawn. Mountains which for centuries have acted as a refuge for wildlife and for the human spirit, are today under threat as never before.

Shaped by Ice *The smooth outlines of these Scottish mountains are typical of an ancient landscape. They have been moulded by glacial ice.*

1 Mountains in the Landscape

Stone Works *Folds within the rocks reveal the powerful forces that built mountains.*

Unseen forces brewing deep within the smouldering furnace of the Earth's core have moulded the crust of our planet with a slow but violent intensity to create the mountain ranges. Exposed to the elements, the mountains are then eroded and sculpted by the forces of water, ice and gravity, scoured by glaciers and carved into by ancient river courses. The mountains in their turn mould wind and water, generating the flow of rivers and the biting force of mountain winds, while whipping the air around their peaks into swirling masses and complex, dancing wave forms that can generate strange illusory effects among the clouds above.

Volcanic Cone *Mount Cotopaxi towers over the Andes.*

How Mountains Are Made

For all their grandeur and solidity, mountains are as ephemeral as clouds when considered against the great expanses of geological time. They rise up from the land, only to melt back into it again as gravity reclaims its own.

Imagine a force so powerful that it can compress a rounded granite pebble, squeeze and stretch it like clay, then draw it out gradually to thirty times its original length – a long, slender rod of rock. This is the force that built the mountain ranges. Such elongated pebbles are to be found in certain rocks of the European Alps, packed together with other former pebbles, all stretched out in the same extraordinary way.

If we could turn the clock back 200 million years, to a time when the dinosaurs thrived and the strange bat-winged reptiles known as pterodactyls flew through the air, we would find this same granite pebble, compact and rounded, lying on a beach, glinting in the sun, with the waves of a long-vanished sea lapping gently over it from time to time. No boat ever sailed on this ancient sea, a vast expanse of shallow, briny water that stretched across southern Europe and much of Asia. Modern geologists, who see it only in their minds' eye but can trace its shores and sediments in surviving rocks, call it the Tethys Sea.

The pebble's long journey from the shores of the Tethys Sea to the summit of the European Alps, begins undramatically with the breaking of a slightly larger wave on the beach.

In the Beginning *The peaks of the Swiss Alps soar out of the fog at sunset. These same rocks once lay on the bed of a sea, now long vanished.*

The wave catches the pebble and claws it down below the waterline. The pebble rolls and tumbles beneath the receding wave, finally coming to rest nestled under water among other pebbles.

Later in the day a storm brews up inland. The heavy rain continues all night and streams burst their banks. A torrential rush of floodwater brings huge quantities of sandy soil down to the shore. This torrent rolls all the shoreline pebbles much deeper down, far from the water's edge. When the flood subsides, the storm-transported sediment settles thickly over the pebbles on the seabed, encasing them in a heavy pall of sand and grit. The pebble, and others around it, are set forever in place, destined to lie alongside one another and share the same fate for the next 200 million years.

With the passing of time, more sediments settle in the waters. More layers follow, year after year, millennium after millennium. The weight of sediments above grimly pressing down, combined with other unseen forces, causes the lower layers of sediment to sink, very gradually, creating a shallow depression in the Earth's hard surface far beneath.

This sinking keeps the sediments covered by the shallows of the sea, which allows more sediments to form above. The downward pressure grows ever more intense on the sand around the pebble, and in time its grains are forced together, compacted into a soft, gritty rock. (This type of rock, with large pebbles encased in finer sedimentary rock such as sandstone, like raisins in a cake, is called a 'conglomerate'.)

More aeons pass – an almost unimaginable length of time in which further layers of sediment are piled on top of the pebble, and it sinks deeper and deeper towards the heart of the Earth. The temperature around the pebble increases very slightly as the warming effect of the Earth's red-hot interior is felt.

Fire Down Below

It is in the fiery interior of the Earth – or more precisely in the half-molten outer layer, or mantel, known as the asthenosphere – that the forces which will stretch and distort the pebble have their origin. The asthenosphere begins about 45 miles (70 km) below the surface, and the semisolid material it contains can move and flow, very slowly, as warm putty might.

There are powerful currents in the asthenosphere, driven by the even more intense heat below. These slow, surging currents in the half-molten rock disturb the solid surface of the Earth, taking helpless sections of the Earth's hard crust (known as plates) on long, enforced journeys, like rodeo riders in slow motion. The pace is so funereal that the plates only move about ½-8 in (1-20 cm) a year, no faster than the speed at which a human fingernail grows.

The forces that move the plates may be slow but they are implacable, and their colossal strength is shown where two plates meet, carried into a headlong collision by the currents of the asthenosphere. This is what was taking place 200 million years ago, many miles beneath the point where the pebble lay in its shroud of sandy rock: a titanic collision between two plates of the Earth's crust, the African plate and the Eurasian plate.

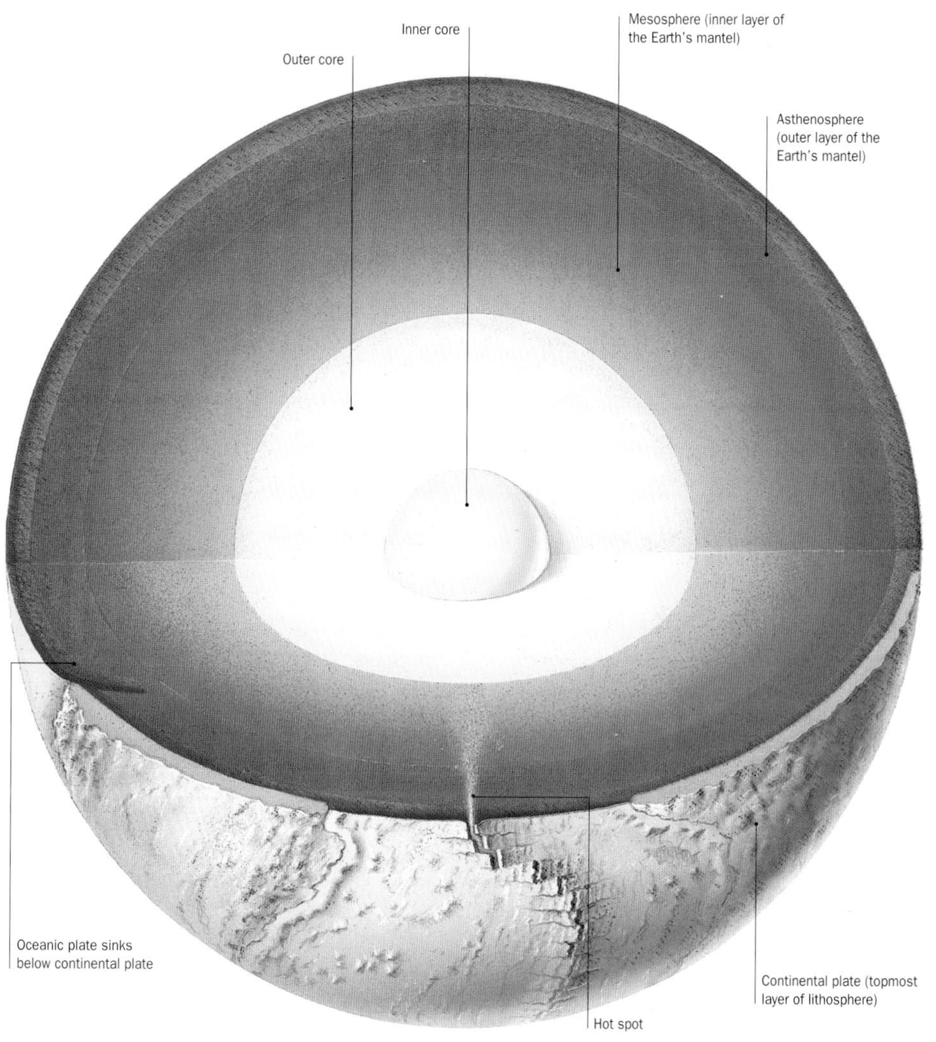

Liquid Rock ***In the asthenosphere, rock is hot enough to liquidise, but not so compressed that it cannot flow. Currents in the asthenosphere are the force behind mountain-building.***

As the plates collided, they squeezed the shallow Tethys Sea out of existence. The sea basin slowly vanished as its southern shore was carried northwards, gradually creeping closer to the opposite shore, turning the great expanse of water into an ever narrower channel.

In modern times, this slow collision continues, and all that remains of the immense

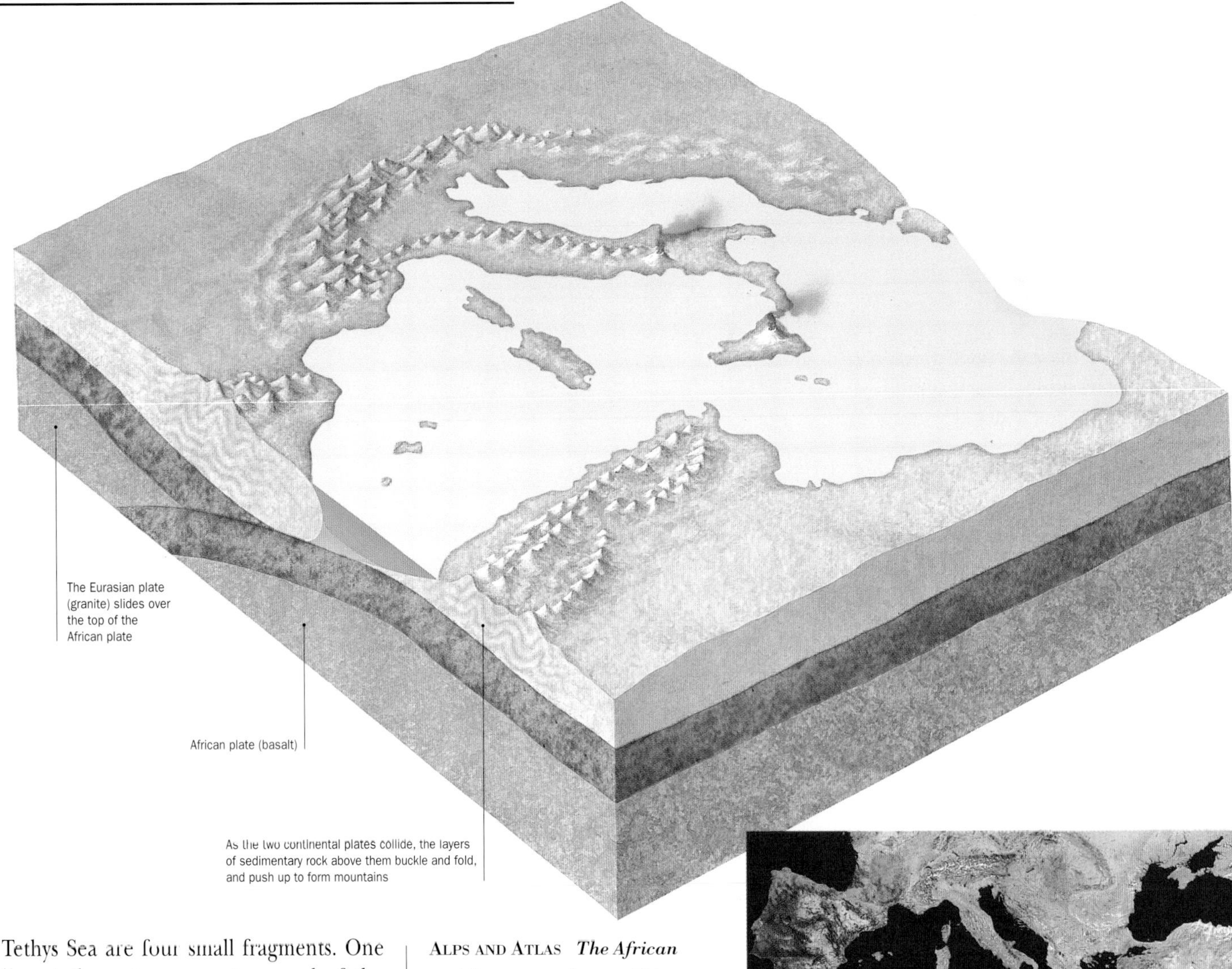

Tethys Sea are four small fragments. One lies at the extreme western end of the Tethys, pinched off into an elongated basin that we know as the Mediterranean. The others – the Black, Caspian and Aral seas – are smaller; the Caspian and Aral seas are landlocked and the Black Sea virtually so.

Alps and Atlas *The African and European plates collide. Right: A satellite picture shows the mountain areas (in green) around the Mediterranean and Black Sea, remnants of the ancient Tethys Sea.*

The Mountains Are Born

It is now 10 million years ago: the dinosaurs and pterodactyls have long vanished from the scene, and the fated pebble, still encased in its shroud of sandstone, is beginning to rise from beneath the sea. The Tethys Sea has now narrowed almost to nothing, and the immense pressure of the colliding plates has started to push up low hills along its northern edge, compressing rocks so that they rear upwards.

Far beneath the sediments in which the pebble lies is a layer of hard basalt called the 'oceanic crust', the leading edge of the African plate. As it travels northwards, it slowly rams into the 'continental crust' of the European plate, which is made of granite. Granite is lighter than basalt, and this difference in density is to have important consequences. The impact pushes together the layered sediments that lie above the crust, sediments laid down under the Tethys Sea. These layers of sedimentary rock begin to buckle like so many sheets of metal, crushed by opposing forces into concertina folds. Somewhere deep in those folds lies our pebble, still spherical in its bed of sandstone, but now far above sea level, forced upwards into the budding mountain chain.

Sedimentary rocks fold up with relative ease, but deeper down, where the two crustal plates themselves meet, the confrontation is resolved in a different way. Neither granite nor basalt is inclined to fold, but because the granite of the continental crust is less dense than the basalt of the oceanic crust, the latter simply sinks below the continental crust and plunges downwards.

The descent of the edge of the oceanic crust continues until it encounters the hot, viscous rock of the asthenosphere. Even before it contacts this zone directly, the basalt is affected by the extraordinary heat and begins to melt. Although no human being has ever penetrated this deep into the Earth, the liquid basalt so produced is familiar to us – it is the magma that flows from volcanoes. As this magma forms beneath the emergent folds of the new mountain range it expands, and being of a different composition from the rocks around it, surges upwards through the overlying continental crust.

In some mountain ranges, the magma surges up unstoppably, fighting its way through all the buckled sediments to spew out at the surface as a fiery volcano, or to create an eruption of volcanic ash – as at Mount St Helens in Washington's Cascade Range. In other mountain ranges, the magma stops well before it reaches the surface, welling up unseen into the buckled strata of the mountain, forcing itself into cavities and lodging there. The only sign at the surface may be a hot spring or a geyser formed by groundwater that is heated by the magma.

Sometimes the magma stops even lower down, heating the sedimentary rocks around it, bringing warmth to the very heart of the young mountain range. Such heat, combined with the enormous pressure from the movements of the Earth's crust, can make some rocks more pliable, while others are changed chemically as if in a furnace, heated to the point where their chemical structure breaks down and they then recrystallise in new forms. When this happens to a sedimentary rock, such as sandstone, it becomes harder and changes colour. The product is called a metamorphic rock, because it has changed fundamentally, or 'metamorphosed'. Marble, for example, is formed from metamorphosed limestone.

The Elastic Pebble

It was heat and colossal pressure that turned the spherical pebble into a long, thin cylinder. These forces transformed the sandstone around the pebble into a metamorphic rock, while the pebble itself grew so hot that it lost some of its former rigidity and became more responsive to the pressures exerted on it. In this case, the pebble lay at a point where the layer of rock was folded back on itself. In the making of the European Alps the rock layers were folded and compressed to an extraordinary degree, many of the folds doubling over again, like the crests of breaking waves. At the turning point, the rock had to bend around an unaccustomed curve, and this imposed a massive tension and stretching force, which distorted the rock enormously along the crest of the fold. In this way, the compressing force of the two colliding continental plates was transformed at certain places within the new mountains into a localised pulling and shearing force of immense power. This localised force tugged remorselessly at the pebble and its companions, stretching them, over the millennia, into fine cylinders of rock.

At the time that this occurred, the pebble was deep within the Alps, but it did not remain there for ever. As soon as any mountain chain begins to rear up, the forces of erosion start to bear down and chisel it away. After many millions of years of erosion, the layer of rock with the elongated pebbles finally came to light as the last of the overlying layers vanished. And so the pebble emerged into the sunshine once again, 200 million years later, thousands of feet higher up, cemented firmly into metamorphic rock and transformed almost beyond recognition.

These changes taking place in the European Alps were mirrored by mountain-building on the southern shore of the Tethys Sea, which created the Atlas Mountains of North Africa. Both the Alps and the Atlas Mountains were just the western outposts of a far larger mountain-building event that gave birth to the high ranges of Turkey, Iraq and Iran, the Caucasus, the Hindu Kush and the Himalayas. All these ranges are formed from rocks that once lay smooth and flat beneath the Tethys Sea. In the East it was – and is (for mountain-building continues) – the Australian-Indian crustal plate that produced the northward drive, butting into the Eurasian plate and producing the highest peak in the world, Mount Everest, by its relentless compression of the ancient Tethys sediments.

In South-east Asia, the northward movement of the Australia-Indian plate resists the south-westward motion of the Pacific plate, producing the highlands of New Guinea. It may seem strange that the Pacific plate is generating mountains at distant margins, as if it were advancing on all fronts, but this is exactly what is happening – the Pacific plate is spreading in several directions at once. Although it is consumed at all these margins (its heavy oceanic crust slipping beneath the lighter continental crust as it pushes up mountains above), new plate is generated at the same time,

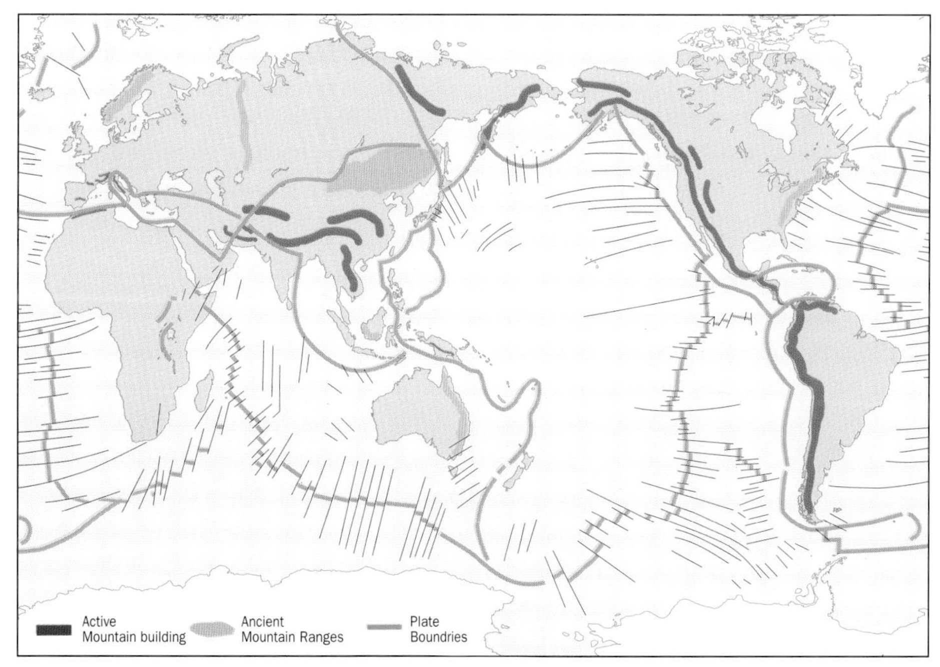

Restless Earth *Throughout the world, the continental plates are moving, forcing up mountains and creating areas of volcanic activity.*

Going Down *Like the autumn leaves, the Appalachian Mountains are near the end of their life, old peaks worn away by erosion.*

deep beneath the Pacific Ocean, and this fuels the continued expansion.

All of these are young mountain ranges, the products of ongoing plate movements. Older mountain ranges such as the Urals, the mountains of Scandinavia and Scotland, the Altai and Pamir ranges of Asia, and the Appalachian Mountains of North America are usually devoid of volcanic activity and hot springs, because the plate collisions there are long since over and the colliding plates have fused into one. These peaks are also less spectacular in height, because erosion has worked on them for millions of years since the uplift activity ceased.

Are the Himalayas Hollow?

The idea that the Himalayas could be hollow may seem laughable, but it was once seriously proposed as the answer to a puzzling problem. During a land survey of India in the 19th century, an accurate measurement was made of the line, theoretically vertical, through the centre of the Earth, using a plumb line – a lead weight on a cord. Calculations had already been made to compensate for the sideways pull of the Himalayas on the lead weight, since mountain ranges are large enough to exert a significant gravitational attraction of their own. When the measurements from different parts of India were compared, it was evident that something was amiss – they did not tally. After careful reworking, it became obvious that the Himalayas were not 'pulling their weight'. Could they indeed be hollow?

The original calculation was based on the known weight of the rocks in the Himalayas, but it assumed that immediately beneath them were the heavier rocks of the Earth's crust, and then a succession of other dense layers. This was the mistake in the calculation. Geologists now know that when the intense folding activity associated with mountain-building occurs, it does so in both directions – upwards *and* downwards. The layers of sedimentary rock that are bunched up by the pressure of the colliding plates push down into the Earth as well as up into the sky. They force the underlying crust and the dense, solid rock beneath it (collectively called the lithosphere) out of the way, making a depression in the semi-solid asthenosphere which lies below.

So mountains have roots going deep into the ground, like the long, hidden roots of a tooth. It was these roots, made of relatively lightweight sedimentary rocks, rather than the high-density materials of the lithosphere, that had reduced the sideways pull of the Himalayan region from that calculated.

In old age, the roots of a mountain can emerge at the surface once again. As erosion eats into a mountain range, wearing away its peaks, so its total mass declines. Relieved of the pressure, the lithosphere bounces back, very gradually, and the mountain range is lifted a little. In areas such as Scandinavia, the melting of the formerly huge ice-shield since the end of the last Ice Age has also contributed to this lifting effect. With each loss of weight from above, the lithosphere rises a little more and the mountain range rises too, so that the erosion of young mountains only reduces their height above sea level by 700 ft (200 m) per million years, despite the fact that 3000 ft (900 m) of the peak has actually been eroded in that time.

In northern Canada, to the south and east of Hudson Bay, there are the ghosts of mountains past, mountains that once – about 3000 million years ago – were as

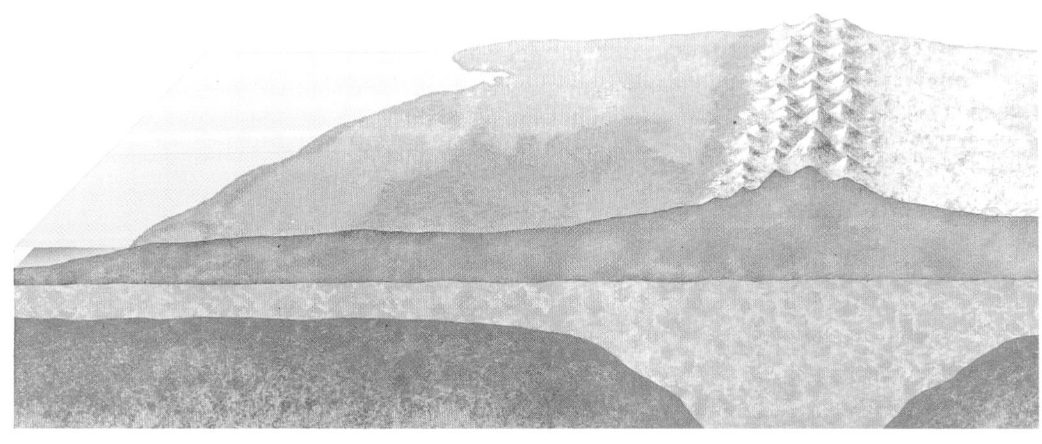

Rocky Roots *The forces that push mountains up also send folds of rock down into the Earth, creating 'roots' below the mountain peaks.*

young and soaring as the Andes or the Himalayas today. Erosion has worn these peaks away to nothing. This is flat, rocky, infertile wilderness, cut by thousands of lakes and swamps, and ridden with mosquitoes. An aerial view reveals a chaotic swirling mixture of granite and different types of metamorphic rock, cut by innumerable snaking ridges and narrow irregular depressions, branched and twisting, in which water has collected.

This seemingly random and inexplicable landscape is now recognised as a cross-section through the deepest roots of a vanished mountain range. These ridges and lake-filled hollows are the remnants of violent folding in ancient sedimentary rocks. Erosion then brought the mountain roots

The Past Revealed *The terrain around Hudson Bay represents a cross-section through the roots of ancient and long-vanished mountains.*

to the surface and subsequently wore away the least resistant of the metamorphic rocks, leaving twisted, elongated hollows that have become swamps and lakes.

This extraordinary terrain is the central part of the Canadian Shield, and it is surrounded by the remains of other eroded mountain ranges, not of such great antiquity but all dating from over 1000 million years ago. To the farmer, the Canadian Shield is worthless; to the early pioneers it was a confusing mass of impassable lakes and swamps; but to the geologist it is an unrivalled opportunity to see into the very roots of a mountain range – roots that were once buried deep in the Earth – and to comprehend more fully the powerful forces that give birth to the Earth's mountains.

Carved from Granite

In the Sierra Nevada mountains of California, the 'middle age' of mountains can be seen, a halfway stage between the tall, youthful peaks of the Himalayas or the Andes and the extinct eroded plains of the Canadian Shield. The Sierra Nevada mountains are carved from a huge block of granite known as a batholith, which once formed the heart of an ancient mountain range generated by folding and uplift over 150 million years ago. There were upwellings of red-hot liquid magma into the newly folded mountain chain, as happened with the European Alps; but in the ancient Sierra Nevadas, this upwelling was on such a colossal scale that it created a single gigantic mass of solidified granite in the core of the range.

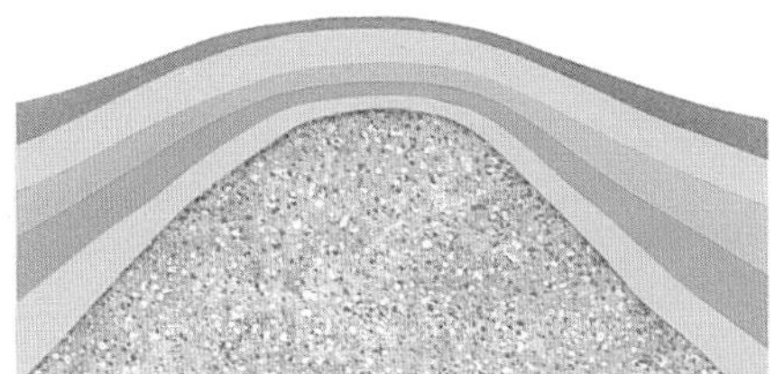

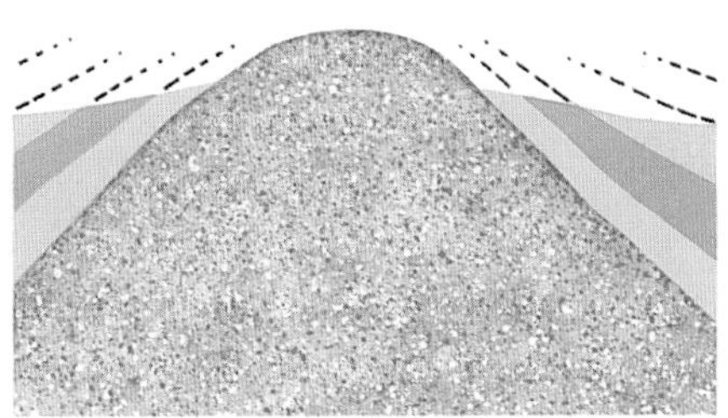

Batholith *Volcanic upwelling can create a mass of granite in the heart of a mountain (top). Erosion will expose this to form granite peaks (above).*

In time, rain, wind and ice stripped away the folded sediments above and exposed the granite. Subsequent disturbances of the Earth's surface have tilted and elevated this great mass of granite, raising its eastern flank high above the adjacent land and thereby causing further erosion. Succumbing to the forces of erosion itself, the hard volcanic rock has broken down into valleys and peaks, the tallest of which, Mount Whitney, scales 14 495 ft (4418 m).

Batholiths are the largest rock bodies in the Earth's crust, and few can rival the dimensions of the massive block of stone from which the Coast Range of western Canada has been sculpted. At the surface it is 185 miles (300 km) wide, more than 1250 miles (2000 km) long and rises to almost 13 000 ft (4000 m). But its true depth is at least seven times as great – 18 miles (29 km) or more – because it extends deep into the Earth's crust. The forces of erosion have cut this mighty slab of rock into hundreds of small peaks and ridges, while rising sea levels have drowned its western valleys to create fiords. The Bitteroot Mountains and Salmon River Mountains of Idaho are shaped from another great batholith, as are

RAIN CUTS *Rainwater has run into the lines of weakness in this batholith in Arizona, cutting the rock into regular straight-edged masses.*

the hills and low mountain ranges of Baja California.

Smaller intrusions of volcanic rock into folded mountains can create many strange landforms. In the New England Tableland of northern New South Wales, Australia, granite blocks near Glen Innes appear to be stacked one on top of another. The earliest European settlers thought they were prehistoric monuments, and called them 'Stonehenge' after the ancient man-made stone circle in southern England. Closer study revealed that the granite was formed by volcanic intrusions into narrow, pipe-like vents in now-vanished sedimentary rocks. Erosion stripped away the softer sedimentary layers, but left the granite as thin columns. As granite crystallises it establishes a pattern of blocks and joints, and the exposed joints are vulnerable to erosion. The gouging out of these narrow lines of weakness in the granite has created the impression of separate blocks stacked up by hand.

Some sedimentary rocks permit the magma to flow out horizontally and form hard, resistant layers of volcanic rock within the sedimentary layers. In Tasmania this has occurred extensively, and the sheets of volcanic dolerite embedded in the rock have influenced the landscape through their resistance to erosion. Many mountains are table-like, where the dolerite provides a flat protective 'hat' and resists the erosive forces that would otherwise shape it into a pointed peak. The dolerite is also responsible for the spectacular 4000 ft (1200 m) high Great Western Tiers, whose hard-topped volcanic cliffs run along the northern and eastern boundaries of Tasmania's western Central Plateau.

RISING FROM THE DEAD

Like a phoenix from the ashes, new mountain peaks can rise from the worn-down relics of old mountain ranges. The many mountain ranges of Nevada and eastern Utah, known to geologists as the Basin and Range Province, have been formed by a complex process from a rock layer that was once the root of an ancient mountain range. Having been eroded to flatness and covered for long periods by water that laid down fresh, flat sediments over the old gnarled roots of the vanished mountains, this vast region was then pushed up again, elevated forcefully from beneath by an arching of the Earth's crust. This arching placed great tension on the rock, stretching it intolerably so that it split in many places. Such splits are known to geologists as 'faults', and they run in a north-south direction throughout this region.

Faults result in a sharp displacement of the rock on one side of the fault, which either slips downwards or is forced upwards, leaving a cliff face exposed. This sheer cliff face is called an escarpment. Like other mountain-building processes, this movement proceeds at an imperceptible speed but eventually, over the millennia, achieves an impressive change in height of many thousands of feet. Long before the movement is complete, however, erosion has begun. Trickles of water cut into the bare, near-vertical face of the escarpment, making little gulleys that eventually widen to valleys and finally split off a row of separate peaks from the original scarp face.

Some of the ranges in the Nevada-Utah region owe their origin to a single fault, so the peaks are asymmetrical: steep and jagged on the faulted side, but sloping away more gradually on the opposite flank. Other ranges originated with a double fault, a block of rock slipping down between the two fault lines. Technically known as horsts, or block mountains, these uplifted ridges erode into mountain peaks that are equally steep on both flanks. The repeated faulting that cut the landscape of Nevada and western Utah thus led to a series of parallel mountain ranges running from north to south.

In time, erosion eats such peaks away, as it does with all mountains. In Arizona and northern Mexico, the tail end of that process can be seen – the worn-down stumps of parallel ranges that once stood as high as those of Nevada, and were formed by the same process of faulting, slippage and erosion.

THE ANGRY MOUNTAIN

The Chogga people, who live in the foothills of Mount Kilimanjaro in East Africa, have a legend about the three peaks that loom above their villages. The central one, Kibo, is the perfect cone familiar from photographs of Kilimanjaro. It dominates two far smaller peaks, Shira in the west, and Mawenzi in the east, a tattered, broken remnant of a volcanic cone. The Chogga legend says that, long ago, Mawenzi was in far better shape, but one day he came to Kibo, saying that the fire in his hearth had gone out and asking for a burning ember to rekindle it. Kibo gladly gave him not only fire but also a bunch of bananas, in the generous, neighbourly tradition of African villagers. The next day Mawenzi returned, saying that his fire had again gone out. Kibo obliged again with both fire and bananas, but when the request was repeated the next day he grew impatient, and on the fourth day, when Mawenzi asked again, Kibo lost his temper and attacked his neighbour with a club, battering him into the jagged remains that are seen today.

Is this tale pure fantasy, or did some long-dead inhabitants of the region witness

FAULT-MADE MOUNTAINS
Faults in the Earth's crust give rise to upraised and depressed sections that form mountain ranges. The mountains are then shaped by the forces of erosion.

Above: The block sinks – known as a rift valley

Below: The block is raised – known as a horst

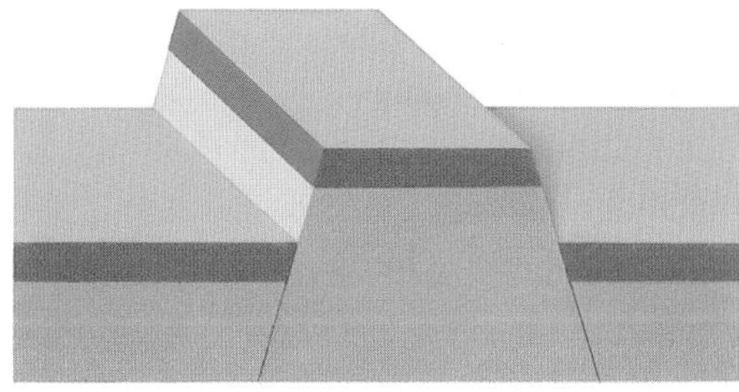

Block faulting (right) occurs when movement causes the crust to divide into rectangular blocks between parallel fault lines

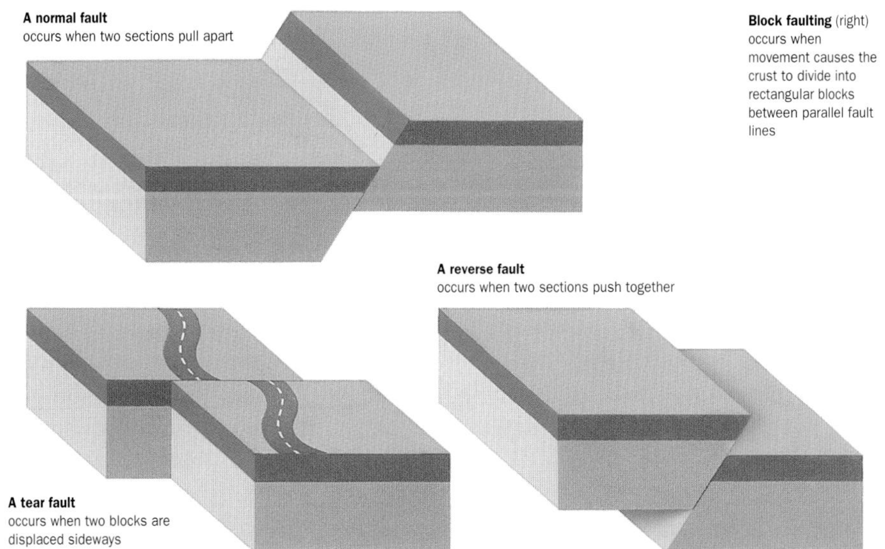

A normal fault occurs when two sections pull apart

A reverse fault occurs when two sections push together

A tear fault occurs when two blocks are displaced sideways

Uplifted blocks can be tilted – known as tilt blocks

Faulty Towers *The Grand Teton range, in the US, sits on a long fault. Land slipped on one side, exposing a towering edge of rock to erosion.*

the last great eruption of Kibo, which perhaps damaged the adjacent cone, about 36 000 years ago? Or, more plausibly, did some ancestor of the Chogga, a mere 200 years ago, witness the last plume of ash from Kibo and elaborate this event into the legend? Whatever the story's origin, we can be sure that people who differed little from ourselves, at least in physique, watched every stage in the formation of Mount Kilimanjaro: at a mere 1 million years old, this mountain is far younger than the human species.

Volcanic cones such as Kibo are unique among mountains in that their basic shape owes little to erosion: they are the only mountain peaks whose primary shape is a product of purely constructive forces. Magma – molten rock – surges up from the Earth's interior and spills out to make the cone. Some volcanoes intersperse eruptions of magma with eruptions of ash, the successive

Mountain Legend
The peak of Kibo, central cone of Mount Kilimanjaro, is depicted as an angry giant by local legend.

layers accumulating into a cone. The process can be remarkably quick, as Kilimanjaro shows: despite its youth, it stands 19 340 ft (5895 m) above sea level.

Kilimanjaro is just one of a string of volcanic peaks that run down the eastern side of Africa. For over 30 million years, this fragile portion of the Earth's crust has suffered the effects of subterranean forces operating at the divide between the African plate and the Somalian plate, and tending to pull the plates apart. Tensions in the rock have produced the giant cracks that created the Great Rift Valley, while the restless, molten interior of the planet has erupted through the weakened surface at regular intervals. The volcanic ash tends to blow and wash away at great speed, and even solid lava is readily eroded, much of it being porous and vulnerable to rainwater. Owing to erosion, innumerable volcanic cones have vanished in those 30 million years. The current landscape of East Africa, dotted with peaks such as Kilimanjaro, Mount Meru, Mount Elgon and Mount Kenya, is simply a snapshot in time. Given another 10 million years, this landscape will again have changed completely, new peaks springing up as the old ones disappear.

Faulting also takes place within folded mountains, such as the Andes and the

Volcanic Growth ***Volcanic cones are built up by successive eruptions. The shape varies, depending on the consistency of the molten lava.***

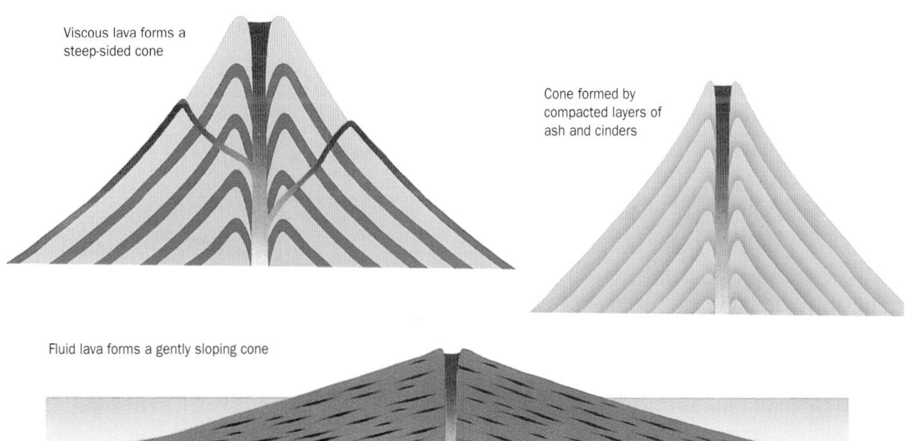

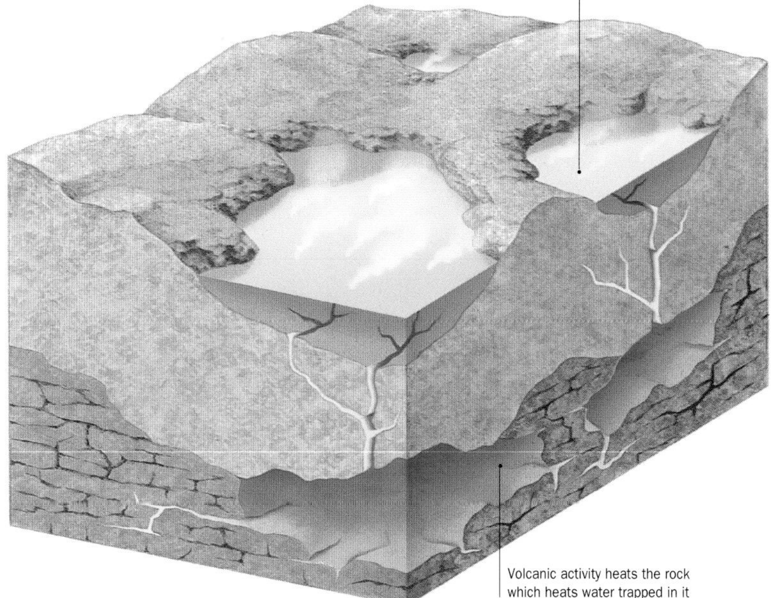

Red-hot Monkeys *Japanese macaques, or red-faced monkeys, warm themselves in a hot spring in the Japan Alps. Above: Thermal springs form as a result of volcanic activity, where water is heated in hot rock fairly close to the surface.*

Himalayas, when tensions in the rock become too great and 'something snaps'. These faults create sheer escarpments and add to the chaotic jumble of peaks and valleys already created by upthrust, folding, erosion and volcanic activity.

Faulting has played a major role in the Kaikoura Range of New Zealand, and the highest peak in the range, Tapuaenuku, has been eroded out of the fault escarpment. Here erosion has reached the 'mature stage', where there are distinct and virtually symmetrical peaks, and the neat incision of the fault scarp is no longer obvious except to an educated eye.

Steaming with a Monkey

In the Japan Alps, it is not unusual to share a hot bath with a monkey. The bath is an outdoor one, in a natural hot spring valued by Japanese walkers and mountaineers for bathing away the aches and strained muscles of a strenuous climb. The red-faced monkeys, also called Japanese macaques, that live on the lower slopes of the Japan Alps have used the hot springs for many thousands of years, long before the climbers came here. The warmth of the waters helps the monkeys, whose ancestors were inhabitants of the tropics, to survive the icy mountain winters.

As with hot springs in other mountain ranges, those of the Japan Alps derive their heat from contact with rocks deep inside the mountains. The rocks themselves are warmed by red-hot magma seeping up from the Earth's fiery heart. The same volcanic activity that warms the water also built the mountains – and much of the Japanese landmass besides – though large areas are now eroded to a lower and more level surface.

Japan lies over a point where, once again, different sections of the Earth's crust are in conflict. Here the Pacific plate and the Philippine plate have both been pushing westwards for millions of years, pressing against the Eurasian plate. At the point of contact, the crust of both plates is an oceanic crust; there are no thick layers of sediment above (as there are at the edge of a continental plate). Instead, one ocean crust

Peak of Perfection *The perfect volcanic cone of Mount Fuji, always coated with snow and ice, is inspiration for much Japanese culture.*

slipped beneath the other, melting as it descended, and the molten rock percolated upwards to emerge as volcanic eruptions. These major eruptions, which gave birth to the Japanese archipelago, began about 40 million years ago and were so colossal that the islands they created, once solidified into rock, became a massive obstacle to the continuing movement of the oceanic plate below. The volcanic rocks were, in consequence, squashed and deformed by the subsequent movements of the plate. The Japan Alps are not, therefore, a set of neat volcanic cones, but volcanic deposits that have been further lifted, compressed and distorted by the movements of the plates far beneath them. Mount Fuji, a perfect cone and the highest mountain in Japan, is a later addition, built up by successive eruptions between 80 000 and 5000 years ago. It stands slightly apart from the Japan Alps and reaches 12 389 ft (3776 m), almost 2000 ft (600 m) higher than Yari and Hotaka, the loftiest peaks of the Alps themselves.

If Mount Fuji could be set beside the largest volcanic peak in the world, it would be dwarfed. Mauna Loa measures 32 000 ft (9750 m) from base to summit – more than two and a half times the height of Mount Fuji. Yet its peak is only 13 677 ft (4169 m) above sea level, because Mauna Loa springs from the deep bed of the Pacific Ocean to form part of the Hawaiian archipelago. Displaced to dry land, Mauna Loa would tower over the tallest terrestrial volcanoes, such as Mount Kilimanjaro – 19 340 ft (5895 m) – and would even outstrip Mount Everest at 29 022 ft (8846 m).

Ice Work *Water seeps into cracks, freezes and fractures the rock into small fragments, or scree (above). Left: Scree builds up at the base of a cliff.*

GLACIER SPEEDS

The fastest glaciers in the world are found in Central Asia and travel at 2625 ft (800 m) a year, more than $6\frac{1}{2}$ ft (2 m) per day. An average glacier only moves about 165 ft (50 m) a year – about the speed of the hour hand of a watch.

It is not by chance that the highest volcanic peak sits on the ocean bed rather than on land. Indeed, the Atlantic and Pacific oceans are peppered with volcanoes that rival Mount Everest in height. Unlike their terrestrial counterparts, these oceanic peaks do not suffer the constant attack of Earth's most powerful rock-destroyer: ice.

Death by a Thousand Cuts

Ice is the major erosive force in the mountain peaks. Even in the tropics, a cap of unmelted snow sits on peaks such as Kilimanjaro above about 15 000 ft (4500 m), and during the ice ages there were even ice caps on the highlands of tropical New Guinea. The destruction of mountain summits by ice is 'death by a thousand cuts', as water seeps into the tiny fissures and pores of the rock by day, then freezes at night. In freezing, it expands and so pries the rock apart. The repeated process of water penetration and freezing, day after day, finally loosens the outer flakes of rock, which fall away exposing fresh cracks and pores in the untouched rock beneath. These are now accessible by water, and fall prey to the same destructive process.

Taking a whole mountain range, there are billions of these tiny blades of ice slicing at the rocks every night and day, carving their way into the peaks, little by little. The falling chunks and flakes of rock accumulate in 'scree slopes' or 'talus slopes', bleak expanses of bare rock debris in which the friction between the separate fragments only just holds them in place – narrowly balancing out the gravitational pull that would drag the scree farther down the mountain slope. It is a delicate balance, as many mountaineers and travellers have

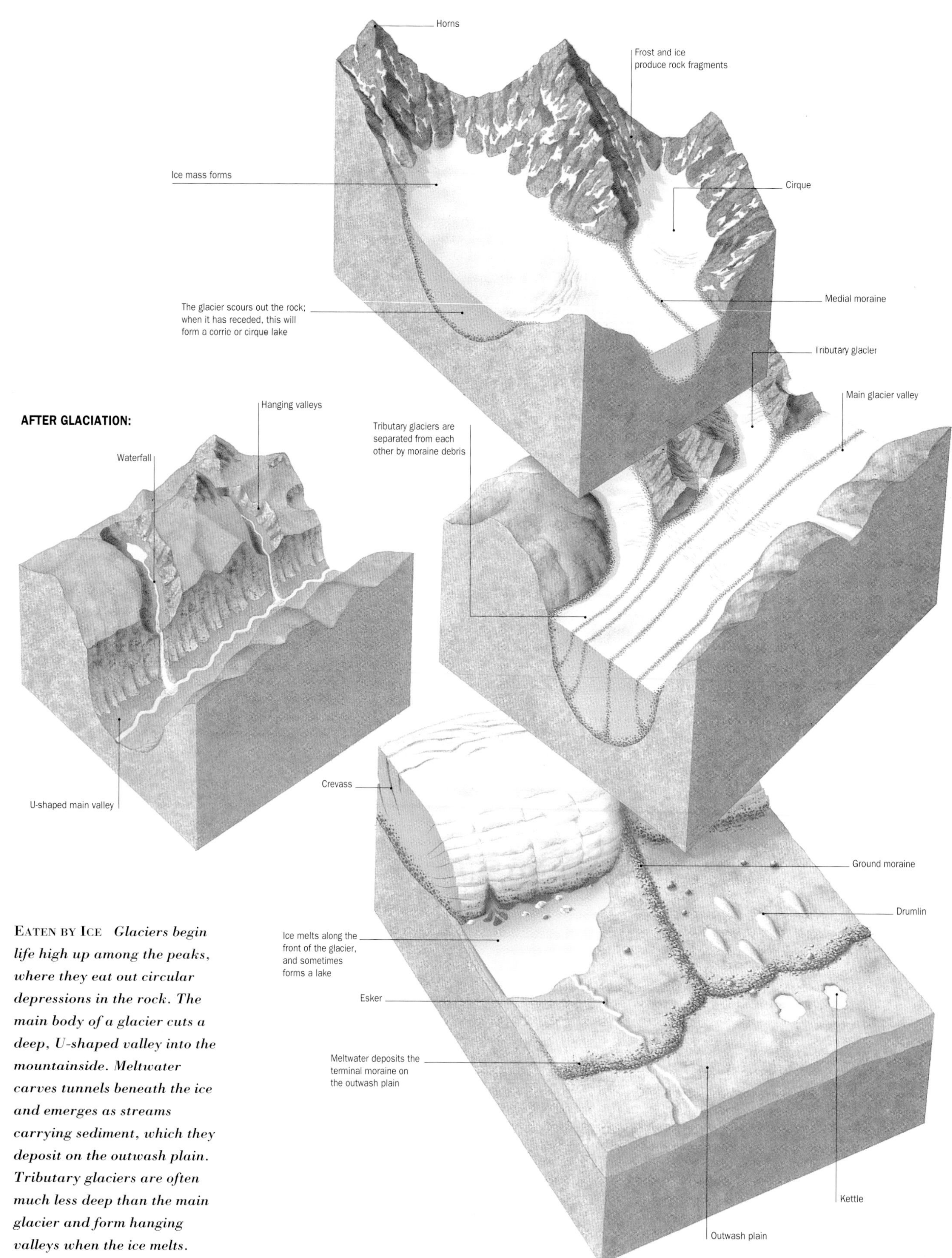

Eaten by Ice *Glaciers begin life high up among the peaks, where they eat out circular depressions in the rock. The main body of a glacier cuts a deep, U-shaped valley into the mountainside. Meltwater carves tunnels beneath the ice and emerges as streams carrying sediment, which they deposit on the outwash plain. Tributary glaciers are often much less deep than the main glacier and form hanging valleys when the ice melts.*

found. The slight pressure of a human footfall on a scree slope can tip the balance the other way and animate the stones into a sudden torrential avalanche.

Rivers of Ice

The billions of tiny, knife-like slivers of ice that dissect a mountain summit from within are assisted, in many mountain ranges, by the far more conspicuous rivers of ice known as glaciers. Whenever snow accumulates and compacts in an upland valley, remaining unmelted during the summer months, a glacier can develop. The weight of more snow bearing down from above forces out the air between the snowflakes and produces an intermediate stage known as *névé*, or *firn*, which is midway between snow and ice. On close inspection, it looks like a jumbled mass of half-broken hailstones. More compression expels most of the air, and the snow becomes ice.

If solid ice forms in what was once a river valley, it produces a profound change in the dynamics of that valley. The water of a mountain stream flows at about 3 ft (1 m) per second. A glacier, by contrast, takes nearly 8 hours to cover the same distance – it is moving 30 000 times more slowly. Inevitably the ice builds up behind, the glacier grows, and the pressure on the valley itself increases exponentially. The inherent erosive power of ice is augmented by this colossal dammed-up pressure, and the glacier enlarges the valley relentlessly over the coming years.

Although the valley becomes wider, much of the enlargement takes place out of sight at the base of the glacier, which gouges deep into the bedrock. It creates a valley with a typical U-shaped cross-section that extends far into the mountainside. The pieces of stone rubble that are produced by this erosion, rather than falling as scree, become embedded in the ice, and this transforms them into agents of further destruction, giving the advancing glacier a saw-toothed surface that scratches and scours the rock walls farther down the valley.

Licked by Ice *The leading edge of a glacier resembles a giant icy tongue lapping its way down a mountainside (right). Small stones scoured from the surrounding rocks are carried downwards and deposited in lines known as moraines (above).*

When the snout of a glacier finally reaches the warmer zones of a lower mountain slope and begins to melt, the larger rock debris that it plucked from the high valley walls is deposited as a line of rubble, called a moraine. Moraines may be so substantial that they block valleys, forming a natural dam that prevents water flowing out of the valley and so creates a lake. Lake Wakatipu in New Zealand is held back by a wall of debris called the Kingston Moraine, which is up to 1000 ft (300 m) deep.

The importance of glaciers in sculpting mountains can be seen most clearly in regions where the glaciers have now departed. In north-eastern Tasmania, only one peak was tall enough for glaciers to form during the last Ice Age. This peak, named Ben Lomond by homesick Scottish settlers, is distinctly different in form from the less lofty peaks around it, with far steeper cliffs, more bare rock stripped of soil by glaciers,

Ice Sculpture *A glacier in Patagonia shows the effects of strains within the glacier combined with melting by the sun and nocturnal refreezing.*

and more rock debris around the feet of the mountain, swept there by the rivers of ice. In addition, there are small, circular lakes of the kind known as cirques or corries, which form high up on mountain peaks in the bowl-like depression where a glacier originated. Finally, Ben Lomond is peppered with the rounded, ice-scoured rocks known as *roches moutonnées.*

All these distinctive features are the handiwork of valley glaciers, the agents also responsible for the angular, gnawed-out spire of the Matterhorn and for the majestic pinnacles of Mount Everest. Today, valley glaciers are the only kind to be found on most mountains, but during the ice ages there were also continuous sheets of ice on some high mountain ranges, covering peaks and valleys alike. This type of ice cover produces a completely different kind of landscape when the ice recedes. Rather than carving out jagged peaks and deep valleys, it has a flattening effect, rubbing sharp edges and peaks away with its frictional force and leaving a more uniform scoured terrain.

Where ice survives in the mountains today, it creates its own magical scenery. In the high Himalayas the climber can be surrounded by gigantic walls of solid blue-green ice, with dramatic overhangs and cornices, often sculpted by the wind into bizarre curves and hollows, or hung with silvery stalactites of ice where meltwater has refrozen as it dripped downwards. The granite spire-like peak of Mount Nilankatha (itself carved out by larger Ice Age glaciers, as its shape reveals) is guarded on all sides by sheer ice walls.

In this region, 'ice tables' and 'ice mushrooms' are occasionally found: slabs of granite rock supported on a clear column of ice, the last vestige of a melted glacier. They develop when a stone slab carried on a glacier protects the ice immediately below it from the warm rays of the sun.

Mud Slides

Water does not bite into rock as viciously as does ice, but it, too, inflicts great destruction. Or rather, it is the combination of water and gravity that erodes the mountain ranges. Gravity pulls downwards, while water both lubricates and gives added weight to gravity's insistent force, so that particles of rock and soil come tumbling down to the lower slopes.

Much of this erosion is gradual, unseen and undramatic. Known as 'creep', it produces a slightly thicker layer of soil at the base of a mountain slope than at its upper limit. Creep may tilt trees away from the summit by stealing the soil from among the roots on their downslope side. To compensate, and to achieve a vertical stance once again, the tree curves its trunk upwards. The activity of earthworms and other burrowing creatures speeds up the process of creep, which denudes mountains of millions of tons of soil every year.

Creep can produce dramatic mud slides, often following heavy rainfall, particularly in arid terrain where a great deal of dry rock debris has accumulated in a gully, providing the raw material for the mud slide. All it takes is a downpour to soak this debris, turn it to mud, then loosen its tenuous hold on the steep slope. One massive mud slide in the San Juan Mountains of

Frozen Fantasies *Once carried by a glacier, this rock now shades the frozen glacier remnants beneath it from the sun, forming an ice toadstool.*

HOW GLACIERS SHAPE MOUNTAIN PEAKS

Because the effects of the last Ice Age are still highly visible on the Earth's mountain ranges, especially in the Northern Hemisphere, glaciated mountain tops are the most familiar type and have provided the stereotyped image of a mountain peak (as, for example, in the logo for Paramount Pictures).

Before the last Ice Age, however, many of the mountains of the Earth would have had more rounded summits. As temperatures plunged, valley glaciers formed in the river valleys of these rounded summits and cut deeply into the rock, clawing out rock debris from the sides of the valleys and eventually leaving sharp-edged, precipitous ridges between them. In time, the valley glaciers extended backwards towards the summit, and this sculpted angular peaks such as the Matterhorn and Mount Everest.

Ice-Age Legacy ***The summit of the Matterhorn was shaped by ice.***

Colorado, known evocatively as the Slugmullion Mud Flow, created a new lake – Lake San Cristobal – by blocking a branch of the Gunnison River. The mud had flowed for 6 miles (10 km) before coming to rest in this river valley. Mud slides are also frequent in the Himalayas and New Zealand, and the deforestation of mountainsides greatly increases their frequency. Mud slides with the consistency of thick custard can buoy up huge rocks, and even lift houses from their foundations, carrying them forwards for a while like ships in full sail. Some mud flows are over 300 ft (100 m) thick, an irresistible wall of destruction.

POOLS OF BOILING MUD

In the Rotorua district of North Island, New Zealand, the presence of hot magma deep down in the mountains announces itself at the surface with pools of boiling mud, geysers and other types of 'hot spring'. The mud is derived from volcanic rock, decomposed by the very hot, acidic spring water, then agitated by the restless bubbling of the water. A thick, glutinous mud is the inevitable result. As the water in the mud turns to steam, the mud splutters like pea soup. At some springs, small mounds of mud called 'mud volcanoes' accumulate around the mouth of the spring.

Many of New Zealand's geysers are also muddy. Waimango geyser, the largest ever recorded but now no longer active, in its heyday would spurt a fountain of black boiling water 1500 ft (500 m) into the air. Muddy water is the sign of a young geyser. As the geyser grows older, a layer of glassy deposit, called sinter, develops on the vent where the geyser is produced, and this keeps the water clean.

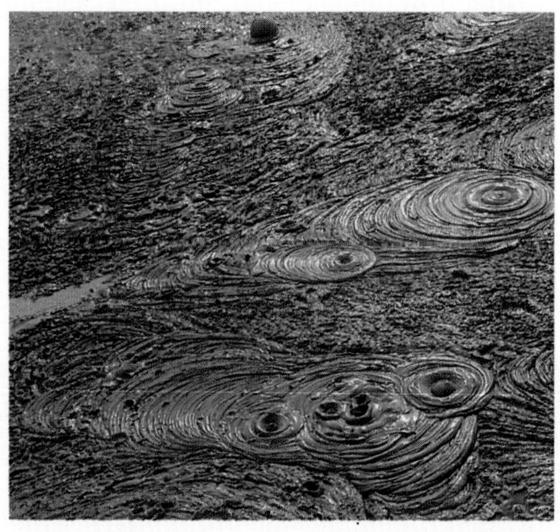

Mud Glorious Mud ***The boiling mudpools of Rotorua in New Zealand are a sign of the volcanic ferment taking place deep in these young mountains.***

Landslides and Rockfalls

Dry rock debris can also be involved in dramatic and catastrophic falls when an accumulated mass becomes unstable. The tremors of an earthquake can sometimes be the trigger for a landslide or landslip, as regularly happens in the Andes. If the volume of falling material is great enough, and the tremor large enough, the landslip can behave almost like a liquid, despite the fact that it is made entirely of dry fragments. It can achieve huge speeds, 'washing' down into a valley and breaking against the far side like a wave. This type of fall is described as a 'catastrophic debris stream'.

When material descends in free-fall from a near-vertical surface, the term 'rockfall' is used rather than landslide. Rockfalls can be small or large, and often originate with ice-damage to the integrity of the rock above. Once ice has repeatedly widened small cracks, huge chunks of rock can break away. One of the largest rockfalls of all time occurred in Alberta, Canada, in 1903. In the space of 100 seconds, 7.5 million tons of rock split away from the face of Turtle Mountain and fell thousands of feet. Although it consisted of one huge wedge as it began its descent, the rock disintegrated on impact with the ground, entirely burying the mining town of Frank, as well as the surrounding farmland – 3200 acres (1300 ha) in total. The town was covered by 100 ft (30 m) of rubble and the Crowsnest River was dammed, creating a small lake. What triggered this catastrophic rockfall is unknown, but mining activity in the locality could have created earth tremors, destabilising an already weak mountain escarpment.

Hewn by Water

If rivers had memories the Brahmaputra would have a strange tale to tell, for it has seen the highest peaks in the

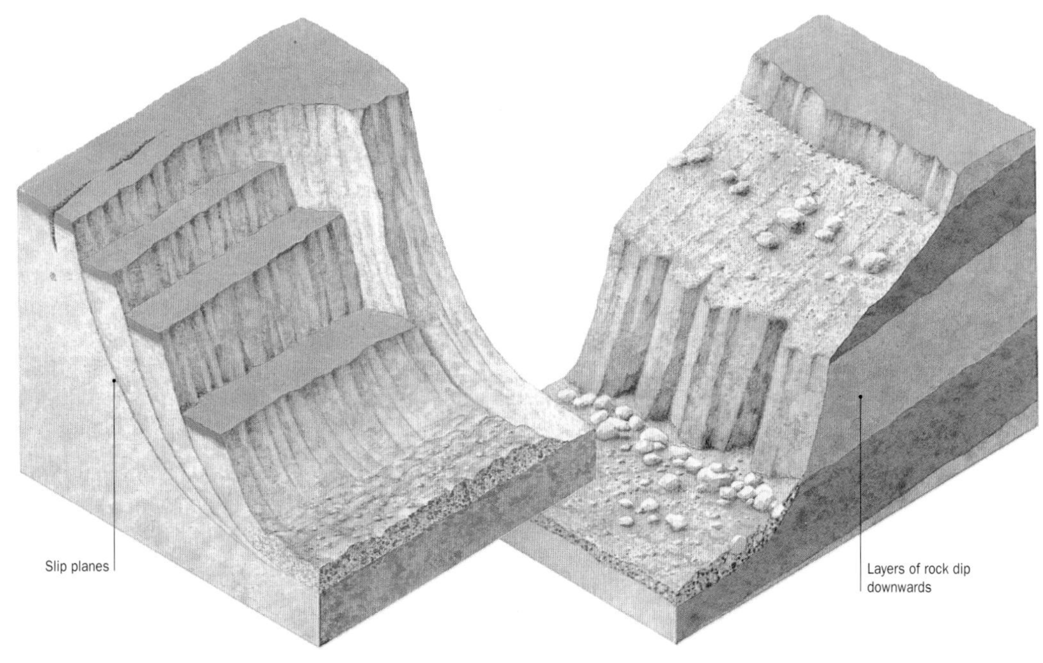

What Goes Up ***Landslips occur when loose rock and mud slump down under the pull of gravity along slip lines (far left). Rockfalls occur when part of a cliff-face slides away (left).***

world rise from nothing. Today, this river has its source in a small ice-cold stream running off a glacier in the Chemayungdung Mountains, part of the western Himalayan range. This source is over 16 800 ft (5120 m) above sea level and the river then flows due east along the northern side of the Himalayas for over 775 miles (1250 km), becoming deeper and wider as it goes, and effectively separating the Himalayas from the mountains of Tibet. Running through Tibetan territory here, it is known by its Tibetan name of Zangbo, which simply means 'river'. The name is apt for it is incomparable, the river of all rivers.

At its easternmost point, the Brahmaputra swings north, then runs in a tight hairpin bend around a mountain called Namjagbarwa Feng, which stands 25 446 ft (7756 m) above sea level. The Brahmaputra then cuts south, slicing through the Himalayas and tumbling down into the Assam valley. Flowing south-west into Bangladesh, it then swings round again and flows south-east to join the Ganges before pouring into the Bay of Bengal.

The strangely devious course of the Brahmaputra, which owes little to the logic of the landscape, gives a clue to the river's history. Another can be seen in the spectacular gorges it has cut on three sides of Namjagbarwa Feng – gorges that are 10 000 ft (3050 m) deep at one spot known as Pei. The river at Pei stands 6562 ft (2000 m) above sea level. About 75 miles (120 km) upstream, it stands at 9843 ft (3000 m) above sea level, whereas 25 miles (40 km) downstream it has dropped to 2843 ft (866 m). In the space of just 150 miles (240 km), the river not only doubles back on itself, but also descends a full 7000 ft (2133 m).

The illogical course of the Brahmaputra and the precipitous gorges, both point to the same truth about its origin: it flowed across this land *before* the Himalayas were raised. Its path – or perhaps the path of several ancient rivers that are now combined to form the Brahmaputra – must have made sense in the context of some long-vanished landscape. It was a strong river even then, powerful enough to eat down into the rock beneath it, as the land was compressed and forced upwards by the collision of the Earth's crustal plates. Each time the Himalayas rose, the

Old Man River
The Brahmaputra River begins high in the Himalayas and follows a course older than the mountains (right). In Tibet (below), it gathers its waters from melting snow and ice.

river sliced down into the rock a little farther, keeping pace, inch for inch, and so preserving its age-old course amid the newly forming mountains. Indeed, it helped create some of the mountain peaks; it was clearly responsible for carving out Namjagbarwa Feng, and its sister peak Jialabaili Feng, which stands on the opposite side of the river and reaches 23 460 ft (7151 m). Measuring from their peaks down to the bottom of the gorge at Pei, it is clear that the Brahmaputra has cut down through at least 20 000 ft (6100 m) of rock here since the Himalayas began to rise.

TUMBLING WATERS *In a hanging valley in the Sierra Nevada, a waterfall marks the place where a small glacier once flowed into a larger one.*

BORN-AGAIN MOUNTAINS

In the Appalachian Mountains, the rivers follow a course as illogical as that of the Brahmaputra, but their history is entirely different. These mountains have a far longer and more complex past than the Himalayas. They were first lifted more than 200 million years ago, producing a series of folds that run roughly south-west to north-east. Erosion gradually wore away these mountains to low ridges of resistant sandstone, interspersed with softer valleys of shale and limestone. Then the sea rose, flooded the land and remained there for millions of years, during which time thick layers of ocean sediment were deposited over the earlier ridges and valleys, smoothing out their surface into flatness.

Movements in the Earth's crust then pushed some sections of the area upwards again, and the sea level fell. At this stage, rivers established themselves on the low, smooth surface of the newly emerged sediments. These flowed eastwards to the sea.

Crustal movements continued and the land rose farther, forming a low mountain range. The erosive forces of the rivers, combined with wind and rain, gradually raked away the relatively new ocean sediments, and exposed the ancient sandstone ridges and their intervening valleys once again. In this way, the eastward-flowing rivers were superimposed on a much earlier landscape with ridges running diagonally across the river courses: an incongruous mixture that had somehow to be resolved. The resolution depended on the erosive forces of the young rivers cutting through the sandstone ridges at their weakest points to make short gorges. The shale and limestone of the intervening valleys were eroded far more efficiently, and thus moulded the river system into a new 'trellis' pattern, rather like a fruit tree trained along a wall. (It was the strangeness of this trellis pattern that first alerted geologists to the complicated evolution of the Appalachian Mountains, although it has taken many decades for their intriguing past to be understood.) In time, most of the newer sediments were carved away, leaving the ridges of the ancient mountain system, now raised anew and etched into sharper relief by the novel and complex river system.

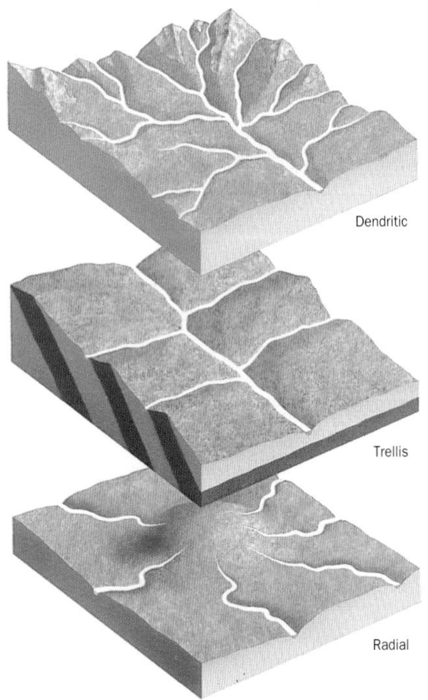

PATTERNS OF THE PAST *A typical river system (top) flows from the peaks into the valleys. A trellis pattern (centre) indicates a succession of uplifts of old mountain ridges. Around a volcanic cone (bottom), water drains away in all directions.*

Not all rivers sit so at odds with the shape of their mountain landscape. On the south side of the Himalayas, for example, young rivers flow down from the high peaks and into the Assam valley to become tributaries of the Brahmaputra. These are rivers that have grown up with the mountains themselves. Some began as rivers then turned to glaciers during the last great Ice Age, only to become rivers once again when the world grew warmer.

Even logical rivers can have strange courses. Mighty rivers that originate on the west side of the Indian subcontinent, rivers such as the Godavari and the Krishna, although they arise only a short distance

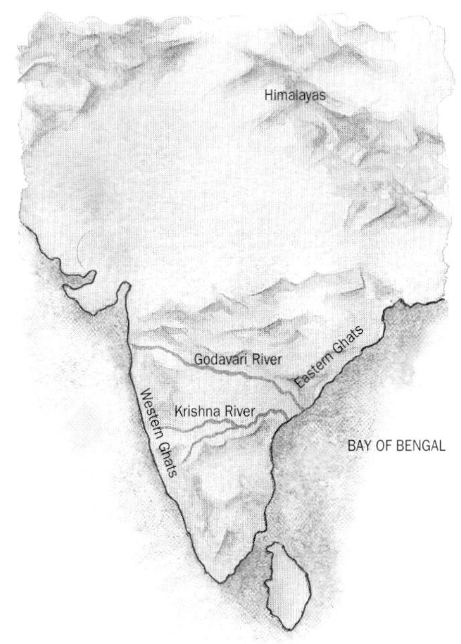

Incredible Journey *Because of the pattern of the mountain ranges, the Krishna River flows the whole width of the Indian subcontinent to reach the sea.*

from the Arabian Sea, flow eastwards across the entire span of the subcontinent, to discharge into the Bay of Bengal. The reason for this long journey is that the rivers rise on the eastern slopes of the Western Ghats, a range of low mountains and hills formed by faulting and erosion, which extends along India's western margin. A similar pattern is shown by the Amazon in South America, which drains its waters from tributaries high in the Andes, then plunges eastwards to discharge into the Atlantic. In North America, rain and snowmelt from the Rockies travels down tributaries into the Missouri, then into the Mississippi and finally out into the Gulf of Mexico. Each of these epic voyages is dictated by a mountain range, giving rainwater the impetus to travel thousands of miles across a continent.

In many parts of the Northern Hemisphere, mountain rivers now flow in valleys that were gouged out by glaciers, and these have characteristic features. Particularly striking is the difference in depth between main valleys and the valleys of tributaries – smaller glaciers do not cut so deeply into the rock. Once the glaciers melt and vanish, and rivers flow in their place, this discrepancy becomes strikingly evident as the side valleys sit stranded, high above the main valley. These 'hanging valleys', as they are called, create spectacular waterfalls at the points where tributaries drop down to join the main watercourse. Stunning waterfalls of this kind are seen in the Himalayas, especially along the tributaries of the Ganges such as the River Alakanda and River Mandakini, where some waterfalls are over 300 ft (100 m) in height.

Opposing Forces

Erosion and uplift, uplift and erosion – almost all mountains are the outcome of these opposing forces, one creative, the other destructive. They combine to shape the myriad peaks, ridges, crags, escarpments, ravines and valleys of the Earth's mountain ranges.

Exceptions to the rule are rare and intriguing – volcanic cones, such as Mount Fuji in Japan or Cotopaxi in the Andes, whose forms are the outcome, primarily, of creative forces alone. Diametrically opposed to these are the mountains made by erosion alone, such as the Catskill Mountains of New York State, or the bizarre limestone peaks of karst landscapes in China, South-east Asia and New Guinea. These low summits have been created by the erosion of surrounding rocks in what was originally a flat plain.

Disregarding the exceptions, we can see how the struggle between uplift and erosion sculpts the mountains' craggy summits with constant change and reshaping, so that no mountain is exactly the same size and shape today as it was yesterday. Material that is now at the very core of a mountain range will one day become loosened and set free by erosion to tumble downwards. In time its particles, whether large or small (perhaps reduced to rock dust or fine grains of sediment), will become part of new rocks, and these may well rise up again as part of a new and nameless mountain chain many millions of years hence.

Karst Country *The Guilin hills in China are unusual in being formed by erosion alone, as rain and rivers cut away the soft limestone rock.*

THE POWER OF MOUNTAINS

Mountains dominate the landscapes in which they are set, creating eddies of wind and water vapour about their peaks and dividing the water that falls on them with unjust measure, deluging the land on one flank, parching it on the other.

When the hot, dry Santa Ana wind blows into Los Angeles, the mood of the city changes. As crime writer Raymond Chandler put it: 'Meek little wives feel the edge of the carving knife and study their husbands' necks.' The homicide rate rises by as much as 50 per cent when the Santa Ana blows, and it was once accepted in California that 'crimes of passion' should be dealt with more leniently if the Santa Ana was in full force on the date of the crime. So obvious was its mood-altering effect to all residents of the city that this odd legal loophole went unquestioned for decades.

The Santa Ana is named for a canyon in the surrounding hills through which it sometimes blows, but its place of origin is farther away, in the high mountainous plateau of the western United States, where small changes in weather conditions can produce a heavy upland body of air sitting above layers of less dense air in the lowlands. This triggers a downhill rush of the heavier air, pulled by gravity, a phenomenon that is known as a katabatic wind.

As it rushes towards the coast and Los Angeles, this katabatic wind must travel around the hills and mountains behind the city, including the San Bernadino Mountains which reach heights of around 11 500 ft (3500 m). This upland barrier compresses and dries the wind, heats it up and, by channelling it tightly through narrow spaces, gives it added vigour. It arrives in Los Angeles like the blast from a blowtorch.

The chinook winds that often blow down the eastern slopes of the Rockies, and the föhn winds that sometimes rasp the valleys of the European Alps, are also hot, dry winds with similar origins. Each arises from a complex interplay of different factors, but there is a simple common denominator: as cool, moist air blows over a mountain range it turns into hot dry air. This

SLEEPING GIANTS *Mountain ranges are passive but powerful; they cool, heat and divert the flow of air, affecting the local climate in many ways.*

strange metamorphosis is brought about by a succession of forces, each of which can be explained by basic physics.

As the cool, moist air impacts on the mountain it is forced upwards, where pressure is lower, leading to expansion and simultaneous cooling. This affects the water vapour in the air, which condenses into rain or snow. As these fall on the mountain slopes on the approach side, the airstream rushes on, purged of its moisture, flies over the summit and down into the lowlands beyond. Pressure rises during the descent so the air is compressed, and this makes its temperature rise. Because dry air warms up more effectively than moist air, the wind makes an overall gain in temperature in its eventful journey over the mountain. Given the right conditions, there is a rise of 1°C (1.8°F) for every 330 ft (100 m) that the air falls. The rate at which ascending wind on the approach side of the mountain cools down is far slower – only half the rate of warming – so there is an overall gain in temperature. This is called the 'föhn effect'. Chinook winds in the Rockies are so warm that they can melt snow on their descent and so strong that they can trigger avalanches.

Recent research has shown that the airstream changes in other, more subtle ways during this journey over mountain summits. All air contains electrically charged atoms, called ions. Some carry a positive charge, others a negative charge, and the relative numbers of positive and negative ions gives the air itself an overall charge. Most air has a mild negative charge, and the negative charge is augmented by the sea, beside waterfalls and on mountain peaks – all places noted for their ability to raise the spirits. By contrast, the Santa Ana, the chinooks, the föhn winds and others of their ilk are loaded with positive ions, which are suspected of causing ill-effects.

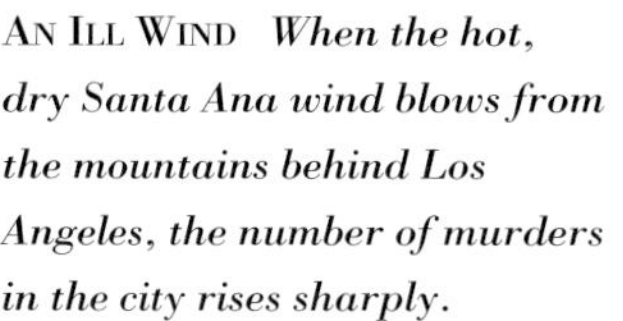

AN ILL WIND *When the hot, dry Santa Ana wind blows from the mountains behind Los Angeles, the number of murders in the city rises sharply.*

German and Swiss scientists have studied the effects of the föhn winds on human behaviour and found that reaction time is badly affected. This may explain the 50 per cent rise in road accidents in Geneva when the föhn winds blow. Human physiology is also affected, as shown by the increase in deaths after major surgical operations – not the fault of the surgeons themselves, affected by the mood-altering effects of the föhn, but an outcome of the patients' changes in blood clotting and other physiological reactions. Patients often die from blood clots or, paradoxically, excessive loss of blood. Some hospitals in Alpine areas of Switzerland and Germany have a policy of deferring major operations rather than

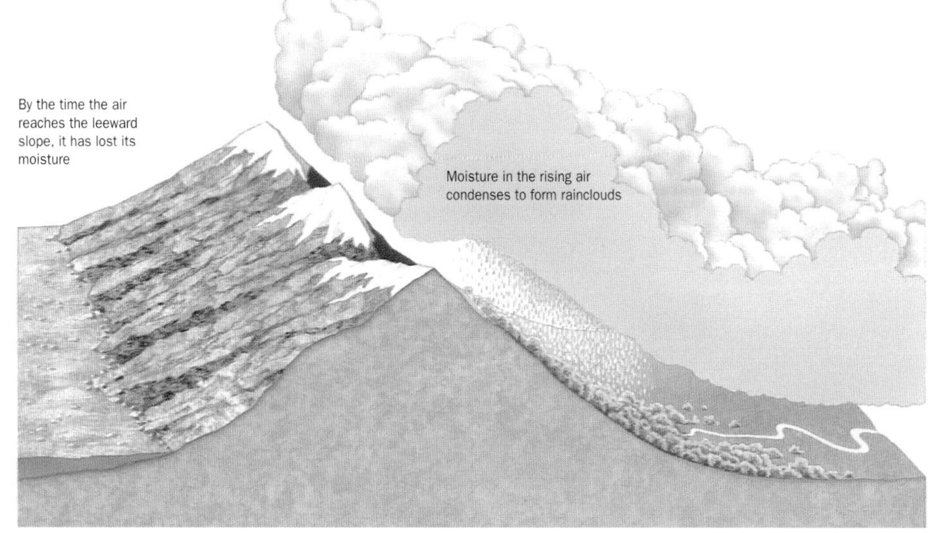

AIR WAVES *Air loses its moisture as it rises over mountains; as it flows down the other (leeward) side, its temperature rises, creating a hot, dry wind.*

Peak Power *In California, wind farms exploit the hot, dry winds blowing down from the Sierra Nevada mountains and generate electricity.*

carry them out when the föhn is in full spate.

Exactly why positive ions affect us in this way is unknown. Some of the positively charged particles are oxygen atoms, and their change in electrical charge may make the absorption of oxygen from the lungs more difficult, putting our breathing under stress. The positive ions are also known to affect the levels of a chemical messenger substance called serotonin, which circulates in the blood and brain. Since serotonin is known to affect our mood, our sleep patterns, and some aspects of blood circulation and clotting, it could be the common factor in all the strange effects of the hot, dry mountain winds. So characteristic are these winds that they are often referred to as 'föhn winds', regardless of where they occur throughout the world.

Not all mountain winds are hot, however. Quirks of geography can produce localised wind effects, such as the cold, dry wind that runs down from the Caucasus Mountains to the coasts of the Black Sea and Adriatic Sea. Blowing only in winter, it brings ice and snow down from the high peaks and churns the relatively warm, placid waters up into violent waves. Locals call this cold cruel wind the 'bora', and dread its arrival each winter.

Occasionally the mountain winds prove useful. In California, where persistent winds blow down the slopes of the Sierra Nevada mountains, wind generators are set up on the farms to transform the power of the airstream into usable electricity.

In addition to regularly recurring winds such as the Santa Ana, mountains can also generate freak winds by compressing an unusually fast-moving body of air and forcing it through a narrow gap. Such winds must often go unrecorded, but one that blew over Mount Washington in New Hampshire in April 1934 was measured: it achieved a speed of 230 mph (370 km/h). Winds such as these can lift the roofs off houses, or demolish them completely.

Rain Shadows

In the high Andes there are places where a walk of less than an hour takes you from dense cloud forest, where the small trees are hung with mosses and ferns that thrive in the damp air, to an utterly different landscape, parched and stony, with little vegetation except harsh, thorny scrub. The dramatic contrast occurs because one side of the mountain receives the full brunt of the winds that discharge the moisture they are carrying as they encounter the mountain peaks. Having spent all their rain, the winds have nothing left for the next stage of their journey, so a 'rain shadow' exists on the opposite side of the peak.

This small-scale effect on a single Andean peak is repeated on a far grander scale across the wider landscape. The northern and central Andes separate dense moist evergreen rain forests on their eastern side from a bleak coastal desert on the west. Here, rain-bearing winds come from the Atlantic, carrying moisture across the Amazon basin, whereas the prevailing winds of the Pacific all veer away from the South American coastline, leaving it parched except for cold sea fogs. The southern Andes cast a rain shadow in the opposite direction: here the prevailing winds are from the west, and the western flank of the continent is pelted with rain or snow and shrouded in cloud for much of the year, while to the east lie the dry, windswept uplands of Patagonia.

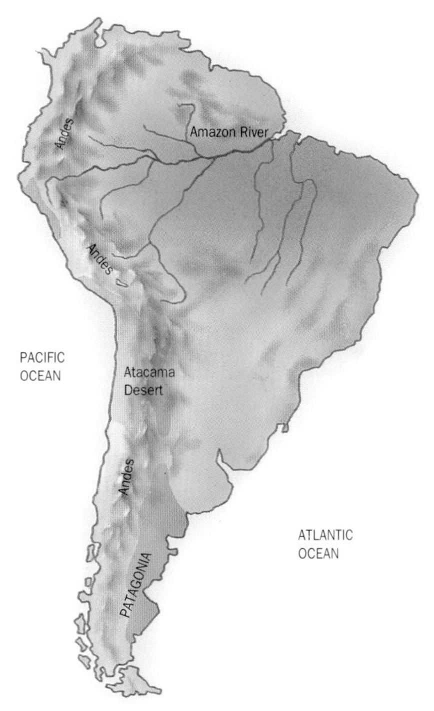

Rain Barrier *The Andes block rain-bearing winds blowing from east to west in the north and centre of the continent, and from west to east in the south.*

In effect, mountain chains are like giant hands dividing the waters, bestowing rain in generous amounts on one flank, while denying it to land on the opposite side. The Himalayas cast their rain shadow to the north. As the monsoon winds of the Indian subcontinent sweep up from the south-west between June and September they drop their moisture in great sheets of life-giving rain, sometimes as hard and unbroken as if a waterfall were coursing down from the sky. Much of the rain has been spent by the time the winds confront the sheer rock ramparts of the Himalayas, but what is left hammers down on their southern slopes in a last great outpouring, swelling the mountain streams on the lower slopes or settling as snow on the high peaks.

By the time the winds have passed over the 'roof of the world', they have been robbed of all moisture, and they blow parched and feeble down into the valley of the Zangbo (the Brahmaputra) on the northern side of the Himalayas. If it were

Rain Shadow *The barren coastal region of the Atacama Desert on the west of the Andes is in stark contrast to the green forests on the eastern flank.*

WELL-WATERED SLOPES *A valley on the fertile southern slopes of the Himalayas has terraced fields to help retain the soil and reduce the effects of erosion.*

not for the waters of the Zangbo, this valley would be barren.

The difference in rainfall between the southern and northern sides of the Himalayas has striking results. The Himalayan valleys on the southern side are moist, green and fertile. Farmers' fields are lush with grass and in the woods wild strawberries grow in thick, sweet clumps. The pervasive moisture also encourages leeches, which slither across the wet foliage of the trees and drop onto people and animals below. These bloodsucking parasites are so numerous and persistent that it is impossible to prevent them from creeping through openings in protective clothing, and even through the lace-holes of shoes, to reach the warm skin below: the only effective defence is to soak trousers and socks thoroughly in salt.

On the northern aspect of the Himalayas, and in the Zangbo valley, no leeches slither from the trees – indeed there are no trees in most places. Here the terrain is largely bare and stony with a scattered covering of scrubby bushes. Only along the margins of the Zangbo and in the deep river gorges are there trees or dense vegetation.

Properly managed, the power of mountains to intercept rain can have untold benefits for the surrounding land. The trick is to even out the distribution of rain around a mountain range. In south-eastern Australia the Snowy Mountains, or 'Australian Alps', are bordered by four huge reservoirs, stocked by meltwater flowing from the high, snow-covered peaks in spring and summer. Left to its own devices, most of the meltwater from the Snowy Mountains would flow down the Snowy River and out into the sea. Massive engineering work, begun in 1949, has diverted some of the water to the Tumut River and the Murray River, which flow towards the dry interior, supplying irrigation systems on lowland farms in the dry, rain-shadowed lands inland from the mountains. Some of the water is carried over the western slopes of the range, which are immensely steep and allow the cascading energy of the water to power hydroelectric turbines providing electricity for New South Wales and Victoria.

OVER THE TOP *A small hydroelectric generator diverts water from one side of Australia's Snowy Mountains to the other.*

FLOODS FROM THE MOUNTAINS

Springtime swells the waters of the Ganges, and pilgrims trekking north to the source of the river along India's Pilgrim Road must ford the tributary streams that pour their small offerings of water into the holy river. These tributaries are impassable from midday until midnight, when snow and ice, melted by the day's sunshine up in the mountains, swell their waters to a torrent. Pilgrims must wade across before the sun is up, when the ice-cold waters run lower.

The combination of monsoon rains and the immense altitude of the Himalayas is reflected in the great size and powerful flow of both the Ganges and the Brahmaputra. The floods from these two mighty rivers, rolling across the flat plains of Bangladesh, can sometimes be so violent that they destroy villages and human lives, leaving the survivors prey to famine and epidemics.

Even in the good years, there is loss and destruction. The twisting underwater currents of the Brahmaputra, which owe their energy to its long and eventful descent from the mountains, tend to erode the banks from below, with no visible sign of damage until a whole section collapses into the river, often taking a waterside pathway and its pedestrians with it. The influence of the far-off Himalayas can also be felt in the temperature of the river water. When spring comes and the snow melts on the high peaks, the waters of the Brahmaputra grow noticeably colder.

Even more dramatic and unpredictable floods are produced by the mountains of Iceland. Known as *jokulhlaups*, they are a unique feature of landscapes where ice forms continuous caps over high mountain peaks. Where such an ice cap sits atop a volcanic peak, the eruption of the volcano beneath the ice can induce the ice to melt and lead to flooding on a colossal scale. Jokulhlaups in the Katla region of Iceland sometimes achieve a flow rate of 3.5 million cu ft (100 000 m³) per second – the same as that of the Amazon.

Floods from as long ago as 1362 have left surviving marks on the Icelandic landscape in the form of huge rocks, some over 1765 cu ft (50 m³), carried down onto the lowlands by the floodwaters. Volcanic ash carried down by the floods has thickened the sediments in lowland river valleys by several feet.

In the Grimsvotn area of Vatnajokull there is a lake beneath an ice cap that has produced some of the most spectacular jokulhlaups. The lake sits in the crater of a volcano, with an air space immediately above, covered by a thick sheet of ice. Volcanic activity periodically warms the ice up, and as it melts it trickles into the crater lake, whose water level rises. Five or six years pass before the crater is full to the brim. At this point, the water either floats the ice cap off the mountain, or melts it partially along its lower edges, forcing about a dozen channels beneath the ice. Many of these channels run for 30 miles (50 km) under the ice before the water emerges into the open. The combined discharge of these dozen channels produces a flood of terrifying proportions. Once the floodwater has flowed out of the crater lake, calm prevails again, but the lake begins slowly filling for the next great flood, some five years hence.

FROZEN FLOODS

Just as gravity brings huge volumes of water down from the mountains, so it can bring the great torrents of snow known as avalanches. In some areas these can pose a threat to the surrounding lowland area, as at Juneau, the capital city of Alaska, which is at sea level but is menaced by avalanches from the precipitous slopes above. Avalanche experts have warned against the expansion of Juneau's suburbs into the areas at maximum risk, but these warnings have been ignored, and some believe that there is a major disaster 'waiting to happen' in Juneau.

Villagers in Switzerland take a more cautious approach, and there are government regulations that prevent building in high-risk zones. Even so, many villages are

DISTANT DISASTER
Severe floods in the Brahmaputra delta region of Bangladesh, possibly due to the effects of deforestation in the Himalayas, bring destruction with increasing frequency, washing away crops and submerging whole villages.

HOW MOUNTAINS CREATE 'FLYING SAUCERS'

FLYING SAUCERS IN THE ANTARCTIC ***A lenticular cloud forms over the peaks of Coronation Island in the South Orkneys.***

Moving airstreams can behave in strange ways when they encounter mountains. One of their more unusual effects is to create lenticular clouds, some of which catch the sun and have a luminous quality, giving them a striking resemblance to 'flying saucers'. Indeed, lenticular clouds could have been at the root of the first flying saucer 'sighting', made in 1947. This occurred over the Cascade Mountains in the north-western United States, where a pilot saw a procession of nine brightly lit, saucer-shaped white objects, spinning along: a convincing description of a typical set of lenticular clouds.

Mountains spawn such clouds when an airstream passing over the peaks somehow produces a vertical oscillation in the air on the far side. This column of air is literally bobbing up and down for a short while, and with each upward bounce it projects warm moist air into the colder zone near the summit. Condensation occurs at the top of the air column, and a saucer-shaped lenticular cloud is born. As the column of air moves up again, it forms another lenticular cloud beneath the first, and so on. Piles of these neat little clouds may be stacked up one beneath the other, or the first one may move off before the next cloud forms, carried along by air currents in a procession, like ducklings following one another.

Sometimes lenticular clouds have circular rings around them, which increases their resemblance to the classic flying saucer of 1950s comics. Lenticular clouds can also acquire a strange spinning motion, suggesting that the air may be twisting in a vortex beneath them. These are called rotor clouds, and reinforce the impression of unearthly, self-propelled vehicles flying through the sky.

at risk, and rely for protection on complex metal barriers built on the slopes above to break the fall of avalanches. Forests are also an effective barrier and some villages have a wedge-shaped forest situated immediately above them, its sharp end pointing up the slope to intercept and diffuse any descending avalanche. Both people and livestock are forbidden from entering such forests, so that the trees suffer no depredations, for their survival is aleady precarious at such altitudes. Known as *bannwalds* – 'forbidden forest' – these green defences show how important trees once were in hindering avalanches, and the extent to which deforestation is responsible for aggravating the avalanche problem.

The wedge shapes of the bannwalds can be reproduced in stone and these are used to protect many Swiss churches and farmhouses, pointing uphill like a phalanx of giant masonry arrowheads, one behind each building.

A snowflake is the epitome of lightness and delicacy, and snow settles soft and thick in the mountains, but in an avalanche snow is utterly transformed into a substance of terrifying, life-crushing mass. It is speed that makes the difference. The fastest avalanche ever measured travelled at 217 mph (349 km/h). This extraordinary speed was recorded in 1898 at Glarnisch in Switzerland, where the avalanche crossed a valley a mile (1.6 km) wide at the bottom of the slope and hit the opposite side with such force that it shot up the valley wall for some distance, then thundered back down into the valley again. While this was an exceptional avalanche, speeds of 200 mph (320 km/h) are not uncommon. They can occur because the avalanche literally 'takes off', rising from the ground and travelling downhill on a cushion of air, which releases it from the drag of frictional forces and allows it to accelerate unchecked. The tremendous speed pushes air ahead of the avalanche, generating a shockwave as powerful as that from an exploding bomb. It can pick up solidly built adults and send them sailing through the air, and lift a small truck and flatten it against a tree. The shockwave can demolish sturdy buildings, paving the way for the avalanche to do further damage.

Japanese scientists have measured the force of the snow as it collides with obstacles, and found the impact to be as much as 13.5 tons per sq ft (145 tonnes per m^2).

WHITE DEATH *A small avalanche descends from a peak in the Himalayas (left). Deforestation in the European Alps has increased the damage caused by avalanches each year and anti-avalanche barriers are needed (above).*

One-fortieth of this force would be sufficient to flatten a modern frame-built house.

Internally, that colossal momentum is sufficient to force out every molecule of air when the snow finally comes to a halt and the avalanche is over. This is why avalanches set into solid ice, as hard as concrete, making it impossible for victims to scrabble their way to the surface, even if only buried by a few feet of 'snow'.

But how does an avalanche begin? It almost invariably involves snow that has built up in several successive layers over a period of time. The crucial weakness that starts an avalanche rolling is the formation of a more mobile interface between two of the snow layers. This can happen if the surface of one day's snow is partially melted by the sun, then refrozen as ice before being covered by more snow. The thin ice layer is as good as oil in lubricating the point where the separate layers join.

Meltwater seeping between an old, well-compacted layer of snow and a thick, fluffy new layer above it can also mobilise the upper layer, as can feathery hoar-frost crystals formed on the surface of an earlier snow layer during very cold, clear weather. Each of these is a potentially treacherous source of instability that may lie deep below fresh layers of snow, like a time bomb ticking slowly on, until the moment when the overlying snow reaches a critical mass and is triggered into motion by some slight vibration. A lone skier can be sufficient to trigger the fall, or even a loud noise. When, in 1800, Napoleon took his troops across the Alps into Italy, he cautioned the scouts ahead not to 'cry or call out for fear of causing a fall of avalanches'.

The greater the vibration, the bigger the potential avalanche. In 1970 an earthquake in the Andes generated the largest recorded avalanche, which descended on the town of Yungay in Peru, instantly entombing it in ice and taking 18 000 lives. A similar death toll occurred in 1916, during fighting between Austrian and Italian troops in the Dolomite Mountains. The shellfire directed at the opposing front was loud enough to trigger occasional avalanches, and when the troops noticed this, both sides retrained their gun-sights on the snow-laden slopes above, and deliberately

began setting off avalanches. The direct fire produced ever larger falls of snow, and 18 000 troops were buried alive in prisons of ice. Bodies were still being recovered from the site almost 40 years later.

Life to the Lowlands

The chill waters that flow from the mountains are often responsible for bringing rejuvenating sediment to the tired soils of agricultural lowlands. In North America the average rate of land loss through erosion on the plains and lowlands is estimated at 1/2 in (1 cm) per thousand years, whereas on the steep slopes of mountain peaks it can be 10-20 times as high. Rates of erosion are higher on those mountains with heavier rainfall and on mountains with steeper slopes and more dissected rocks. Among the highest annual rates in the world are those in the Japan Alps, at 1/12 in (2 mm) per year, while the mountains of New Zealand often rival this figure. This sediment all comes to rest somewhere: on the lower slopes, on the plains below, or under the sea. Where it comes to rest in river valleys, or over the surrounding lowlands during widespread flooding, the sediment creates productive agricultural lands.

The southernmost point of the Red Sea narrows down to almost nothing: it is a sea that has constantly to fight for its outlet to the wider ocean. To the south lies a huge flat expanse of dull, greyish gravel and sand, crossed by innumerable rivulets and temporary streams, whose pattern changes with every wet season. As the swollen rivers writhe about the plain in response to the torrential flows of rain, so fresh cargoes of sediment, too heavy to remain waterborne, are unloaded onto the land. The plains grow year by year, spreading silty tentacles of land into the sea and threatening to clog up the narrow channel from the Red Sea into the Gulf of Aden.

Looking westwards, the origin of all this new land can be found – the Semien Mountains. The Semiens are part of the great Ethiopian Dome, a granite mound of fantastic size and height built up by successive upwellings of molten lava, a viscous type of lava that is too thick and sluggish to erupt into volcanic cones, but repeatedly surges up and spreads over the pre-existing granite to build layer upon layer of greyish-black rock.

The last spurts of red-hot rock were added to the Ethiopian Dome 4-5 million years ago, and then all went quiet. But

Down from the Mountains *Erosion of the fragile volcanic rocks of Ethiopia's Semien Mountains brings life to the plains below, where the soil is enriched by the annual influx of sediment. Deposited sediment at the southern end of the Red Sea has reduced the exit to a narrow channel (above).*

rivers had already begun cutting into the most susceptible points on the high granite surface. Then came the ice ages, when glaciers formed on the coldest zones and gnawed more determinedly into the hard granitic mass. By the time the glaciers retreated, there was devastating damage to the summit of the Ethiopian Dome, and the thick silts now being washed down onto the plains below are easily scraped from the dissected and vulnerable surface by the annual rains. The mountains are, in a sense, passive players in this great drama of rain and river, but their silent and colossal presence affects the land for hundreds of miles around, shaping the coastline, pinching up the outlet of a sea, and providing fresh, fertile sediments on the adjoining plains.

2 Living Mountains

Day Begins *Hunched on a rock, a pika soaks up the early morning sunshine.*

Broad-winged ravens, eagles and lammergeiers float upon the unseen air currents and thermals generated around the highest crags on the Earth's surface. Down on the ground, mountain ranges are the haunt of burrowing rodents such as marmots, pikas and chinchillas, a precarious home for those sure-footed acrobats of the rocks, the mountain goats and sheep, and a welcome refuge for persecuted species such as wolves, bears, lynxes and mountain lions. Climbing the mountainside, each zone has its own distinctive vegetation, yielding in the highest peaks to an alpine zone where only the very hardiest shrubs, mosses and lichens can survive.

Fiery Blooms *Colorado's rimrock paintbrush.*

FROM FOOTHILLS TO SUMMIT

The journey up a high mountain is like a voyage through many different worlds. From the shelter and luxuriance of low ground to the punishing conditions much higher up, each level makes its mark on the shape of living plants.

The world's smallest trees, as stunted and gnarled as Japanese bonsai, grow wild on high mountain slopes. They are conifers such as pines and spruces, their trunks bent over to grow horizontally, their branches snaking away low over the ground, intermeshed with those of neighbouring trees. They are pruned not by human hands, but by extreme cold and mountaintop winds.

This dwarf forest, no more than a mat of woody vegetation standing just a few inches clear of the ground, is known by its German name *krummholtz*, which means 'twisted wood'. It is found along the tree line in some parts of the European Alps and in many other mountains around the world. Krummholtz occurs at the point where the survival mechanisms of trees – even these, the hardiest of conifers – are finally defeated by the worsening climate which accompanies increasing altitude.

Krummholtz is living proof of the adaptability of trees, as a simple experiment shows. If a forester takes a seed from the small woody cone of a krummholtz pine, carries it down to the foothills of the same mountain range and plants it there, it grows straight and strong, eventually reaching 60 ft (18 m) or more – the normal height for its species. This tall young tree shares the same anatomy and physiology with its tiny stooping parent. But the parent was moulded and modified in its youth, almost beyond recognition, by the harsh temperatures and vicious winds of the high mountains. A few feet higher up the mountain and the krummholtz trees finally disappear, giving way to the low hummocky vegetation of the alpine zone.

Return to the krummholtz in winter, and the trees will be entirely covered with a thick undulating blanket of snow. Prostrate trunks and intermeshed branches create a springy platform on which the snow can rest and accumulate. Here lies the key to the survival of these trees. While winter winds howl around the peaks, reducing the effective temperature for living beings to such low levels that little can survive their icy blast, the krummholtz trees are insulated by the snow, under which the temperature is a steady 0°C (32°F). Their needles and delicate buds are protected, and the environment within this miniature forest assists the survival of animals as well. In the space beneath the snow-covered krummholtz canopy, lit by a

FLAILED BY THE WIND *Growing at over 10 000 ft (3000 m), these Rocky Mountain conifers face a constant and relentless adversary: the wind.*

SOUTHERN SPLENDOUR *In the highlands of Tierra del Fuego, lengas (southern beeches) glow with autumn colour. Winters here are long and hard.*

diffuse white light, voles and shrews scuttle like squeaking giants, their backs rubbing against the lowest branches of the trees.

Mountain winds blow all year round, not just in winter. These blasts of desiccating air kill the buds on trees on the side that habitually feels their full impact. Buds on the other side, with their minimal shelter, can usually survive and develop. It is this which makes the trees bend over to one side: in fact, they are growing on one side, while dying on the other. (The same effect creates bent-over trees near the coast, where constant sea breezes shape trees.) The wind is coaxing the tree into its distinctive shape as skillfully as any topiarist.

The protective effect of snow, meanwhile, combines with the wind to miniaturise the krummholtz trees. Any trunks or branches that grow upwards and therefore protrude from the cover of winter snow are annihilated by the wind. In this way, the blanket of snow both creates the krummholtz and ensures its survival.

Farther down the mountain slopes taller trees have the same bent-over shape. These are called flag trees, and while they are far larger than the krummholtz, they are still considerably smaller than the tall straight trees on the forested slopes below. They do not bend at such a young age as the krummholtz trees because they are partially sheltered by their neighbouring flag trees and by the forests below. For the walker ascending the mountain, flag trees are like signposts, pointing to the tree line just ahead. They mark the point at which trees are beginning to lose the battle with the altitude.

ZONE ABOVE ZONE

The transition marked by the tree line is just one of many changes in vegetation encountered during the ascent of a mountain. There are several distinct zones at different levels, typically ranging from forest in the foothills to sparse alpine vegetation near the summit. The tree line is unusual in its sharpness, however: the transition from one zone to another is not distinctly marked elsewhere and one type of vegetation grades imperceptibly into another.

Climbing a mountain is equivalent in many ways to walking away from the Equator towards the polar regions. In the lowest of the foothills, the vegetation will be like that of the surrounding countryside – forests of beech, oak and other broad-leaved trees around the Alps, tropical rain forest around the Mountains of the Moon in Rwanda, monsoon forest around the southern Himalayas, juniper and pinyon forest in the southern Rockies. Ascending a little higher, these forests give way to those of hardier trees, often conifers such as pine and spruce. Such coniferous forests are typical of the Alps, the Rockies and the Himalayas, and are roughly equivalent to the boreal (northern) coniferous forest that covers Canada, Scandinavia and Siberia. Above the tree line, the alpine vegetation is similar to that of the tundra zone in the Arctic, with tough grasses and sedges, and low mounds or 'cushions' of cold-resistant flowering plants. Finally, there is snow and ice on the mountain summit, a virtually lifeless terrain like that of the polar ice caps. An ascent of 2500 ft (760 m) is equivalent, in terms of vegetation changes, to travelling about 400 miles (640 km) towards the North or South Pole.

Vegetation zones on mountain slopes were first recorded scientifically by the German explorer Alexander von Humboldt, who noticed the gradual changes in plant life while scaling the Andes between 1845 and 1862. However, these multiple zones had long been known, and skillfully utilised, by native mountain people in the Andes and elsewhere. They grew their different arable crops at the most favourable levels, journeying down the mountainsides to collect wood from the forests, and travelling up to the high open meadows to graze their livestock.

Humboldt's scientific work was continued in the 1890s by an American geographer, C. Hart Merriam, who studied the San Francisco Mountains of northern Arizona. These mountains encompass a dramatic range of different environments. They are

Privileged Position
On the lower slopes of the Rockies, pines and aspens grow tall and straight. At higher altitudes, the same trees look very different.

Natural Resilience *The alpenrose flourishes near the tree line. Its tough evergreen leaves are built to survive wind and frost. Overleaf: A moss campion bursts into brief summer brilliance on an Alaskan peak.*

surrounded by hot sagebrush desert, and this is the vegetation which clothes their lower slopes. As the altitude increases, desert gives way to dry, low-growing juniper-pinyon forest, then to mixed forest of ponderosa pine, gambel oak, quaking aspen and other species. It is the power of the mountain slopes to intercept rain-bearing winds and relieve them of their cargo of moisture that allows lush forest to grow here, on a mountain surrounded by desert. Ascending farther, rainfall is still plentiful but the temperature falls, and conifers begin to predominate. This zone, where the pines, firs and spruces take over, is equivalent to the northern boreal forest of Canada, and Merriam called it the 'Canadian zone'. Next comes the 'Hudsonian zone', named for northern Canada's Hudson Bay. This zone includes the timber line, with tough species such as the Engelmann spruce and subalpine fir growing just below and on the line, sculpted by the wind into flag trees and krummholtz. Finally, above the timber line, is the arctic-alpine zone, with its grasses, sedges and wild flowers. At its upper limit, only a few lichens, clinging fast to wind-scoured rocks, are able to survive. Right at the top, the vegetation gives way to snow on the highest peaks. Far below this frozen landscape, but only a few miles distant, the desert swelters in temperatures of 32°C (90°F) or more.

HEAT IN HIGH PLACES

For every 600 ft (180 m) up a mountain, the temperature drops, on average, by 1°C (2°F). Despite this, it can sometimes be much hotter by day on a mountain peak than it is far below, if the peak projects above the clouds and is warmed by the sun.

There are many local variations in mountain vegetation zones. In the European Alps, a zone of shrubby bushes lies between the tree line and the low alpine vegetation on many mountain slopes. This includes bush-forming species such as dwarf mountain pine, hairy alpenrose (a type of rhododendron), spring heath, dwarf alpine willow and green alder. Higher still, ranging above 6700 ft (2000 m), are low woody heaths with shrubs such as cowberry, bilberry, dwarf azalea and dwarf juniper. An unusual type of vegetation known as 'hedgehog heath' is found on dry mountain peaks near the Mediterranean – including the southern slopes of the Pyrenees, the *sierras* of central and southern Spain, Italian mountains such as the Apennines and Mount Etna, and fabled Greek mountains such as Parnassus and Olympus. Hedgehog heaths are also found in the mountain ranges of North Africa, such as the Atlas Mountains, revealing the ancient connections between these two landmasses. In hedgehog heath, the shrubs grow in compact low mounds and protect themselves against grazing animals such as ibex, chamois and domestic goats, by long sharp spines. Those more delicate plants without spines, growing between the spiky cushions, are laced with toxic or foul-tasting chemical substances.

Lodgepoles and Quakers

Many plants show special adaptations to the unstable nature of their environment, where rockfalls can change the face of a mountain in moments. In the Rocky Mountains, areas of forest are regularly flattened by avalanches or windstorms. The first trees to recolonise the cleared area are often quaking aspens or lodgepole pines. Quaking aspens almost

Hugging the Ground *By spreading out close to the rock, mountain juniper avoids the worst of the wind. In winter it is protected by a layer of snow.*

always regenerate from hidden roots, which spread under the ground and can throw up new trees when the opportunity arises – a speedy option that gives aspens the edge over other trees. An aspen grove may include 100 or more trunks but just one root system from which they all spring. Few aspen seeds germinate successfully today, but botanists believe that the climate in the Rockies a century ago was wetter and more favourable to germination, so that all the aspens now living may originally have come from seeds which germinated at that time.

RECORD NUMBERS

The largest number of vegetation zones occur on high mountains in the tropics. On some, the journey to the summit is equivalent to walking from the Equator to the North or South Pole. Other mountains are remarkable for their unique plant species. Mount Olympus in Greece has 20 such species, called endemics. These are typically found on lone peaks where they have evolved in isolation.

BIRTH BY FIRE *These lodgepole pines have to endure cold, heat and sometimes summer fires. Paradoxically, forest fires help the pines by triggering the release of their seeds.*

SURVIVORS *In Bolivia's Sajarma Valley, at over 16 000 ft (4900 m), cushion-shaped* yareta *plants have to resist both sunshine and cold.*

Lodgepole pines benefit from a different sort of disaster – forest fires, which occur naturally in the Rockies, though many today are of human origination. The cones of lodgepole pines are thick with sticky resin and open to liberate their seeds only after exposure to the heat of a forest fire. The seeds are then released into a clear space, with a dressing of fresh nutrient-rich ash to fertilise the soil.

Above the tree line, there is a similar survival value in the low cushiony mounds which are the natural growth form of many alpine plants. This shape offers some protection against the sort of damage that tumbling rocks and scree might inflict on a more spreading twiggy plant. The cushiony outline, with its dense foliage and the vulnerable buds buried deep within the mound of leaves, also protects against the damaging effects of ice and cold winds. What is more, it helps to trap soil and its own discarded leaves around the plant, thus providing itself with fertile growing conditions and resisting the forces of erosion on a steep slope.

Many cushion plants have a covering of fine fuzzy hairs that trap a layer of air around the plant and improve its insulation. Others have a waxy surface to resist the dehydrating effects of wind. Long taproots are also a common feature of these cushion plants. As well as giving them access to water, which may be scarce on steep slopes where the rainfall quickly drains away downhill, a taproot provides stability and a solid anchor, which helps them to resist uprooting by the wind, and to withstand the occasional violent movements of scree and soil on the surface. Moss campion, a successful mountain plant in both Europe and North America, has a deep taproot and the slow growth that is typical of cushion plants, adding only a few millimetres of growth and one or two leaves to each stem in a year. Many clumps of moss campion are over a century old.

The brilliant flowers of mountain meadows, and the large showy blooms of many small alpine plants such as the mountain gentian and the edelweiss, are an adaptation to the shortness of the summer growing season in the mountains. With such a brief opportunity to fatten their seeds before

VYING FOR ATTENTION *A myriad of blooms compete for the attention of pollinating insects in this Rocky Mountain alpine meadow. They have only a short time to produce seeds.*

winter returns, mountain flowers have no time to waste in attracting pollinators such as bees and butterflies. In the Rocky Mountains, the list of potential pollinators also includes various species of hummingbird which fly up from South America for the breeding season, and sip nectar from the vivid red blooms of the paintbrushes and gilias, the purplish bonnets of the Colorado columbine, and other mountain flowers.

No mountain, even the most conical of volcanoes, is a perfectly regular environment, identical on all sides. The irregularity of mountains – in shape and climate – disturbs the basic pattern of the vegetation zones, producing a complex patchwork. The sun is an important factor. In the Northern Hemisphere, south-facing slopes receive more sunlight than north-facing ones. The sunlight warms the soil and plants on these slopes, allowing many kinds of vegetation to creep up much higher than they do on the northern slopes. Overlying this pattern is the effect of the prevailing rain-bearing winds, which make the windward slopes far more moist than the leeward slopes.

A Complex Patchwork

Even this pattern is far from simple. In southern Tibet, the terrain is for the most part parched and bleak, because the Himalayas act as a barrier, intercepting the monsoon winds. But where rivers cut across the Himalayas in a north-south direction, the rain-bearing winds can penetrate, and there are surprising pockets of lush forest with junipers, silver firs, larches, birches and brilliantly flowered rhododendrons, red and yellow, growing up to 60 ft (18 m) tall.

Adding to the complexity of the pattern are the many intricate movements of the winds around the peaks, scouring some slopes and making them hostile to plant life, while sparing others. The state of the soil, whether acid or alkaline, the steepness of the slope, and its stability or instability, all introduce further levels of variability.

In the Alps and other European ranges, the long history of human exploitation has left its mark. There are few places where the original tree line is intact, and virtually no unmodified native forests. Many of the mountain areas that were once forested have been converted to shrubby vegetation, or to heath or hedgehog heath, by human activities such as tree-felling and the grazing of domestic animals. In many areas, goats have kept the tree line at an unnaturally low altitude for millennia.

In more recent times manmade pollution has taken its

SNOW-PATCH PLANTS

In the European Alps, late-lying patches of snow, such as those which collect in slight hollows or in areas shaded from the sun, have a decisive effect on plant life. Snow patches protect plants from periods of bad spring weather on the one hand, but they also prevent plant growth. Yet when the snow does finally melt, it provides extra surface moisture which may help the plants to grow. By looking at the types of plant present, a botanist can estimate how long the snow patch persists. An abundance of mosses indicates that the period without snow is less than eight weeks: flowering plants cannot grow here because there is not enough time to flower and seed. Dwarf willow, alpine buttercup, scree saxifrage and blue arabis indicate that there is three to four months without snow cover. Not all plants are held back by snow, however: in the Himalayas, primulas with their buds and young leaves shielded by scaly sheaths, force their way up through the unmelted snow to open their yellow, blue or purplish flowers.

Flowers among the Snow *In the European Alps, glacier crowfoot often grows near patches of late-lying snow. Its flowers turn pink as they age.*

toll. More than 4 million cars drive through the St Gotthard Pass in the Swiss Alps every year. The roads approaching the pass are now under increasingly serious threat from avalanches and the cars themselves are part of the impending problem.

Air pollution, from industrial emissions and traffic fumes, is weakening the coniferous forests of the European Alps. It is opening the trees up to attack by insects and fungi, and leading to the premature death of many trees. The thinning out of the forests has reduced their ability to catch avalanches and prevent them from falling onto roads and villages below. Throughout the Alps, there is a steadily increasing toll of damage from avalanches.

Alpine Highway *A road snakes its way over the St Gotthard Pass, while a road tunnel passes beneath it. Both have increased pollution from traffic.*

Deforestation

Switzerland has experienced severe deforestation before. In the 19th century her forests became so depleted by felling that the number of avalanches increased sharply. Great communal efforts were made to replant and maintain special forests, called *bannwalds*, that would protect settlements. The efforts were successful, but in the past few decades air pollution has debilitated the forests, and over half the trees are now thought to be unhealthy. Many are terminally ill, and the bannwalds are now being replaced or supplemented by steel barriers to hold back the snow.

Switzerland is at the advanced end of a process of devastating deforestation which is just beginning to gather momentum in many other mountainous areas of the world. In the clear, thin, scentless atmosphere of the high plateau in northern Nepal, a line of mules or yaks passing by on the trails will, suddenly and unexpectedly, fill the air with the rich smell of pinewood. The smell seems extraordinarily strong and exotic in the cold atmosphere of this area.

The aromatic loads, covered by sacking on the animals' backs, are hauled up from the southern slopes of the Himalayas. The timber comes not from plantations, but from primeval native pine forests. The demands for timber – for construction materials and fuel, tools and tent poles, kitchen utensils and decorative objects – comes from communities above the tree line as well as from those who live among the forests, so the mountain trees have long been under immense pressure. Steadily, over the centuries, those forests have been dwindling in size, but the effects were gradual enough in the past to be accommodated by the environment and the human population. Even though the forests were not being replanted, there was some natural regeneration. With the new demands of the modern era, the pace of forest loss has quickened considerably with disturbing effects.

A traditional system for the management of the Nepali forests once helped to protect them from over-exploitation. Among the peasant farmers there was a limit on how much wood and forage each family could extract. This restraint by the peasantry was in marked contrast to the attitude of the Nepali kings, who, from the 9th century AD onwards, ordered the felling of trees on a large scale to provide timbers for their temples, monuments and palaces.

Despite these onslaughts on the forests, sufficient areas remained around the villages

Fuel from the Forest *Porters carry pine wood to a tourist hotel in Nepal (left). In this part of the world, wood for fuel is a rapidly shrinking resource. In Nepal's Saganartha National Park (right), a warden checks a batch of trees. These blue pine saplings will help to regenerate the park's forests.*

LIFE ON THE TREE LINE

The tree line varies with latitude, because tropical and subtropical climates allow trees to thrive at greater heights. The closer to the poles a mountain is, the lower the tree line occurs. Other factors also come into play, such as rainfall and snowfall, wind speeds and soil characteristics. In the European Alps, the tree line varies between 6000 and 7000 ft (1800 and 2100 m). Some tropical mountains have no tree line – many of the peaks in New Guinea for example are forested right to the summit. In the Himalayas and the Andes, the tree line stands at around 12 000 ft (3600 m), whereas on Mount McKinley in Alaska it is no higher than 3000 ft (900 m). The highest forests in the world are found in Tibet, extending to 15 000 ft (4600 m). Although the Rockies are at about the same latitude, their tree line only reaches 11 000 ft (3300 m).

FOREST'S EDGE *On a mountain in Washington State, scattered trees grow among alpine flowers. Instead of being fixed, the tree line around a mountain top is a living boundary that is always on the move.*

for the peasants to continue their age-old management system satisfactorily. What destroyed the system was, ironically, a government measure designed to protect the forests. To curb the seizure of forests by the rich and powerful, all forests were nationalised in 1956, and the size of holdings limited. Properly administered the scheme might have worked, but there were too few staff to map the forests properly, and the laws were easily manipulated by the affluent classes to exploit the forests for timber even more intensively than before. As the peasants in the villages saw this happening, with the apparent backing of the new laws, their own restraint began to seem pointless. They abandoned the traditional limits on extracting timber and foliage.

By 1978 it was clear that the nationalisation programme had badly misfired, and new laws were passed granting forests to

Gap in the Forest *In the North Cascades in Washington State, a rectangle of bare mountainside shows where an area of forest has been clear-cut. This form of logging greatly accelerates erosion.*

community ownership. Slowly the old management system is being revived, but the people of Nepal are discovering that it is much easier to destroy traditions than to rebuild them.

The demands of the modern tourist industry are responsible for adding greatly to the current wave of deforestation. Every year Ghorapani, one of the busiest tourist villages, plays host to 25 000 Westerners on trekking holidays, who pass through and spend a night or two here, accompanied by about the same number of guides and porters. Wood is needed for cooking the trekkers' meals, and for providing daily hot showers – a Western luxury that is inappropriate in an area where fuel is so scarce.

Other demands also contribute to deforestation. The leaves of certain trees have long been harvested for use as animal fodder, mainly for goats. With the thinning of the forests, the few remaining trees are raided for leaves again and again. Some now have just a few green sprouts from their highest branches, but, with hungry herds to feed, the villagers still climb these skeletal trees and pluck the only remaining leaves. For a few seasons, the trees can draw on their reserves and push out new leaves, encouraging the villagers to believe that this relentless harvesting will not kill the trees. But in time the trees become exhausted by the constant marauding and die.

When mountain slopes lose their covering of trees, they are far more susceptible to mud slides and rockfalls. The rate of soil erosion increases sharply, and this in turn leads to further losses of trees and other vegetation, as well as a loss of terraced agricultural land, since terraces are often swept away in mud slides or deeply buried.

The soil and mud which rushes down the denuded slopes ultimately flows into a river, and this can have devastating effects on fish and other forms of life. Deforestation of steep slopes in the Cascade Mountains, and other areas of the north-west Pacific coast of Canada and the USA, has led to the pollution of streams, estuaries and coastal regions by soil particles. This in turn has damaged the salmon that once swam in from the sea, and travelled up these same streams – formerly clear and sparkling – to reach their breeding grounds. Similar stories of river and coastal pollution come from deforested mountain regions in many other parts of the world. With mountains, as with all natural habitats, human interference often has far-reaching effects.

Loosened Grip *Tree roots help to keep loose rock in place. On this hillside in Nepal, clearance for farming has triggered a landslip.*

Wildlife of the Mountains

For animals, life in mountains has it rewards. There is abundant space and freedom from many of the competitors that live on lower ground. But mountain life also exacts a price: the need to struggle against an often hostile climate.

Watching a herd of ibex escape across a mountain slope in the European Alps, it sometimes seems as if they are flying in the face of gravity. With a miraculous agility and surefootedness, they can traverse smooth slabs of rock, run swiftly across ice-covered crags, leap apparently impassable gullies and ravines, and ascend precipitous cliff-faces where no footholds are visible. Even a herd of young ibex with their mothers can perform such feats, leaping 12 to 15 ft (3.7 to 4.6 m) with each bound, travelling unhesitatingly along razor-edged ridges, around blind corners, down narrow 'chimneys' between two cliff-faces, and up rock walls without seeming to look before they leap. Rocks and boulders loosened by their hooves may thunder down into the valleys below, but the ibex race on. They are apparently oblivious to, and somehow immune from, the dangers of going down with boulders that fall beneath their weight, or of being hit by a rock-slide which an ibex farther up the slope has unleashed. Often the ibex have disappeared from view a long time before the thunderous rocks have come to rest amid their echoes far below.

The spectacular climbing abilities of the ibex depend on hooves that are as hard as steel, with rough undersides for traction, and soft rubbery pads in the hollow part which provide a grip on ice or wet rock like that of a rubber suction pad. The distance between the two parts of the cloven hoof is not fixed. They can be splayed apart and then brought closer together to clamp onto a rough surface, or kept tightly together for insertion into a narrow foothold, or they can be manipulated in a variety of other ways as the nature of a particular terrain demands.

The 'dewclaws' on the back of each leg come into play when the animal encounters a vertical surface. The dewclaw is vestigial, as it is in other hoofed mammals – it is the remains of one of the digits which evolution has dispensed with in the development of the two-digit hoof from a five-digit paw. But this dewclaw is not totally useless, because it can help the ibex to brace itself against the rock behind it as the animal descends a precipice.

Horned Might

Male ibex must perform these perilous acrobatics with the handicap of a pair of horns; they have to maintain their balance despite this additional weight on the head. The backward-curving and heavily ringed horns are up to 33 in (84 cm) long in the

Quick Descent *Using its rear feet as brakes, a chamois, a smaller, daintier cousin of the ibex, runs down a rocky slope, proving itself no less an acrobat than its relative.*

Show of Strength *Spotlit by afternoon sunshine, two male ibexes show off their horns. This is the first stage in establishing which of the two is the dominant male. Unlike antlers, horns grow throughout life.*

ibex of the European Alps, and they are even longer on some of its close relatives, such as the Siberian ibex whose horns can be more than 55 in (140 cm) long. These fantastic natural weapons are used principally to intimidate other males, not for protection from predators. The fully mature and dominant males have the largest and rely on their impressive size to overawe younger males during the breeding season from October to December. They turn their heads sideways-on to their rivals, to demonstrate the size of their horns by presenting them in silhouette. If the rival does not accept defeat at this stage, there may be a violent fight in which both males rear up on their hind legs, charge at each other and clash their horns angrily against one another.

By these displays and fights, a dominant male with large horns asserts his ownership of a harem of females and drives away any other males to ensure sole mating rights for himself. His genes, which are passed on extensively to the next generation, mean that future generations of male ibexes will have horns at least as large. The price for this sexual success is the great weight of the outgrowths themselves, and males often try to rest them against rocks to relieve their aching neck muscles. They may even sleep on their feet if this allows the horns to be supported by a rock.

The horns of the male ibex have been their downfall in a world where human predators can kill at a distance. Trophy-seeking hunters have greatly reduced the numbers of ibex in almost every part of its range, which includes the Iberian peninsula, the European Alps, the Caucasus, central Asia, Arabia and North Africa. The species was virtually exterminated in the Alps by the end of the 19th century, leaving only a small population in the Valle d'Aosta of the Italian Alps. To prevent this herd's total disappearance, the hunting of ibex was banned and, in 1922, the Gran Paradiso National Park was set up to protect it. By that time, numbers were already increasing, to the extent that ibex could be removed and taken to Switzerland and other parts of the European Alps – a highly successful reintroduction which has produced populations of ibex many thousands strong.

Hunting of ibex is still banned in the national parks of the Alpine region. Apart from golden eagles, which may take some newborn kids, there are few predators and most ibex die of natural causes, often falling victim to avalanches and blizzards. In the Gran Paradiso National Park, more than 100 ibex can be killed by bad weather in a single winter, and in the Pamir Mountains of central Asia, 10 per cent of the ibex population is thought to be killed each winter by avalanches. Ironically, it is often the ibex herds themselves that have set off the avalanches, by walking across unstable snow-covered slopes and causing vibrations that loosen the upper layers of the snow.

Ibex are exposed to the hazards of avalanches in the European Alps because they live above the tree line, ranging up as far as the snow line and feeding in the most exposed parts of the mountains. Their food consists of grasses, sedges, the small tough leaves of shrubs, and some lichens which they scrape from the rocks. In some mountainous regions, however, ibex do descend into the forest during the worst of the winter weather.

Rocky Defences

In the mountains of southern Africa, such as the Drakensberg and Brandberg ranges, there are no wild indigenous goats or sheep such as the ibex. Instead, a small antelope, the klipspringer, has evolved to fill the niche they occupy elsewhere. Its name means 'cliff jumper', and the klipspringer can leap up near-vertical surfaces to escape predators such as leopards, landing with all four feet together on a ledge of rock no bigger than a large coin. Standing on the top of an unscalable crag, it is able to stare down nonchalantly at its enemy. Klipspringers have a thick coat of hair, with an unusual mossy texture, which is thought to help them to withstand the bruising impact of the rocks as they vault about in their mountain environment.

Their reliance on their nimbleness in rocky places is shared by the mountain sheep and goats, whose first impulse when threatened is to rush for the most inaccessible crag and to climb it as fast as possible. American scientists have studied the Rocky Mountains' bighorn sheep, using implanted devices which measure heart rates and transmit the findings electronically. They have shown that the animals' hearts begin to beat faster – a sign of stress – when they are 400 ft (120 m) or more from a vertical surface. The farther the creatures are from a cliff, the more their hearts race. This information has helped conservationists to

RED CELLS GALORE

The blood of the vicuña, an Andean grazing mammal which is found between altitudes of 13 000 ft and 18 000 ft (4000 and 5500 m) in the Andes, has three times as many red cells per drop as the blood of an average human. This adaptation to altitude enables the animal to absorb oxygen more efficiently.

On the Lookout *Sensing trouble, a herd of Sind ibexes (left) watch for signs of danger. Huge horns mark the leader of the herd, seen here in the centre. African klipspringers (opposite) lack the ibex's bulk and its formidable horns, but they too have nonslip hooves. They stand on tiptoe.*

restore a landscape after a large-scale opencast mining operation. By working out the needs of the Rocky Mountain bighorns, they could design a landscape that made the animals feel secure.

Some mountain sheep and goats divide their time between the craggy heights and the forested slopes slightly lower down. The chamois, found in European ranges such as the Alps, Pyrenees and Carpathians as well as in parts of Turkey, inhabit the altitudes around the tree line. During the winter chamois always descend into the forests, often to the beech woods of the lower slopes, to find more plentiful food and to escape the weather and the risk of avalanches. Their winter food consists of mosses, lichens, buds, bark and leaves.

Some of the adults, particularly the males, may stay in the forests in summer, but the females and young head up to the alpine pastures. Pregnant females separate from the rest of the herd, and each goes off alone to find a haven on some inaccessible cliff-face, safe from lynxes and foxes, and concealed from birds of prey beneath a gnarled old juniper or tucked away inside a small cave. Here, she gives birth to one or two kids, which pull themselves to their feet within an hour of their birth, and are soon following their mother as she leaps from rock to rock. A few weeks later, they rejoin the herd of females and young to graze on alpine herbs and grasses. If the midday sun grows too hot, they find a late-lying patch of snow on which to recline until they have cooled down.

Soaring in the Heights

Mountain birds, meanwhile, include the majestic golden eagle and another magnificent and widely distributed specimen: the lammergeier. This scavenges on the carcasses of klipspringers in the Drakensberg and those of ibex in the Himalayas. It is

Lofty Domain *A golden eagle surveys its mountainous habitat in north-west America. A single nesting pair can occupy a territory covering 50 sq miles (130 km²).*

LIFE IN A LAYERED HABITAT

Snowcock Flock *The Himalayan snowcock's plumage blends in well against bare rock. Snowcocks often nest at the entrances of caves.*

Making the most of habitats at different heights is a key part of survival for many mountain animals: a mountain is something like a department store, with different items available on different floors. Thanks to their powers of flight, birds are well placed to make use of such a complex environment. In the Himalayas, flocks of white and grey feathered snow pigeons feed in the cultivated fields around the villages at altitudes of about 15 000 ft (4600 m) during the day, picking up seeds and other morsels of food. As the sun sinks beneath the mountains each evening, they take to the wing, wheel about over the houses and fields as they form up into a flock, and then fly up several thousand feet to rocky cliffs above the snow line where they roost for the night. At these roosts, they are safe from golden eagles, their main predators, which rarely fly as high as this.

Snowcocks, much larger birds, the size of small turkeys, also make a daily vertical migration. They feed at higher altitudes than the snow pigeons, well above the villages, grubbing for plant tubers and other nutritious, fleshy roots. Their daily descents are made in search of water, which they drink from small ice-cold mountain lakes.

found in the mountains of Tibet, Ethiopia, Iran and Turkey as well, and once ranged throughout the European Alps; now, however, it has only a few isolated European refuges in Greece, the Pyrenees and the mountains of southern Spain. Although it belongs zoologically with the vultures, the lammergeier is not solely a scavenger: it will also seize small live prey such as monitor lizards and tortoises.

The latter are cracked open using the same technique which the lammergeier applies to large bones from carcasses. Seizing a bone in its talons, the bird soars upwards to about 300 ft (90 m), then dives a little way and drops the bone onto the rocks below, turning sharply and swooping downwards to retrieve the broken pieces from which it sucks out the nutritious marrow with its tongue. If the bone does not break the first time, the lammergeier tries again – up to four attempts have been recorded for a single bone. Favourite spots for smashing bones are used repeatedly, even though the lammergeier may have to fly several miles from its carcass to reach the place.

Distances such as these are, in any case, trivial to a bird such as a lammergeier. With a wingspan of up to 9 ft (2.7 m) and a powerful diamond-shaped tail, it can exploit the natural air currents and thermals of the mountains with extraordinary ease, flexing its wings slightly to sink 1000 ft (300 m), then effortlessly changing the angle of the tail to rise again by 3000 ft (900 m) or more and vanish over a ridge. Walkers on the

Flying High *Like its cousin the lammergeier, the Andean condor is a mountain vulture.*

high mountain pathways may hear behind them a low howling sound as the wind blows through a lammergeier's long wing feathers. Turning, they find the giant bird flying level with them, suspended as if weightless over the chasm below, its unnerving yellow eye with the bright scarlet rim staring curiously at the human intruders into its mountain world.

Lammergeiers are supremely adapted to the mountains, and never descend to low altitudes. They have been observed flying at 30 000 ft (9000 m), a height that would take them over the summit of Everest with plenty of room to spare. Somehow their lungs and general physiology are adapted to the thin atmosphere that makes this altitude so hostile to human beings. Because lammergeiers live permanently above the tree line, rocky ledges and caverns are the only nesting and roosting places available to them. The rich orange colour of the bird's breast and head feathers comes from these rocks. Iron oxide and other pigments impart the colour, and the lammergeiers deliberately rub the pigments into their feathers, for reasons that are not fully understood.

Lammergeiers have sometimes been observed swooping down on chamois and other species of mountain goats, apparently trying to make them lose their balance and so send them tumbling down the mountainside. A few travellers in the Himalayas have reported the same sort of attack on themselves. Although no one is known to have fallen victim to these tactics of the lammergeier's, it seems possible that this unusual vulture may use the perilous mountain terrain as a weapon to kill prey for itself, rather than simply feeding on carrion. There is a historical report of golden eagles using the same tactic. Thomas Johnson, a botanist who travelled in the mountains of north Wales in 1639 collecting plants, could not persuade anyone to take him up to the more remote crags: 'Our rustic guide feared the eagles nesting there, for they are accustomed to swoop crosswise on swift pinions before the faces of the cattle feeding on the precipices, and by suddenly frightening them, make them fall down the rocks and become their prey.'

BORNE ON THE WIND
Soaring effortlessly on almost motionless wings, a silhouetted lammergeier scans the ground below for signs of food.

These are not the only stories of threatening behaviour by mountain birds of prey. For centuries there have been tales told of eagles snatching babies or small children. Zoologists maintain that this is impossible, except perhaps for a newborn baby, since birds of prey cannot lift more than their own weight, and none weighs more than about 12 lb (5.4 kg). An experiment with a tame golden eagle showed that it could not take off with an 8 lb (3.6 kg) weight attached to its talons. Yet there are many detailed and convincing stories from a number of mountainous regions in different parts of the world – the French Alps, the Swiss Alps, central Anatolia, the mountains of Norway, the Italian Apennines, the Scottish Highlands and the Rocky Mountains. These tell of children up to the age of eight being abducted by eagles, lammergeiers or other large birds of prey, often apparently frenzied with hunger. Other observers have seen eagles carrying off goat kids and half-grown deer whose weights greatly exceeded the limit set by zoologists. Perhaps it is the desperation for food that permits a bird of prey to exert far more muscle power than it would normally do.

UNDERGROUND FAMILIES

Birds of prey thrive in mountain regions because they are not hindered by the difficult terrain. In fact, the complexities of intermeshed valleys, peaks and ridges can be turned to their advantage, allowing them to swoop suddenly over an outcrop of rock and down onto a peaceful grassy meadow, appearing as if from nowhere and seizing their prey within seconds. In response to this constant threat of surprise attacks, many of the vulnerable creatures of the

SENTRY DUTY *An alpine marmot stands on its back legs as it keeps watch. As well as looking out for predators, dominant males also watch for intruding rivals.*

mountains have evolved a system of sentries, posted on high lookout rocks, whose warning cries will send other members of the species running for cover.

Chamois whistle when alarmed by the appearance of an eagle, and so do the marmots, solidly built and thickly furred rodents, with short tails and a habit of standing upright on their haunches in a bear-like posture. This stance is the one favoured by the sentries, since it gives them the widest possible view over the mountain slope. Their alarm whistles, shrill and piercing, are heeded by chamois, ibex and other mountain animals, as well as by the marmots themselves, which disappear in seconds into their burrows. This system of lookouts is remarkably successful, for marmots rarely fall prey to winged predators, even the swift and powerful golden eagles.

Marmots live in extensive underground burrows which accommodate a large family, including two or more generations of young. They have separate burrows at a lower altitude for winter use. These are often very deep, their main living areas located between 4 and 10 ft (1.2 and 3m) below ground level, underneath a large boulder. The winter burrows include special latrine areas and a central chamber where the marmots hibernate in a huddle. Before hibernation begins, they block up the entrance to the burrow from the inside using stones, earth and dry grass. This blockade extends as far as 6 ft (1.8 m) underground from the entrance, to exclude predators while the marmots are at their most vulnerable.

Marmots eat only fresh green food, and it is the absence of such food that determines their period of hibernation. Those living in the more arid regions of Alaska's mountains have one of the longest hibernation periods of any mammal, retiring in the middle of June when the grass begins to wither, and sleeping until March or April of the following year. In the Rockies and the European Alps, marmots do not go into hibernation until September or October when the frost turns the leaves brown.

HIGH AND LOW

Marmots in the Tibetan region of the Himalayas venture as high as 18 000 ft (5500 m). Pikas have been recorded even higher, at 20 000 ft (6100 m) on the slopes of Everest. At the opposite end of their range, pikas are also found at sea level in far north-western Canada.

Unlike marmots, pikas – rat-sized creatures related to rabbits and hares – can eat dry vegetation and do not need to hibernate in winter. They occur in the Rockies and the Cascade Range of North America, and throughout Asia, including the mountains of Iran, the Hindu Kush and the Himalayas, and the ranges of Tibet, Mongolia, China and Siberia. During the summer they harvest grasses, flowering plants such as iris and cinquefoil, and even the lower branches of trees, which they lay out on sun-baked rocks to dry.

The resultant hay is perfectly preserved, retaining its natural colours and sweet smell, with no trace of mould on the leaves. The pikas store their hay in well-ventilated crevices among the jumbled piles of rocks, known as moraines, left long ago by retreating glaciers. The sites are carefully chosen for their shelter from snow and rain, so that the hay stays dry and fresh all winter. It is not only the pikas that benefit from these stores in winter. Seed-eating birds such as choughs, larks and mountain finches nest in the pikas' burrows and feast on the seeds that fall from the rodents' hay.

Pikas are small nervous creatures that

MAKING HAY *A pika arrives with a mouthful of grass ready to be turned into hay. Each hay pile can weigh up to 13 lb (6 kg) – 25 times as much as a pika.*

can scale near-vertical rock surfaces and are so numerous in some areas that the ground seems to be alive with their fluffy grey-furred bodies. They are the highest resident animals in the Himalayas. When severe winter blizzards confine them to their burrows, the pikas survive by eating the hay, and by tunnelling under the snow to find green plants.

Above the Snow Line

Even on a mountain's highest slopes, beyond the snow line, there is life. On the surface of the snow lives a layer of red algae, a primitive type of single-celled plant. These algae are distantly related to red seaweeds and share their pigments. Although each individual alga is extremely small, and can be seen only under a microscope, the whole patch of algae, consisting of millions of separate cells, may give a reddish tint to the snow. The algae migrate up to the surface of the snow during the day in order to absorb the maximum amount of sunlight, and then migrate downwards again at night to escape the cold.

The animals that live on the snowfields are largely scavengers, miniature insect equivalents of the vultures, preying on other insects that have been blown up onto the snows by unfavourable winds. So violent and unpredictable are the air currents of mountain regions that many small creatures – not just insects but also spiders and other small invertebrates – are sometimes blown off course in this way. Some are swept up there from far distant lowlands, including large swarms of grasshoppers and aphids which probably originated on arable crops. Minuscule young spiders, which disperse from their place of birth by becoming airborne on long strands of silk, are also vulnerable to being blown off course and ending up on the snowfields.

Migratory insects such as bees, hoverflies and butterflies may need to traverse mountain ranges in the course of their travels and to do so they fly through the same passes used by human travellers. In the Himalayas, this may involve flying to altitudes of 19000 or even 20 000 ft (5800 or 6100 m). During such migrations, freak winds can push the migrants off course and force them to land on a glacier or snowfield.

All these creatures, frozen to death on their last long journey, are meat and drink to the scavengers, which include centipedes, spiders, springtails, woodlice and beetles. Strangest of the scavengers are the grylloblattids, an order of insect that shows some resemblance to crickets and some to cockroaches, and which may be a 'living fossil' closely related to the common ancestor of these two insect groups. Few in number and confined to the icy wastes of mountains, the grylloblattids were unknown to zoologists until the early 20th century, when they were discovered on the snowfields of the Canadian Rockies.

THE EXTRAORDINARY TORRENT DUCK

The fast-flowing waters of a mountain stream are often rich in food, being so clean and well supplied with oxygen that insects such as caddis-fly larvae thrive there in great numbers. But this abundant food is difficult to get hold of because of the racing currents that sweep any unanchored animal away. One species to have risen to this challenge is the torrent duck, which lives at heights of between 5000 and 10 000 ft (1500 and 3000 m) in the Andes. It has unusually large webbed feet with which to power itself against the raging waters, and a long stiff tail which has many uses. It can be pressed downwards and used as a 'third limb' when scrambling out of water onto a slippery rock; while in the water, it can be employed as a rudder, or a hydrofoil, to deflect the pressure of the current and stabilise the duck's position. The swimming powers of this remarkable bird are so well developed that it can maintain a stationary position in a seemingly irresistible mountain torrent, and can even swim upstream, keeping its whole body out of sight under water. If danger threatens, torrent ducks often allow themselves to be swept downstream and over a waterfall, where they hide next to the rock face behind the curtain of water until they feel that it is safe to emerge.

Conquering the Current *A family of torrent ducks sets off to find food. Strong legs and feet help them to make headway upstream.*

LIVING SNOW *Stained a watermelon colour, this patch of snow teems with tiny algae. These remarkable organisms thrive at freezing point.*

Not all insects make a one-way journey into the mountains. Surprisingly, some species seem to make a deliberate migration to the high peaks in order to pass the winter, descending to the lowlands again the following spring. Several kinds of ladybirds do this in the Himalayas, flying into the mountains even if the prevailing wind is against them and heading purposefully for certain peaks where they congregate at time-honoured hibernation spots, often nestling down among dead and still-frozen ladybirds from previous years. A single site of about 10 sq yd (8 m²) may contain as many as 2 million ladybirds. The cold temperatures – a sharp contrast to those on the Indian plains from which the ladybirds originate – may allow the ladybirds to slow their metabolism down so that they can survive the winter without food. Their Himalayan retreats may also offer security from predators, although even here they are not entirely safe. Brown bears have been seen turning over rocks to reveal the huddles of ladybirds, and eating thousands of them in a few quick mouthfuls. Grizzly bears in the Rockies also feed on hibernating ladybirds.

Grasshoppers that land on snowfields and glaciers may survive the winter there, returning to the lowlands in the spring. But it is not certain that they deliberately migrate into the mountains to overwinter, and their high mortality makes this unlikely. A particular combination of migration routes, wind patterns and mountain passes regularly brings down huge swarms of the American migratory grasshopper at the same spot in the mountains of Montana, where they quickly become too chilled to be able to take off again, and so are entombed in the ice of a glacier. Some of the grasshoppers refrigerated in the glacier are believed to be more than 350 years old, and new batches are added every year. When the glacier surface melts a little in the spring, thousands of dead grasshoppers flow out in the meltwater. The frozen insects are so numerous that the glacier earned the name 'Grasshopper Glacier' from early explorers.

For those insects living permanently above the tree line, one solution to the problem of the winds is simply not to fly at all. This is the evolutionary path that more than half the insects in this zone have taken, dispensing with their ancestral wings altogether. Even many of the winged insects, while capable of flying, rarely do so.

HIGH-FLYING BUTTERFLIES

One butterfly, the diaphanous-winged apollo, lays its eggs at altitudes of up to 19 000 ft (5800 m) in the Himalayas, higher than any other butterfly. Butterflies are more abundant in alpine than arctic regions (despite similar degrees of cold) because the alpine regions do at least have relatively warm summers.

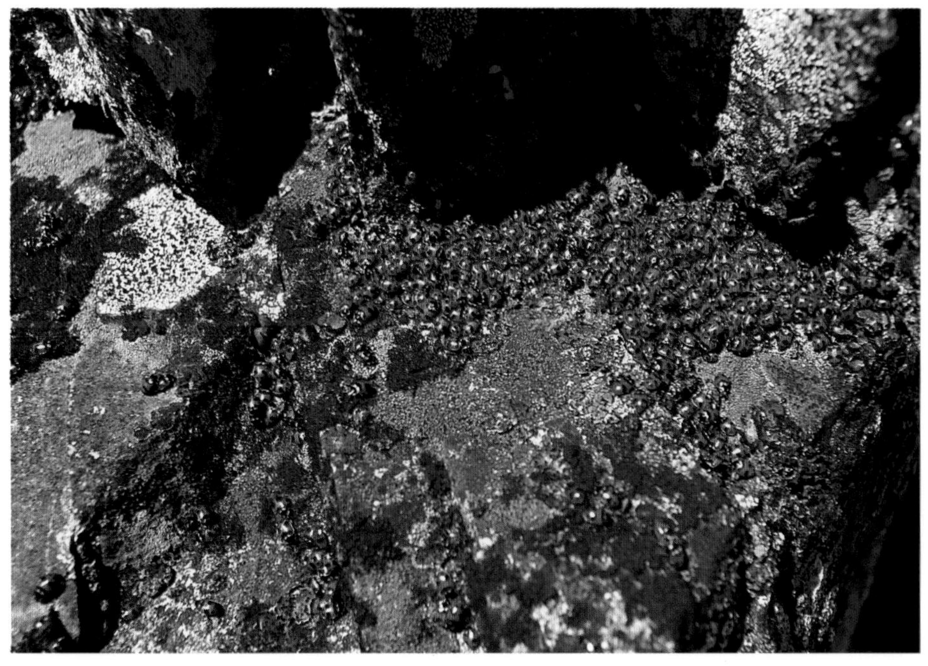

WINTER QUARTERS *Ladybirds cram together in the shelter of a rocky mountain ledge. An unpleasant taste protects them from most predators, but they provide useful winter food when times get hard.*

Islands in the Sky

Mountains impose isolation on their natural inhabitants, but they also offer safety to exiles from lower ground. This preserves unique species that are confined to particular peaks and provides protection from an increasingly crowded world.

Describing his explorations of the north-eastern region of South America in 1595, Sir Walter Raleigh wrote of a crystal mountain covered with diamonds which had a colossal waterfall cascading down it. The mountain, he wrote, resembled 'a white church tower . . . and there falleth over it a mighty river which toucheth no part of the side of the mountain but falleth to the grounde with a terrible noise and clamour, as if a thousand great bells were knocked one against another . . .' Raleigh may have seen Mount Roraima, in today's Venezuela, whose east face features an extraordinary outcrop of glittering white and pink quartz crystals, over which a waterfall plummets for thousands of feet. The diamonds were probably an embellishment of Raleigh's, added to encourage investment in further expeditions and to tempt other avaricious young explorers to accompany him.

Mount Roraima is a flat-topped mountain, known locally as a *tepuí*, one of more than 100 similar mountains that rise like rocky fortresses out of the grasslands and dense forest of this part of South America. The tepuis are block mountains or horsts (from the German word meaning 'heap'), formed from an ancient plateau of sandstone by uplift, faulting and subsequent erosion.

Mount Roraima is the tallest of the tepuís, standing 9094 ft (2772 m) high at its summit, as well as one of the most extensive. Cascading down the sheer sides of another nearby tepuí, Mount Auyán, is the world's highest waterfall, Angel Falls, which is 3212 ft (979 m) high. It is named for an American pilot and adventurer, Jimmy Angel, who found the falls in 1935 while searching for a mountain river where he had once been taken by a

CLUBBING TOGETHER *Like an exquisite floating garden, a cluster of plants decorates one of Mount Roraima's rain-filled pools. Dead leaves generate a supply of self-made compost.*

FALLS FROM HEAVEN *The Angel Falls (left) plunge from the edge of Mount Auyán. Near the foot of the falls, plants thrive in the constant spray. On Mount Roraima's summit (above), unique plants live in a chaotic landscape of eroded sandstone. Rain removes anything that does not have a firm grip on the rock.*

gold prospector. In the event, he never found the gold-rich river again, though he searched endlessly amid the confusing welter of tepuís, mist and forest that make up this part of the world.

Where not encrusted with the crystals that Raleigh described, the rock of the tepuís is a forbidding rich red or black. The terrain on the top of Mount Roraima, as on most tepuís, is a nightmare of sharp crests and ankle-breaking gullies, slippery with rain and raked by thunderstorms of incredible violence. If not drenched by rain, the summits are frequently drowned in a sea of mist, and when this clammy mantel occasionally clears, the rocks are baked to unbearable temperatures by the tropical sun that sears through the thin air.

Rain erodes the rocks of the tepuís' summits into bizarre shapes and constantly washes away the soil, leaving little in which plants can anchor themselves. The plants that do survive here are mostly tough little clumps of grasses, the frugal mosses and lichens, or plants that have their own built-in nutrient supply. These include orchids, which rely on fungi growing around and within their roots to secure nutrients from the crumbling rock for them, or sundews and pitcher plants which trap tiny flying insects to gain nourishment. A high proportion of the plants are endemic – found nowhere else on Earth. They have evolved in isolation here, marooned on the tepuís, far from others of their ancestral kind.

STRANGE PLANTS ON HIGH

In this sense, the tepuís are like a string of islands – islands in the sky – and the same description is often applied to the volcanic peaks of east and central Africa, whose highest slopes support a collection of plants every bit as strange as the giant tortoises and marine iguanas of the remote Galápagos Islands.

Ascending one of these African mountains, the evergreen tropical forest of the surrounding lowlands blankets the lower slopes, but eventually gives way to a stunted and gnarled forest, thick with semipermanent mist. This is known as cloud forest, and may include giant tree-like heathers, their branches hung with long strands of soft green moss. Cushiony mosses and clumps of ferns also typically grow in cloud forest, thriving in the abundant moisture.

Beyond the cloud forest there may be a zone of tall bamboos, and then another transition, at an altitude of about 10 000 ft (3000 m), to heath forest, where the tree heathers predominate and the drapery of mosses is so thick that the outlines of the trees themselves are distorted and concealed, producing a forest of fantastic shapes. Reaching heights of about 11 500 to 13 000 ft (3500 to 4000 m), the vegetation becomes yet more surreal, dominated by giant groundsels whose huge spikes stick up like rockets from a rosette of sword-like leaves. Giant lobelias also grow extensively in this zone, and share the same kind of bizarre shape.

DANGEROUS LANDING *Roraima sundews supplement a meagre supply of nutrients by trapping insects. Each flower-like leaf cluster is studded with sticky hairs.*

APE OF THE VOLCANOES

The mountain gorilla is similar to its sister subspecies, the lowland gorilla, but covered with a thicker coat of hair to protect against the cold and damp of the cloud forests. These huge apes live in small bands, led by a dominant male known as a 'silverback' for the saddle of silverish grey hair across its broad, black, muscular back. Mountain gorillas, for all their size and strength, eat nothing but plant foods, principally bamboo shoots which they find in the bamboo zone between 7500 and 10 000 ft (2300 and 3000 m). They peel off the tough outer layer of the shoot and eat the softish white core. More surprisingly, the mountain gorillas consume the nettles which grow in clumps among the bamboo and have such a powerful sting that they can pierce two layers of clothing to cause intense irritation to human skin. As well as eating the wood nettles, mountain gorillas often incorporate them into their makeshift sleeping nests and are apparently unaffected by the stings. Mountain gorillas sometimes travel upwards, above the tree line, to collect blackberries. Although in many ways these gorillas are well adapted to their environment, they frequently suffer from diseases that seem to be related to the cold and damp, such as pneumonia. Zoologists believe that they may not be ideally suited to the altitudes to which they are now restricted due to the expansion of human populations.

Forest Feast *Perched on a plant-laden tree trunk (left), a young mountain gorilla reaches for food. Below: Mature adult males, or silverbacks, head each gorilla troop. Despite their size, they rarely use their strength in anger.*

DAY WARMTH *Giant groundsels (left) and lobelias (above) bathe in the sunshine and mist near Mount Kenya's summit. In this thin air temperatures plunge once the sun begins to set.*

The fact that this plant form is also seen among some mountain species from the Andes suggests that it may have particular survival value at such altitudes. It is probably adapted to the extreme temperature range of the high tropical peaks, where plants are baked by the sun during the day and must then endure temperatures far below zero by night. In at least some of these towering plants, and perhaps all of them, the spiky leaves can fold inwards over the central bud at nightfall to protect it.

The giant lobelias add another layer of sophistication to this arrangement. They secrete a sticky liquid which is held in by the circle of leaves. The liquid, which wells up around the central bud and covers it by night, contains natural antifreeze. Although a thin crust of ice may develop during the night, the main body of the liquid remains unfrozen, as does the delicate bud.

Another striking characteristic of these plants is that their dead leaves do not fall to the ground, but stay attached to the plants below the rosette of living green leaves, hanging limply like drooping brown skirts. This dead vegetation likewise protects against the cold by providing insulation for the lower part of the stem. Many species of giant groundsel and giant lobelia also have a dense wool over their living leaves, or a mass of fine spines, which trap air around the plant as effectively as a scarf or sweater. The colder the area in which a particular species of giant groundsel grows, the thicker the layer of insulating fibres, and the fatter the stems and leaves of the plant.

EVERLASTING IN THE PEAKS

The highest vegetation on these African mountains, above the giant lobelias and groundsels, is the alpine zone of mosses, lichens, tough grass and low-growing plants. Among the many exotic species that survive against the odds here are the 'everlastings', with their shiny, hard-petalled daisy-like flowers which survive for months. These ancestors of the everlasting garden plants grown for dried flower arrangements are adapted to achieve pollination, despite the few insects in the cold and mist at high altitudes.

The specialised vegetation of these African 'islands in the sky' is probably a relic of the type of vegetation that occurred over large tracts of the African continent during the ice ages. During those times, the cold-adapted plants and animals could move about from one mountain area to another, because the climate of the lands between was far cooler. With the end of the ice ages about 10 000 years ago, the cold-adapted plants such as the giant groundsels lost territory to tropical vegetation such as rain forest, and became isolated on the separate mountain peaks. With this isolation, independent evolution began, producing the many different endemic species seen today.

LONG LIVES *Everlastings, or helichrysums, turn their flowers towards the sunshine in the mountains of South Africa's Cape Province. With thousands of plant species all crammed into a relatively small area, this is one of the richest floral regions in the world.*

HUMMING IN HIGH PLACES

Several peaks in the Andes have their own species of hummingbird, each of which evolved its unique characteristics in the isolation of that mountain. That hummingbirds should have colonised the high mountains at all is remarkable, given their tiny size (a small warm-blooded creature loses heat far more rapidly than a large warm-blooded creature), their constant and intense level of activity, their high metabolic rate and their huge requirement for food. Whereas lowland hummingbirds rely mainly on nectar for energy, supplementing this with some insects, high-altitude hummingbirds treat insects as their staple diet – the only possible strategy in an environment where flowers are a rarity at most times of the year. This change of diet has allowed hummingbirds to survive at astonishing altitudes, with the highest at up to 20 000 ft (6100 m) on Mount Chimborazo in Ecuador. Hummingbirds here make far thicker and sturdier nests than lowland species, incorporating feathers, wool, cobwebs, fern leaves and cottony or feathery plant seeds to produce a well-padded structure up to 4 in (10 cm) deep and 5 in (13 cm) wide. Within these nests, which are lodged in a rock cavity for further protection from the wind, the hummingbirds go into a state of torpor, a sort of hibernation, each night. Their metabolic rate falls dramatically, as their breathing and heartbeat slow down, conserving vital energy.

HIGH-ALTITUDE HUMMINGBIRD *The red-tailed comet is found only in the mountains of Bolivia and northern Argentina.*

Mountains are not only refuges for the cold-loving species of the Ice Age: they are also, in many parts of the world, small islands of wilderness in a vast sea of humanity, roads, concrete and intensively farmed arable land. Many wild animals, especially large predators such as wolves, bears, lynxes and eagles which have been killed off in most parts of their former range, have survived in the more inaccessible parts of the mountains. Some which were not well adapted to the high mountain peaks have been compelled to retreat from the lowlands and the foothills into these refuges. The European wild cat, the lynx and the brown bear are all, by nature, inhabitants of the coniferous forest or the forest edge, but all have been forced up above the tree line in the mountains of Europe by human incursion. Some such animals, in Europe and elsewhere, continue to suffer persecution in their mountain haunts and have become exceedingly wary of people. The snow leopard, for example, is so elusive that few people have ever seen one alive – and that includes biologists who have studied these leopards in their Himalayan haunts for years, following their tracks but never catching a glimpse of the animals themselves.

ON THE PROWL *Unlike its domesticated relative, the European wild cat (left) is extremely wary, and very rarely seen. The beautiful snow leopard (opposite) is one of the world's rarest cats. It lives in the mountains of central Asia, and hunts at up to 19 000 ft (5800 m).*

Some mountain animals which are largely suited to high altitude living, but once benefited from access to lower-lying areas as well, now find themselves hemmed in by human activities. Mountain species that might have migrated across lowland areas to reach other peaks, in search of a mate or a less crowded living space, are now unable to do so. In central Africa, mountain gorillas were once able to descend from their damp and chilly forests when

Rare Visitor *Once widespread throughout northern Europe, the lynx has retreated to the safety of high ground. It hunts rabbits, hares and birds, mostly by night.*

the weather was especially bad, and to enjoy the better climate of the surrounding lowlands for a while. As the human population has gradually encroached on the forests surrounding the Ruwenzori and Virunga Mountains of Uganda and Zaire, with small farms and villages spreading up the lower slopes, this option has disappeared for the gorillas, making them more susceptible to disease.

Mountain Mysteries

If the mountains give refuge to bears, lynxes and wolves, and hide the snow leopard so effectively, could they also harbour animals that are never seen – or rarely seen – by human eyes? Tales of the yeti, a large ape-like creature living in the high Himalayas, were once almost universally dismissed as nonsense, but with more and more mountaineering expeditions into this zone there has been a steady trickle of 'sightings' by reliable witnesses over the past 40 years. Several climbing expeditions have been woken in the night by animals scavenging outside their tents, and found large human-like footprints in the snow the following morning. Others have sighted powerful ape-like creatures with long reddish fur walking upright or, occasionally, on all fours. Similar reports of a large elusive ape-like creature come from other mountainous parts of Asia, including the Tien-Shan Range, the Altai, the Karakoram Range, the Pamirs and the Caucasus.

Some of the prints reported as those of yetis are undoubtedly the tracks of smaller animals that have been melted by the sun and later refrozen, a process that increases the size of the prints and can make several small ones merge into one large 'footprint'. But not all of the prints can be explained in this way, and with more than 50 reports of tracks or actual sightings, many more people are now hesitant about dismissing the yeti as a mythical beast.

If the yeti really does exist, it probably lives in the rocky, sparsely vegetated zone above the tree line, eating lichens and mosses, and catching marmots, pikas and other small creatures.

FLAMINGOS IN THE ANDES

The James's flamingo is found only in the high Andes, breeding in salt lakes at altitudes above 14 000 ft (4300 m). Although the eggs have long been collected by the local people, it was only in 1886 that this mountain-dwelling flamingo was discovered by western science.

Last Refuge *Despite its lumbering appearance, the brown bear is an accomplished climber. In a crowded world, mountains provide it with the best chance of survival.*

3 Mankind in the Mountains

Spiritual Heights *A Buddhist monastery sits perched on steep Himalayan rocks in Ladakh.*

Some mountain ranges have been inhabited for thousands of years, colonised by people who lived before history began – people who conquered the daunting landscape of the high peaks with nothing more than their own strength and skill and the simple equipment they could make from wood and stone. In the New Guinea highlands, the Andes and the Himalayas, many of their descendants still live in largely traditional ways. They offer a window into the past, revealing the effects of mountain isolation, and helping us to understand how people without modern technology could survive the challenges of life lived at high altitude.

Rugged Splendour *Life is harsh for Tibetan nomads.*

The New Guinea Highlanders

Men who wore wigs of their own or their ancestors' hair; piglets that suckled at women's breasts; a world of near-constant warfare between villages – all this survived undisturbed in the New Guinea highlands until the 1930s.

A short story by H.G. Wells, 'The Country of the Blind' published in 1904, tells of a mountaineer who slips and falls in a mountainous region. Descending a great distance but surviving, he finds himself in a valley that was cut off from the outside world by a massive rock-fall centuries earlier. The inhabitants have been isolated for so long that there is no memory of the outside world. Furthermore, due to an endemic disease, everyone is blind. When the newcomer explains to them that he can see, the inhabitants of the valley cannot understand, having no notion of sight. They conclude that the strange newcomer is insane.

Although fictional, this story tells an essential truth about the mountains – that they are often 'worlds apart'. Indeed, fact proved as strange as fiction during the 1930s when a completely unsuspected population was discovered living in central New Guinea: as many as 200 000 people inhabiting a chain of lush, green temperate valleys suspended between two precipitous mountain ranges. Until then, both map-makers and the colonial administration of New Guinea had assumed that the centre of the island was a single mountain range, its peaks capped with snow and ice, its terrain inimical to human life.

Exploration of the deep interior had been held back by the jagged limestone pinnacles, whose white blades jut vertically through the jungle in many parts of the

Lost World *Dense tropical rain forest covers Mount Bosavi in Papua New Guinea.*

FEATHERY FINERY *Mekeo tribespeople from south-eastern New Guinea bedecked and painted for a 'singsing', a celebration.*

mountains. As well as large obstructive crags, this deeply eroded limestone terrain possesses millions of smaller spears of vertical rock, so sharp and painful to the feet that it is nicknamed 'Broken Bottle Country'. The hostile landscape, combined with the belief that nothing but chill summits lay beyond, kept the white rulers of the island to its coastal fringes. One explorer wrote: 'The rock is honeycombed and stands on end; it forms fissures and craters, large and small . . . We found it impossible to cut a straight course, for in dodging the impassable craters we were turned in all directions. From a distance every timbered elevation looked like a spur of some divide; but at close quarters we found them to be only the rims of more craters.'

Four young Australian gold prospectors finally broke through this barrier in 1933, to make the first venture by white men into the deep interior. Discovery of gold in a river near the coast had drawn them upstream into previously unexplored areas. Braving the difficult terrain, they struggled over the mountains and came upon an astonishing sight – fertile valleys far below, neatly fenced and drained, with rows of beans, sugar cane, sweet potatoes and yams. Pigs rooted in the fields, and from the small thatched huts came wisps of smoke. Larger communal buildings, some as big as churches, formed the focal point of each village.

CULTURE SHOCK

Descending into the valley, they encountered people even more astonished than themselves. The highlanders were initially terrified by these white-faced, pale-eyed men. The theory that they were spirits of the dead who had returned to visit their descendants quickly gained ground. The mountain-dwellers flocked around the four prospectors, crying and laughing, hugging them and stroking their arms, singing and crying out with eerie calls, or playing on their sacred bamboo flutes.

GARDEN OF EDEN *Neat plots, with mounds of compost to protect delicate crops from the frost, caught the attention of the first outsiders to penetrate the New Guinea highlands.*

Small and dark-skinned, the highlanders were naked except for aprons made of bark-cloth and a bunch of large leaves tied above their buttocks. Round their necks were necklaces, and the fantastic plumes of birds of paradise decorated their hair. The prospectors also noticed shells, called *kina*, in the necklaces, indicating that there were trading connections with the coast. It is curious that this trade went on without the existence of the highlanders themselves coming to light. One possible explanation is that the lowland traders had kept the highlanders a secret in an effort to retain control of the trade routes. Alternatively, the goods may have travelled in a series of short hops through local exchanges between dozens of neighbouring groups. Each exchange would have formed a single link in a long chain, but the two ends of the chain never encountered one another.

The New Guinea highlanders tended their productive gardens with tools made of stone and wood: they had no metal. Pigs' tusks were used for scraping skins clean; the leg bones of cassowaries (large flightless birds) made gouges and chisels; sharp slivers of bamboo were used to cut up meat, and rats' teeth were valued for the delicate carving of arrow points, or for etching designs into bamboo.

HEADPIECES *Huli tribesmen (opposite) wearing painted faces and elaborate wigs. The wigs are often made from their own hair, grown when they were young. A highland woman (right), with a* bilum *(bag) on her head, tends a vegetable garden. The pig roots for food and so ploughs the land.*

There were no beasts of burden – everything that needed to be transported was carried by the people themselves, often in long string bags called *bilums* that were slung over the women's heads and hung down their backs. The bags were large enough to take a load of sweet potatoes and a baby or a piglet, for piglets were carried about and cherished almost as children, pigs being a major source of wealth and prestige. (Even today, pigs are widely used as a form of currency in the New Guinea highlands. *Bilums*, too, are still the standard way of carrying things around, even in major towns.)

So valuable were pigs that a weak piglet, or one whose mother had died, might be suckled at the breast of a woman. Christian missionaries – who soon moved into the New Guinea highlands – strongly disapproved of this practice, but the most they could do was to restrict the women to using their left breast for this purpose, the left being the realm of the Devil in their view.

Further areas of the New Guinea highlands were reached in the succeeding years. Explorers discovered tribes who decorated their bodies in an extraordinary variety of ways. Nose and ear ornaments were common and often very large – bones, long feathers, tusks, teeth or lengths of bamboo. The nose ornaments, in particular, gave the highlanders a fearsome appearance. Piercing of the nasal septum to take these ornaments was part of the initiation ceremony for boys. The pierced ears were sometimes used to transport small items, such as musical instruments or paint containers.

In many tribes the men wore gourds over their penises. These gourds – some bulbous and brightly coloured, others up to 2 ft (60 cm) long and straight, others long and curved – were grown especially for the purpose. The gourds, hanging down from vines, would be weighted with rocks to lengthen them, or otherwise shaped while growing to produce a particular style. Each man had several different gourds to choose from, and selected one according to the occasion. Among one group of highlanders, the men wore elaborate decorated wigs made from their own hair, which they grew long when young, so that it could be cut off and transformed into a wig. This wig would then be worn for the rest of their lives, frequently decorated with flowers and feathers. Alternatively, wigs might be passed on from father to son. They were – and still are – valuable items in their culture.

The clothes of the Europeans seemed equally strange to the highlanders. If they had been dressed like us, one highlander remarked later, it would not have been so frightening despite their white skins, but with their trousers and bush shirts they were 'like people you see in a dream'. Shoes, too, were totally unfamiliar. For some of the highlanders, the first signs of the strange outsiders were their footprints in the mud. Like other highlanders, they were highly skilled at reading the footprints of their family, neighbours or intruders from other tribes – all barefooted like themselves. From these prints they could recognise individuals and so trace the comings and goings of other villagers, the clandestine activities of sorcerers or other mischief-makers, and the arrival of outsiders. They were shocked by the strange prints of boots, and interpreted them as belonging to giants whose toes had been amputated. The ridges on the soles

DRESSED TO KILL *A warrior from the Simbu region wears his tribe's traditional battle dress. His pierced nasal septum is decorated with a feather.*

of the boots were taken to mean that these interlopers were skeletons walking on their bare fleshless bones.

Warring Peaks

The landscape of New Guinea has divided its people into a complex mosaic of different tribal groups. No fewer than 250 separate and distinctive languages are spoken in Papua New Guinea, the eastern half of the island, accounting for a third of the Earth's total. Across the border in the highlands of Irian Jaya – the western half of the island, now ruled by Indonesia – are many more tribes with their own languages.

Today, the language barriers of Papua New Guinea are crossed by a form of simplified English known as pidgin English or neo-Melanesian. This has become the common language, allowing the people of different tribes from distant regions of the highlands to communicate with each other.

The divisions of language represent heartfelt divisions among the tribes of the New Guinea highlands. Raiding and conflict between tribal groups, and between villages within tribal groups, was constant before contact with the outside world. Most men bore the scars of battle.

Some groups of highlanders staged elaborate ritual battles with their immediate neighbours, for which the men decorated their bodies elaborately beforehand. These were more about spectacle than bloodletting and deaths were few. But the same tribes, and many others who did not practise ritual warfare, also carried out regular raids on their neighbours in which women were raped or pigs were stolen: these raids would then have to be avenged, and sooner or later vengeance would require that someone be murdered. Once this happened, the ghost of the dead would require the killing of an enemy before it could rest. The fear of ghosts was so much stronger than the fear of the enemy that reprisals were inevitable. Violence was also seen as a mark of manhood, and a belief in sorcery added to the conflict: death from illness, snakebite or an accidental fall would be construed as sorcery, and the suspects (always from an enemy village) would then be murdered.

Revenge raids perpetuated age-old conflicts whose origins were long since lost from memory. In this way, raiding and warfare became endemic. Several highland tribes were cannibals, and the eating of enemies

IRIAN JAYA *Ancient traditions have survived in the mountain villages of Irian Jaya, despite the ruthless efforts of Indonesia to suppress them.*

PLAY FIGHTING *Dani villagers prepare for a mock battle with a neighbouring village. Such battles defuse tension without significant bloodshed.*

was a common occurrence as late as the 1960s. Indeed, human meat (reputed to taste like turkey) was probably an important source of protein for some highlanders.

Sometimes these raids escalated into all-out warfare, with looting and burning of villages. Fatalities were relatively low, because there was never indiscriminate killing. Moreover, the webs of kinship created by intermarriage between groups would be remembered even during times of war, and these created a network of loyalties between members of different groups which continued to be respected because of the fear of vengeance from the spirit world. Despite these checks on wanton killing, the burning of crops during enemy raids caused immense hardship, as the people were forced to flee and wrest a living from the forest.

A war that began in one region over some minor incident – an accusation of sorcery, for example, or a woman leaving her husband for a man in another village – could spread like a forest fire, leaping from one community to another. Other highlanders could be caught up in the conflict, as refugees from one area moved into another and recruited new allies, or the aggressors pursued their enemies into places of refuge. As the fighting moved on, it created new grievances to be resolved. The highlanders often felt themselves to be caught up in conflicts whose origins were unknown, but which were endlessly self-perpetuating.

The practicalities of life did limit conflicts between tribes who needed each other for trade. In general, people were at war with those who lived to the east or the west, whereas they traded with those who lived to the north or south: groups living in zones at different altitudes, with different rocks, climate and vegetation, who were useful as sources of unobtainable goods. These goods included timber of a particular kind used for spears, stone for axes, salt, bird of paradise feathers and shells brought up from the coast.

KEEPING WATCH *In parts of the New Guinea highlands, watchtowers were built to guard against surprise attack by warlike neighbours.*

Mountain ranges often defined the boundaries of territories, and the people beyond were usually sworn enemies. So the peaks and ridges that divided the central valley of the New Guinea highlands were dangerous places, frequented mainly by men for hunting, raiding and warfare, while women were confined to the valleys.

Life has changed somewhat in the New Guinea highlands since the first westerners arrived. Until 1973 Papua New Guinea was administered as Australian territory, and this undoubtedly helped to bring a more peaceful way of life to the highlands. Even so, there is still some feuding between different tribes, and New Guinea highlanders remain reluctant to travel to districts outside their home areas for fear of encountering their traditional enemies.

In other aspects of life, westernisation has destroyed many customs. In Papua New Guinea, whose highlanders have political autonomy and some economic opportunities, the wearing of penis gourds has almost died out and factory-made clothing is widely adopted: the trousers and shirts that once inspired such fear when worn by the white intruders are now, just two generations later, everyday dress in many parts of the highlands. In Irian Jaya, paradoxically, the repressive policies of the Indonesian government and limited economic opportunities for the native highland people have led to their traditional culture remaining more intact.

Mountain Dwellers of Asia

The tides of history have swept across the Himalayas and their neighbouring ranges. They have left a complex scattering of peoples, relying on such creatures as the mighty yak to help them to survive in formidable terrain.

In winter, a Kyrgyz woman of the Pamir mountains – which stretch north-westwards from the Himalayas into the central Asian republic of Tajikistan and into Afghanistan and China – must spend several hours every day melting snow. At over 12 000 ft (3660 m), there is no other source of drinking water at this time of year.

The cold is so intense here that even eating from a metal spoon is hazardous: at temperatures that can fall as low as –30°C (–22°F), the metal will stick hard to the tongue and inside of the mouth. The cold, the biting wind and the needles of sharp ice that fall instead of rain, draw involuntary tears from even the hardiest inhabitant, and those tears freeze instantly in the corner of the eye, before they have time to fall.

The exhaled breath collects on the thin moustaches and beards of the Kyrgyz men and freezes hard. Even their eyebrows bristle with tiny icicles. Only their massive fur hats, felt stockings and thick padded woollen clothes allow them to survive here.

The wool for these clothes comes from yaks and from two-humped Bactrian camels, while the hides of the yaks also supply tough leather for their owners' long boots. So precious are the soft warm fibres of the camels

BRIEF RESPITE *The summer sun shines on high altitude marshland in the Pamir Mountains (opposite). For most of the year this landscape is frozen over. The felt tents or yurts (above) traditionally used by the Kyrgyz, are heated by stoves or open fires burning animal dung and are comfortably warm inside.*

that the Kyrgyz must guard them against marauding villagers of other tribes, who will try to pluck out tufts of wool as the huge animals lie sleeping. Yak hair, more coarse and tough than camel hair, has a special value because its fibres can be twisted together to make a strong rope. It can also be compressed into a thick durable felt which is used for the large circular tents or yurts that house the Kyrgyz . The tents are surprisingly warm inside when heated by a fire, but the felt is also extremely heavy to transport.

MOUNTAIN LIVESTOCK

The yaks and camels, along with sheep and goats, are central to Kyrgyz life in this seemingly impossible terrain of ice, stone and terrifying cold. They crop the scarce winter grass, and fatten up on the lush pastures of summer. Yak dung burns on the fires, driving out the cold from the yurts. The milk of goats and yaks is turned into yoghurt and cheese, and some of the yoghurt is dried for storage. In the depths of winter, this dried yoghurt is mixed to a paste with water and heated to form a thick nourishing 'fondue', called *qurut,* to which fat and chunks of bread are added. It is one of the staple dishes of the Kyrgyz . The flesh of the animals also adds to their diet, and the meat can be traded for wheat grown by farming people of other tribes, such as the Wakhis. Felt for lining the walls of the Wakhis' stone-built houses is also traded in exchange for grain.

Above all, the camels and yaks provide transport for this vital trade. Their expeditions to get grain from the farming villages involve gruelling treks of several hundred miles in the dead of winter, through blinding gales and blizzards, across perilous mountain passes, crossing the icy crusts of rivers and praying that these are thick enough to bear the laden animals' weight. Before taking them across, the head of the caravan walks gingerly out onto the ice, taps it and listens with an expert ear for the noise it makes, cautiously assessing its thickness before leading the caravan across. The Kyrgyz also carry sand or ashes with them to sprinkle on patches of smooth ice where the animals would otherwise slip. The camels, with their soft splayed hoofs, are more sure-footed than the other animals on ice. Each camel carries a load of up to 600 lb (270 kg), while yaks carry 150 lb (70 kg) each. The men themselves ride sturdy ponies.

By travelling in winter, much of the journey can be made along the frozen rivers, avoiding arduous climbs through mountain passes. In addition to their own goods for barter, the Kyrgyz may carry exotic items obtained from foreign traders, goods such

GOATS GALORE *Tajik women milk goats in the foothills of the Pamirs (right, above). Goats are vital to life throughout this region: they can survive in the most unpromising environments and eat almost anything. In the warmth of her yurt (right), a Kyrgyz woman churns goat's milk to make butter.*

as tea and salt, from which the Kyrgyz can make a useful profit, allowing them to obtain more grain.

To the Kyrgyz themselves, tea is so precious a commodity that it is carried in a small bag around the neck. Food for the entire trek must also be carried: a month's supply of bread is specially baked for this purpose by the Kyrgyz women, who add animal fat to the dough to make the bread more nutritious and prevent it from going dry and stale. The grain for this expedition's ration of bread comes from the previous trading expedition.

BEASTS OF BURDEN

The Kyrgyz prize their camels more than any other pack animal. They do so not only for the camel's prodigious strength and stamina, but because the fat contained in its humps – a 200 lb (90 kg) store of food – allows it to go without eating for many weeks. By the end of a long trek the humps have almost withered away, as the fat inside them has been used up by the camel's metabolism. Exhausted and hungry, they then eat their fill and gradually replenish their humps.

Bactrian camels were domesticated at least 4500 years ago in central Asia. They are primarily animals of the dry open steppelands, and a few wild herds remain in parts of Mongolia and China. While they are naturally adapted to a certain degree of cold, as experienced on the steppes, and to a meagre diet, it is remarkable that these huge beasts – which stand 6 ft (1.8 m) tall at the hump and weigh about 1/2 ton – have acclimatised so well to the extreme climate of the Pamir Mountains.

RUNNING ON EMPTY *The small, flabby humps of these Bactrian camels show that they are at the end of a long trek and have used up their food reserves.*

BACK TO BACTRIA

The name of the Bactrian camel is derived from the place where it originated – Bactria, the ancient name for the region of Afghanistan that includes the mountains of Hazarjat. The Bactrian camel is easily distinguished from its Arabian cousin, the dromedary, by having two humps, not just one.

Even so, they do need special care. At the end of a day's journey, however tired they may be, the camels must not be allowed to settle down onto the ground. Their body heat would melt the ice or snow beneath them, allowing water to seep into their coats and freeze. On arrival at the place where the caravan will spend the night, the camels are unloaded, then quickly roped together, head to tail, in such a way that the animals cannot lie down. After two hours, when they have cooled sufficiently, the ropes are untied and the camels can finally rest and sleep.

MURDEROUS MOUNTAINS

The name 'Hindu Kush' has a strange origin. It is thought that these mountains were once called the Hindu Koh, which means 'Indian mountains', by people of the central Asian steppes, who viewed this stark range of peaks which stood to the south of their lands as a gateway to the great Indian subcontinent. The name Hindu Kush seems to have sprung from a punning use of the original name. *Kush* means 'killer', and these mountains had indeed been turned into 'killers of the Indians' by the slave trade which flourished for many centuries. Captives were taken from the Indian subcontinent and marched north over the bleak and savage mountain terrain, for

MOUNTAIN COUSINS

The llama, the traditional pack animal of the Andes, can carry 220 lb (100 kg) loads, covering 16 miles (26 km) a day, at a height of 16 500 ft (5000 m) above sea level. A Bactrian camel, at 10-12 000 ft (3000-3660 m) in the Pamir Mountains, can carry 600 lb (270 kg) loads and covers about 17 miles (28 km) per day. These two animals are more closely related than they might appear: both belong to the family Camelidae and share a common ancestor living about 20 000 years ago. The only other living members of this animal family are the one-humped camels of North Africa and the Middle East, and three llama-like South American animals, the wild guanacos and vicuñas and the domesticated alpacas. Alpacas were domesticated in the Andes, along with the llama, about 4000 to 5000 years ago. Both the llama and the alpaca are descendants of the guanaco: the llama was bred for strength and endurance on mountain trails, the alpaca for its wool which hangs down to the ground in the most valuable breeds. The warmth of alpaca wool has long been an indispensable aid to human survival at high altitudes in the Andes. Camel wool, while not quite as soft, is extremely warm and of great value in parts of the Hindu Kush, the Pamir Mountains and the Karakoram Range. When a camel moults, it does so very quickly and the wool hangs off the animal in large hanks that are easily gathered for spinning into yarn.

IN THE ANDES *Indians load up a llama. These Andean animals are related to camels, and share their endurance, strength and bad temper.*

which they were utterly ill-adapted, to be sold in the bazaars of central Asia.

All that meets the eye in the Hindu Kush are lifeless expanses of bare, greyish-white rock, sharp precipices and jagged peaks. These magnificent but bleak planes of rock overawe the bravest human heart with their evident indifference to life. They are broken at intervals by vast lakes reflecting the blues and greys of the skies, all motionless and silent until the wind rises. The crags, ridges and lakes stretch away into endless vistas of the same surreal beauty. Where the peaks and escarpments are made of schist, they glitter with crystalline slivers of mica. A few tufts of bleached grey-green grass are the only signs of life in a wasteland.

At lower altitudes, on the southern flanks of the Hindu Kush, is a greener, gentler land of oak and cedar woods, irrigated fields and upland meadows known as Nuristan. Here the men hunt wild goat called markhor and hang the goat's stout twisted horns outside their houses as a sign of prestige. Snow leopards, bears, wolves and foxes are also hunted, but it is the markhor which is most prized by the hunter, and is a major preoccupation for Nuristani men. The killing of a markhor is undisputed proof of virility.

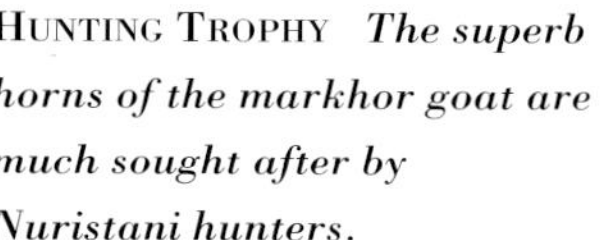

Hunting Trophy *The superb horns of the markhor goat are much sought after by Nuristani hunters.*

The Nuristani men herd domesticated sheep and goats, while their womenfolk grow crops on tiny mountainside fields. The women go barefoot in summer, but bind their legs with strips of cloth to protect against thorny undergrowth. Strong and hardy, they climb high into the mountain forests, collecting firewood, dung to fertilise the fields, and the tender young leaves of certain trees that are used to feed the newly weaned lambs and goat kids. Even in winter, they think nothing of walking many miles barefoot in the snow. Some types of traditional shoes, made of red untanned goatskin, are regarded as 'best' wear, and must be treated with care; if they get damp, the leather will stiffen and be spoiled. It is common for a man or woman visiting another village to walk barefoot the whole way, while carrying the shoes, and put them on only when approaching their destination. For long journeys in winter, a simple form of traditional footwear consists of goatskin wrapped around the ankle and foot, fur side innermost, and tied in place with leather thongs. The toes may be partially exposed but cold does not bother the Nuristanis.

The people are nominally Muslim, but many of their earlier beliefs and customs remain. Their women's freedom of movement is one consequence. Dancing is another: men dance to celebrate weddings and births (their ancestors also danced at funerals) and even beside the beds of the sick to drive out evil spirits. There is still evidence of the ancient cult of the goat, which was once revered as a symbol of both virility and purity. In pre-Muslim days, women wore headdresses with long upsweeping horns to symbolise their purity and prestige. Only one example of such a headdress is known today, preserved in a Norwegian museum. Mass destruction of cult objects in the name of Islam seems to have accounted for the rest. But carved goats' horns, sometimes reduced to an abstract representation, are still seen on old wooden house doors, indicating the status of the inhabitants.

The slave caste, called *bari*, were not allowed to own goats – a law that helped to preserve the fragile mountain environment, where the prodigious appetites and digestive powers of goats can do terrible damage to trees, shrubs and grasses. Today the bari are nominally free, following an edict by King Amamullah of Afghanistan in the 1920s, but they still have inferior social status and rarely own land or animal herds.

On a Higher Plane *The almost lifeless beauty of the high Hindu Kush, seen here at 10 000 ft (3000 m), with the sacred lakes of Band-i-Amir.*

HEAT FOR THE HOME *Crossing a mountain stream on a precarious bridge, a Nuristani woman brings home firewood from a distant forest.*

The free men of Nuristan are warlike individualists, who once had to defend their villages from nomads or neighbouring tribes. A traveller who roamed through this district in 1865 recorded that: 'In order to show how many people they have killed, each man erects a high pole on the outskirts of each village, with a crude figure of a man on top of it. For every man he kills he bores a hole in it and knocks in a peg. If he kills a woman, he bores only a hole, without any peg. A *bahadur* or *surunwali* [someone who has killed many enemies] always occupies the highest place at feasts, and receives a double portion.'

The older Nuristani villages are located on the narrowest possible ledges on the steepest possible slopes, for defence against such marauders. Some are barely accessible. Made of mud brick, their yellowish-brown tones match those of the slope, so that the huddled houses seem to have sprouted from the mountainside, like rocky outcrops or clusters of nests built by giant birds.

Raiding, warfare and blood feuds were once commonplace throughout the region. Major trade routes passed across it, linking China with the Middle East and Europe with India, and helped to foster this warlike tradition. Loot from the caravans, laden with silk, precious stones and other luxury goods, became part of the livelihood of tribes such as the Hunzukuts. The mountainous terrain was ideal for ambushes on lonely pathways or mountain passes, and its secluded valleys and high meadows offered hiding places where raiders might rest up with stolen livestock before returning to their own lands.

Where the danger from feuding and livestock raids has traditionally been greatest, only men are allowed to tend the animals on the high summer pastures. In the less hostile areas, among the Wakhi farmers and other Tajik tribes, for example, women often do the work of herding, while men plough the fields.

GOAT WORSHIP *These images of goats were made by the Kalash people of western Pakistan. Their traditional religion, to which they still cling, is similar to the ancient animist religion of Nuristan.*

To the east of Nuristan in northern Pakistan, traditional houses in the Hindu Kush's Swat valley have windowless, rampart-like walls facing the street, with only one doorway. This entrance often has a wall built immediately behind it, to act as a screen against attack. The centre of the house is an open courtyard, and the rooms obtain their light and ventilation from inner windows. Old settlements in the Nager region are even more heavily defended, with watchtowers and heavy gates. The young men of the village traditionally use the rooms within the towers as a meeting place for dancing, singing and games of skill and strength while they keep watch across the surrounding peaks and valleys for raiders.

Natural enemies can be as destructive as human ones, and the traditional houses were also built to withstand the earthquakes that frequently seize this area of restless, still-growing mountains. A combination of stone walls and solid timbers, hewn from the trunks of colossal trees, provided a structure which could flex and adjust sufficiently to avoid destruction. Roofs were generally made of relatively lightweight materials, such as mud plastered over wooden beams, so that if a roof fell in it did little serious damage. The roof beams also rested on wooden pillars within the house, making them independent of the stone walls, another useful defence against earthquakes.

An Ethnic Mosaic

The enmities between adjacent valleys, or between neighbouring tribes or feuding families, is only part of the long history of hostilities in this region. The powerful tides of international politics have swept through the strategically important mountains of the Hindu Kush, the Pamirs and the Karakoram range, which divide central Asia from both the Middle East and the Indian subcontinent, straddling parts of China, India, Pakistan, Afghanistan, Kyrgyzstan and Tajikistan (the last two formerly republics of the Soviet Union). The invasion of Afghanistan by the Soviet Union, and the devastating war against the invaders by the Mujahidin, is just the latest in a long series of bloody conflicts over territory in the region.

The forces of war and political change have pushed people this way and that, splintering ethnic groups and leaving fragments of old societies stranded far from their homelands. The Kyrgyz, for example, inhabit a large region that straddles the border between China and Kyrgyzstan, but there are small splinter groups living in Tajikistan and in the 'Wakhan Corridor' of Afghanistan, a narrow finger of land connecting Afghanistan with China. The removal of nomadic herding people from their homelands has often left them with no means of feeding their families adequately, and they have turned to raiding for a living, adding to the lawlessness of the mountain ranges.

Traces of more ancient conflicts, stretching back for thousands of years, can be seen in the complex ethnic mosaic of this region. Some of the tribes are Tibeto-Mongolian in origin, with rounded face, high cheekbones and almond-shaped eyes with the upper eyelid hidden by a fold of skin above. Others are Caucasian, with paler skins, less rounded faces and long or hooked noses. While most are brown-eyed, pale green and blue eyes are not uncommon among some ethnic groups, such as the Baluchis, the Kyrgyz and the Pathans. The pale iris often has a much darker ring around the outside and, set against black eyelashes and hair, the effect is striking. Blue and green eyes are commonly attributed to descent from the armies of Alexander the Great, King of Macedonia (now northern Greece) in the 4th century BC. He conquered the Persian Empire and marched onwards to India, but was forced to stop when his troops, possibly weakened by altitude sickness, refused to continue farther than the River Hyphasis. Deserting soldiers, too weary to return to their homelands, or enchanted by the women of the mountains, are thought to have settled in the lower reaches of the Hindu Kush. Other tribes of this region, such as the Chahar Aimaq, claim descent from the armies of Genghis Khan, the

Unshakable *Traditional building methods (left) are still used in the Kalash Valley of Pakistan, where houses have to resist frequent earthquakes. Crammed into an inaccessible vertical niche, a Kafir village (below) in the Hindu Kush is easily defended against raids.*

A LONG PAST *A village in Karakoram, Pakistan, enjoys a time of relative peace. This region has witnessed centuries of conquest and migration as its ethnic mix reveals.*

great Mongol conqueror of the 13th century, who also invaded the region. In an area with such warlike traditions, descent from an invading army is a matter for pride.

A great diversity of languages are spoken in these mountain ranges, indicating yet again the complexities of the past. Among the main groups in the Hindu Kush of northern Pakistan are the Shina speakers, the Kho and the Khoistani. Strangest of all, in the Karakoram Mountains there is a tribal group known as the Burusho whose language, Burushaski, is a 'living fossil', belonging to no present-day linguistic group. The Burusho are similar to the surrounding tribes, known collectively as Dardic peoples, and they share many customs and beliefs with their neighbours. Only their language points to more ancient affiliations. No doubt they were once a distinctive group ethnically, with their own religion and customs, but these have been lost through intermarriage and the exchange of goods and ideas which frequently takes place between neighbouring peoples.

MOUNTAIN OF THE PROPHET

Also living in northern Pakistan are the Balti, who speak an archaic Tibetan dialect, indicating an ancient migration from the east. They are undoubtedly a relic of the time, between about AD 100 and 400, when the region was largely Buddhist (although traditional folk beliefs and animistic religions were still widespread). By 600 Buddhism was in decline, and many of the monasteries that had thrived in previous centuries were in ruins. The cause seems to have been the destructive behaviour of the mountains: a series of earthquakes had unleashed devastating floods, which shook the faith of both the monks and the lay people. A few ancient Buddhist shrines, known as *stupas*, survive, but the faith itself has long vanished. Today the Hindu Kush, the Pamirs and the Karakoram Mountains are almost entirely Muslim, having been converted to Islam from about the 14th century onwards.

In some parts of the region, purdah – the segregation of women from public life – is practised more rigorously than in any other part of the Islamic world. In the Swat Valley of the Hindu Kush, for example, girls are secluded in their houses as soon as they reach adolescence. Women never leave the confines of the house, unless widowed, when some freedom of movement is restored out of economic necessity. Only close male relatives are permitted to enter the women's quarters. The Pathans have a saying: 'A woman's place is in the house or in the grave.' One consequence of these strict laws is that women tend to die at a relatively early age due to ill health, while the men must do all the work of tilling the fields and herding the animals up onto the mountain pastures. For many families, this agricultural work is an impossible burden for the men, and it is only the wealthy who can afford to hire labourers and so observe full purdah.

The process of conversion to Islam continues. Some of the Shina-speaking tribes of the Swat Valley were converted only in the past 200 years and remnants of their earlier beliefs, a local religion with a pantheon of male and female gods, survived well into the 19th century, when goats were still sacrificed to the gods on special feast days.

The way different plants and animals thrive at different altitudes inspired the beliefs of the Shina religion. Different zones of purity and impurity were thought to lie one above the next on the mountain slopes, with spiritual beings, people, animals and plants each having their own level. Purest of all were the mountain peaks, the high lakes and alpine meadows. Here lived the good spirits, envisaged as beautiful winged girls with two peculiarities: eyes set vertically and feet that pointed backwards. Animals living in these highest zones, such as ibex and wild goats, were thought of as holy creatures. Domestic goats acquired special status through their descent from wild goats. Certain high-altitude plants, such as juniper trees and a lichen known locally as *gulgul*, were also imbued with holiness. Malevolent spirits – witches, goblins and giants – dwelt

HIGH AND DRY *A wooden bridge (left) crosses an icy mountain stream in the Swat Valley. Building houses vertically (below), with rock faces for structural support, conserves warmth and saves precious agricultural land.*

at the altitudes inhabited by people, or in deep river gorges and ravines. These low places were considered the most impure. For a shaman, or 'witch doctor', to approach the good spirits in their high places, he must first undergo rituals of purification. Such folk beliefs have now largely died out in the Swat Valley under pressure from increasingly militant and orthodox Islamic beliefs in Pakistan as a whole.

Only a few isolated areas still harbour people who have resisted conversion to Islam. One such group are the Kalash, who live on the western border of Pakistan but have much in common with the people of Afghanistan's Nuristan region to the west. Approximately 3000 Kalash people still live in three high, narrow valleys that are part of the Hindu Kush. The Kalash have fiercely resisted pressures to abandon their old religion, with its vigorous ceremonies. The Kalash drink wine, honour carved effigies of their ancestors, sacrifice goats to their gods, dance with abandon and have a relatively liberal attitude to sexuality. Among their gods are Mahandeo, the god of honeybees; Sajigor, the god of shepherds and their flocks; and Jestak, god of the hearth and family. Supreme over all these is Dezao, the creator.

Dezao was once worshipped throughout Nuristan as well as by the Kalash, but in 1895 the Emir of Afghanistan decided to put an end to this religion and convert the inhabitants to Islam. The whole region was then known as Kafiristan, meaning 'land of the Unbelievers'. In three years the Emir succeeded in a forcible conversion of the whole population, and he coined the name Nuristan or Land of Light (meaning 'the light of Islam') to consolidate his victory. The Kalash escaped this mass conversion because they were subjects – virtually slaves – of the neighbouring, ancient kingdom of Chitral, at that time a British protectorate. They survive as a reminder of what life was once like throughout Kafiristan.

THE HIMALAYAS AND TIBET

Nomad caravans, slow-moving lines of Tibetan men dressed in brown or black, with their yaks, sheep and goats, converge on Lake Drabye in western Tibet. Whipped by fierce winds, they trudge down to the flatlands around the lake, where other nomads are already camped. All around the sapphire-blue water of the lake are vast expanses of white, against which the dark figures of the men and their yaks are silhouetted. It seems at first as if the lake is surrounded by snowfields, but this 'snow' is as hard as rock. The nomads hack out rectangular blocks of this strange substance and stack them into walls to make a corral. They grind down some of the 'snow' by pounding it with a yak horn and pour the fragments into homespun bags, which can later be loaded onto the animals. Occasionally they stop work briefly to taste a little of their haul and check its quality.

This white expanse around Lake Drabye is salt, a commodity so valuable that it is worth its weight in grain on the Nepal border over 200 miles (320 km) away. Here at Lake Drabye, and at other lakes scattered across the high Tibetan plateau, the salt is free for the taking. Handsome profits in grain have traditionally been available to anyone prepared to travel as far as the Nepal border and back through some of the most hostile terrain on Earth, braving winds that are powerful enough to pluck a man from his saddle or bury him under suffocating drifts of snow, and enduring weather that can change in a matter of hours from hot sunshine to a punishing hailstorm: a fall in temperature of 44°C (80°F) has been recorded in a single day.

As well as toughness and stamina, the traders must also have the skill to find food for their pack animals in apparently lifeless expanses of stone, snow and rock. They must know the way over treacherous mountain passes and, on the last leg of the journey to Nepal, be able to cross the raging torrents of the Brahmaputra river without losing the animals or their precious burdens of salt. To the men of the Chang Tang, as the plateau is known, such hardships and skills are simply a way of life, the only life they know.

Salt deposits form on the Tibetan plateau because many of the lakes have no

TIBETAN NOMADS *The drab black tents and clothes are deceptive: these people are cheerful and hospitable.*

outlet: water flows into them from rivers and snowmelt streams, but nothing flows out, and the dryness of the air causes the water to evaporate, leaving behind its load of mineral salts. These minerals consolidate into thick glittering crusts, like white halos around each lake.

There is no grass on this moonscape, and the animals must pause there for the shortest possible time, preferably no more than one night. Usually four or five men out of each nomad band travel ahead of the animal train, reaching the lake in advance and gathering the salt ready for the arrival of the others. They build a corral and excavate the salt. Loading it into the bags, they sew them shut with the sturdy needles that all traditional Tibetan and Himalayan traders carry in special cases on their belts.

By the time the other men arrive with the yaks, sheep and goats, all that remains is to load up the animals. This, however, is far from easy. Yaks are accustomed to being loaded, although they have to be restrained by tying their hind legs together. Loading the shaggy-coated sheep and goats is far more difficult as they continually try to escape, and holding them down long enough for two saddlebags of salt, totalling about 30 lb (14 kg), to be secured on their backs is exhausting work. The men are already tired when they begin the return journey to their village. To ease the journey they leave the sheep and goats loaded up each night when they pitch camp.

They finally reach home a month later to be welcomed by the women and children, who give thanks to the local mountain god, Dargo, for their safe return. Although these Tibetans have been pious Buddhists for 1000 years, this 'new religion' is inextricably mixed with the old Bon religion of Tibet, where each mountain and stream is imbued with its special spiritual power, and ever-present demons meddle with human affairs. Spirits who dwell in particular mountain passes, springs, lakes and other parts of the landscape can readily be annoyed by small offences, or simply develop an unreasonable grudge against a passer-by, who will then be dogged by illness, accident and misfortune.

YAK POWER *No other beast of burden is as strong and hardy as the yak, which can swim across raging icy torrents.*

MOBILE HOME *A Tibetan nomad family pose for the camera in their tent. The children are cared for by everyone and rarely cry, even as babies.*

Symbols of the Bon religion, such as yak skulls, can be seen engraved on wayside rocks next to the Buddhist mandala or wheel-of-life symbol. Many of the ritual features of Tibetan Buddhism are derived from the Bon religion, such as the use of 'prayer flags' – pieces of fabric pinned to poles or guy-lines to signify prayers to the gods. Prayers written on pieces of paper may also be used: these are either thrown into the breeze or lodged in 'prayer wheels', cylinders made of brass and beautifully decorated. The turning of the wheel is a symbolic act, equivalent to saying the prayer, as long as the person who turns the wheel does so with a reverent mind.

The complex rituals of Tibetan Buddhism were once focused on the many monasteries on the Tibetan plateau, often sited on the most inhospitable mountainous terrain, where the sufferings of the body could aid enlightenment of mind and the freeing of the soul.

Although the invasion of Tibet by China in 1950 did not initially undermine the old

way of life on the Chang Tang (Tibetan plateau), the Cultural Revolution of the late 1960s and early 1970s hit the nomads with devastating effect. As well as attempting to reorganise the traditional management of the herds and pastures, making the nomads fence and seed the wild plateau, and forcing them into communes – an ill-advised enterprise that left the Tibetans poorer and often starving – the Red Guards also ordered the closure of the monasteries and compelled the nomads to pull down the buildings. Without the monks and lamas (heads of monasteries), the Chinese assumed that Tibetan Buddhism would die out, but they hadn't reckoned how fiercely the Tibetan people would cling to their religion. Many Tibetans were prepared to go to jail rather than renounce Buddhism: some were imprisoned for up to 17 years.

In the 1980s the Chinese changed their policy and the nomads now once again practise their traditional patterns of herding, according to the old ways, adapting to the capricious weather, scant grass and harsh conditions of the Chang Tang, rather than trying to shape an intransigent mountain world with inappropriate methods. Monasteries are being built once more, and once banned religious rituals are now permitted.

On to Nepal

With the salt from the lake safely stored, the nomads may rest in their villages for a few months, before setting out on the next leg of their journey.

This time they take yaks as pack animals, because only they are strong enough to cross the Brahmaputra River safely. Again, it is a month's hard travelling, the objective this time being the villages of southern Tibet, or even the border with Nepal, where the salt can be bartered for grain. Other goods, such as wool, butter, dried mutton, sheep's fat and livestock may be exchanged at the same time, or on separate

Walking Wealth *To a Tibetan nomad, yaks are his wealth and his source of pride. Herds were confiscated during the Cultural Revolution, but have now been restored.*

trading expeditions. Again, these are bartered for grain, mainly barley, although some wheat flour, maize and rice are also accepted in exchange. For the Tibetan nomads, who still number some half a million people, this age-old trade route is an essential part of their survival strategy. Salt is traditionally their most valuable commodity: they once had a virtual monopoly on it, supplying all the towns and villages of Tibet, as well as the Himalayan kingdoms of Bhutan and Nepal.

Before the Chinese invasion in 1950, each Tibetan trader had a trusted counterpart in Nepal or Bhutan with whom he always traded. The Tibetans, or Drok-pa, were

Material and Spiritual *Prayer flags, their fabric frayed and tattered by the wind, are a sign of the Buddhist faith that predominates in Tibet and much of the Himalayas.*

happy to deal with the Himalayan people, such as the Dolpo-pa of Nepal, because they too were Tibetan in origin. They were also Buddhist, they spoke a Tibetan dialect and followed Tibetan customs. The meeting between the two trading partners would always be a social affair, a chance for the exchange of news and for celebrations and prayers, all blessed with liberal quantities of *chang*, the local home-brewed barley beer. The negotiations over the transaction itself were a minor part of the encounter. The Chinese takeover has changed all that. The exchanges now take place at designated villages within Tibet, so that the trade can be regulated by Chinese bureaucrats. A government official allocates exchange partners, and decides on the rates, as well as the amounts that can be bartered. Much less salt is allowed into Nepal than was customarily traded before the Chinese invasion. Small amounts of sheep's wool, dried mutton and sheep's fat are also permitted. The traders must complete their exchanges within three days, which limits the amount of social interaction between the two groups and has weakened the ties between them.

When the trading is finished, the Tibetans load grain onto their yaks and head for home, while the Dolpo-pa begin the two-day walk back to the border with Nepal. The Dolpo-pa store the salt in their villages until the winter, when they move south to trade with Nepali villagers on the lower slopes of the Himalayas.

The Buddhist lamas decide when they should depart, choosing an auspicious day by divination and blessing the people and yaks before they depart. Women and children often accompany the men on these treks. The yaks' horns are coloured red with sacred earth, and prayer flags are sewn into the shaggy fur along the backs of their necks. Red-dyed yak tails decorate the harnesses like bright feathers, swinging as the animals plod slowly up the trails and out of view of the village. No one looks back, for this is considered bad luck.

The route south takes the Dolpo-pa across a succession of mountain passes at 16 000-17 000 ft (4900-5200 m), as they traverse the tightly folded ridges of the Himalayan range. These passes are the lowest negotiable point in each ridge, a dip eaten out of the high rock wall by the erosion of rain and water over millions of years. The passes were found, and the paths to them worn away, by the people of these mountains thousands of years ago, explorers as intrepid in their time as Columbus or Livingstone. Each year the paths are worn anew by the feet of men and the hooves of yaks, so that the trails are visible from a distance and even when dusted with snow – wavering lines that snake up terrifying slopes, then vanish through a high pass into an unseen valley or plateau beyond. The traders know each pass intimately, much as they know the temper and characteristics of each yak: which animal is likely to gore them, which pass can be blocked by sudden avalanches – information that can mean the difference between life and death.

The ascent to each pass is always an anxious time, as well as exhausting for both man and beast. Ideally the animals should find pasture each night, so it is important not only to get through the pass but to descend to a region with grass that is not too thickly covered with snow. Blizzards and avalanches are a constant hazard, and deaths are commonplace. Coming through a pass safely, the Dolpo-pa give thanks to its spirits, placing stones on the pathside cairns by way of offering, then descend singing joyfully.

Into a Different World

Traversing the last mountain pass, the yak caravan, with its assortment of men, women and children, begins its descent towards the southern slopes. After several days, they come to the forest. For the youngest children making this journey for the first time, this is an extraordinary moment: they have never seen a tree before, let alone a forest. It is an utterly different world, where the sky, normally all around them, is blotted out, where leaves crackle and twigs snap underfoot, where insects buzz and hum, where the air is rich with the smells of rotting vegetation.

Soon afterwards, the caravan reaches the villages of the people of this region, the Rong-pa, who speak a different language and worship different gods: most are Hindus. Traditional trading patterns have survived here, and each Dolpo-pa has a trusted trading partner among the Rong-pa, with whom most trade is done. The Rong-pa welcome the chance to buy Tibetan salt, whose greyish crystals are preferred to the white salt that comes up by lorry from the Indian Ocean into the Himalayan foothills. Livestock, in particular, seem to be healthier and suffer fewer infections when given the Tibetan salt, whereas they develop skin irritation and frequently fall ill when given the sea salt. It is possible that there are other minerals in the Tibetan salt which not only give it its unique flavour but also make up for mineral nutrients lacking in the livestock's other food.

At one time, all the salt used by the Rong-pa came from Tibet, but the restrictions imposed on salt exports by the Chinese government, combined with the programme of road-building by the Indian and Nepalese governments, which has pushed more roads into the lower reaches of the Himalayas, has encouraged the purchase of salt from the lowlands. The end point of the road may still be as much as three months' walk from the Rong-pa villages, but this is close enough by Himalayan standards. The Indian Ocean salt is cheaper, which has forced down the price of Tibetan salt.

It is a price measured not in money but in grain. For centuries the rates of exchange were relatively steady: on the Tibetan border, one sack of salt bought one sack of grain, while in southern Nepal, one sack of salt bought four sacks of grain. This difference in the rates allowed the Dolpo-pa and other high-country traders to make a good profit, enough to keep their families well fed. Today the rates are less favourable and the bargaining is tougher.

An important part of exchange is the provision of winter pastures for the yaks that have travelled south with the Dolpo-pa. In the south, the grass is far more lush than in their arid highlands, and it is a chance for the yaks to fatten up a little. But the lowland life does not agree with them in other ways. They begin to sicken after several months at lower altitudes. The leeches that infest this humid environment are also a menace. Young leeches swim into the noses of animals as they drink and slowly enlarge, gorging themselves on the yaks' blood. Normally, the leech leaves when its home becomes too small, taking the opportunity to swim out again into a stream when the yak

Mountain Market *Trading is a way of life for many in the Himalayas, long a crossroads at the heart of Asia. This market is in Nepal.*

goes to drink. Sometimes, however, the leeches are still in the yaks' nostrils when the return journey to the uplands begins, and faced with a choice between exiting into an icy mountain torrent and staying put in a warm nostril, the leeches stay put. They can sometimes kill a yak by travelling upwards from the nose into the brain.

As soon as the snows have melted on the passes, the Dolpo-pa thankfully load their yaks and drive them out of the Rong-pa villages, up into the high places once again that they call home.

THE BOUNTIFUL YAK

For many in Tibet and the Himalayas, yaks are the key to survival at high altitude. These massive shaggy creatures were domesticated from the wild yaks of China about 2500 years ago. Wild yaks are a type of cattle, but they also have affinities with bison, sharing their humped backs and powerful shoulders. Fewer than 100 wild yaks survive, but domesticated yaks number about 12 million. Wild yaks are all blackish-brown; domesticated breeds come in various shades from white and gold to red or black. Golden yaks are particularly prized and often lead the chain of animals. Yaks share the long horns and warm coats of their wild forebears – essential protection against the ice and snow.

GENTLE SLOPES *On the southern slopes of the Himalayas, fresh green grass is abundant and there are trees and even forests. It is an entirely different world from the harsh cold Tibetan plateau.*

No one could describe the yak as a placid animal: 'domesticated' is a relative term with this stubborn and bad-tempered creature. A yak can suddenly become aggressive and kill its owner or an innocent bystander; hospitals in the Himalayas frequently have to treat yak-inflicted injuries. Yaks are never de-horned because of the need to defend themselves against predators such as wolves and snow leopards.

Yet a yak is hardy and fearless. It can swim across icy streams in full flood, and is undaunted by being fully submerged and carried downstream some distance, struggling on to the opposite bank. A yak can also act as a living snowplough, shouldering its way through seemingly impassable drifts and making a path for caravaners and other animals to follow. A team of yaks working side by side can clear a wide swathe through the snow, and do so with evident enjoyment.

When it comes to a task which the yak does not enjoy, however, or to any enterprise which seems unwise from a yak's viewpoint, such as crossing a flimsy rope-and-plank suspension bridge, it is almost impossible to persuade this animal to cooperate. Obstinacy is bred deep in their bones, and only native Himalayans and Tibetans, born and raised with yaks, have any hope of controlling them.

Pack animals are normally castrated males, castration making them slightly more tractable and cooperative, and only castrated males are actually known as 'yak' in Tibetan. An intact bull is called a *boa* while a cow is a *dri*. The collective name that covers all three categories is *nor*, the same word being used in Tibetan to mean 'wealth'. Indeed, to the nomads, yaks are wealth: a family that owns 100 yaks is extremely prosperous.

Yak cows are milked, though with some difficulty, and they have the advantage of providing milk all year round. A yak provides 16 times as much milk a year as a goat. Yoghurt, cheese and butter are made from the milk. Their butter is of enormous importance in the Himalayas, particularly as an accompaniment to tea: instead of milk and sugar, butter and salt are added. Moreover, the butter is allowed to 'mature' before being used – to Western palates, it tastes distinctly rancid. The overall effect is savoury, a little like soup, but far from appetising at first sip. Seasoned foreign travellers to the Himalayas eventually learn to love the taste and to value its warmth, nourishment and fortification against the intense cold. Native Tibetans and those Himalayan people of Tibetan origin – known generally as Bhotias – may drink as many as 40 cups of this salty yak-butter tea each day.

For the Buddhist populations of the Himalayas, yak butter has a far larger significance, being used in the butter lamps that flicker continuously in many shrines, and for huge butter carvings that are made for major festivals. Among many Buddhist communities, a tribute of butter is collected by the monks from each farmer.

Yaks can be persuaded to cross with domestic cattle, and breeding them is a special skill of the Dolpo-pa and other Bhotias. If a yak cow mates with a bull, the offspring show 'hybrid vigour': males, called *dhopa*, are stronger than either parent, while the females, called *jhuma*, give more milk than either yaks or cows.

CLOSED KINGDOM

Under the rule of the Dalai Lama, Tibet was a closed kingdom, except to those in possession of official permits (mainly Indian traders). There were no secure frontiers, but outsiders were effectively kept out by the fact that villagers could not give food or shelter to anyone without a permit.

Mountain Traders

Trade has long been a way of life in the Himalayas. Wherever natural resources are scarce, trading offers an alternative means of survival. It is also stimulated by the fact that mountains include a number of different climatic regions relatively close together:

HIGH LIVING *Yaks are loaded in Bhutan for the descent to greener pastures. Yaks are so well adapted to high altitude that they eventually weaken and fall ill on the lower slopes.*

THE SACRED MITHAN

In the north-eastern Himalayas, a different cattle species known as *mithan* is kept by highland peoples such as the Nishi of Arunachal Pradesh. The mithan is a domesticated form of the wild cattle called gaur. The mithans have a special status among the Nishi, who follow their own age-old animist traditions. Mithans are not milked nor used to pull ploughs or carry loads, but are killed for meat and in religious rituals as sacrifices. Before a mithan is sacrificed, the Nishi priest will call upon the gods in chants and prayers that last for many hours. The mithan is then beheaded. Mithans and their meat play a crucial role in Nishi society: they are used in payments to compensate for injuries, and they form the central element of any bride-price.

ANCESTRAL BULL *With its huge shoulders and sturdy horns, the wild gaur is ferocious in defence of itself and its young.*

sugar; cumin and garlic; spices grown in the lowlands, such as ginger; tea and tobacco (used mainly for snuff) from distant locations in India or China; amber from the Baltic; turquoise, lapis lazuli and silver from the Middle East or from centuries-old mines scattered throughout the Hindu Kush and the Himalayan region itself.

Political tensions and the closure of international frontiers since the 1940s, notably the border with Tibet, have destroyed much of the traditional trade in this region. Some traders now go to extraordinary lengths to obtain Tibetan hand-made goods that are still in demand locally, such as woollen robes, boots made from leather, and felted yak wool, snuff and Tibetan-style tea which is sold as whole leaves compacted into an oblong 'tea brick'. Nepali traders sometimes travel up to 2000 miles (3200 km) by truck

fertile lowland valleys, wooded foothills, treeless upland slopes, mountain pastures and high plateaus. What is lacking in one area may be produced abundantly in another, creating the potential for lucrative trade.

The lowlands and mountain valleys supply grain to the very high-altitude zones where cereal farming is impossible. The wooded foothills have timber to offer to those above the tree line for construction or for fuel. The high uncultivated slopes, where animals can graze, yield wool, meat, fat and butter for trade with farmers at lower altitudes. Woven cloth for everyday clothes, felt for tents, felt hats and boots, leather, cushions and carpets – often in beautiful rich colours and exquisitely made – are also carried along the trade routes from one part of the great mountain range to another.

Herbs with medicinal properties collected in one region of the Himalayas may command a good price in regions where these plants do not grow. Marijuana, which grows wild in parts of Nepal, is one of the medicinal plants traded – oil extracted from the plant is rubbed into aching muscles to relax them. Traditionally, little use was made of this plant as a mind-altering drug, although it was used to treat insomnia.

Even rocks may be tapped for traditional medicines. In the valley of Sinja in northern Nepal, some of the rocks have seams of a black tar-like substance which oozes out and can be collected. This oily residue was formed from the bodies of billions of microscopic sea creatures which lived over 200 million years ago in the ancient Tethys Sea, a vanished body of water from whose ocean-bed deposits all the rocks of the Himalayas are derived. The black tar of Sinja is believed by Nepalis to purify the body and promote health, and because this belief is shared by Indian folk-medicine, discs of the tar can be profitably sold to traders from India.

Traditionally, more exotic goods have also come into the Himalayas from farther afield:

HIGH AND LOW *Sherpa women display produce at a market. Trade in items that originate at different altitudes is important in the life of the Himalayas.*

Four-legged Trucks
Without animals such as yaks and mules, trade in much of the Himalayas would be impossible. Even sheep and goats are used to transport goods.

or train into India to buy such goods at bazaars where they are available, having been imported into India by permitted routes: the same items were once obtainable a few days' walk from their villages, at the Tibetan border. Trading patterns have also been altered by the incursion of roads into the Himalayas, bringing cheaper manufactured goods such as aluminium cooking pans and printed cotton fabrics.

Carrying the Loads

Even in earlier times, the cost in human toil and suffering of bringing in exotic goods was extraordinarily high. Chinese traders coming over the Karakoram Pass had to climb to an altitude of 18 290 ft (5575 m) amid blizzards and biting winds. There was no danger of getting lost, since the way was lined with the wind-scoured bones of traders and their pack animals who had perished en route. The journey took about 35 days from southern China to the mountain kingdom of Ladakh, where the goods were sold in the great bazaar at Leh, a point where the major trade routes of Asia converged. Human suffering on this trade route was matched only by the suffering of the pack animals. The thin air at the highest point of the route made it difficult for them to breathe, and the Chinese caravaners were forced to slit the nostrils of some of the ponies and mules to allow them to get enough oxygen.

Trade requires transport, and the traders who make a living from satisfying the material needs of other Himalayan peoples have special skills in choosing the right pack animal for the time of year and for each route, or part of a route: yaks for the highest passes and colder terrain; mules at lower altitudes with broad paths and relatively little ice or snow; goats or sheep for perilous paths scarcely visible to the untrained eye. Many

TO GOD, THE EASY WAY
Himalayan porters display legendary strength and endurance. Here a porter carries a Sikh pilgrim, his trainers and legs just visible, to a holy site in the mountains.

of these paths are so narrow and the surface so unstable that a heavy animal such as a mule or yak would always be at risk of tumbling over the edge, taking its load with it. On such paths, the solution is to use large numbers of sheep or goats, each one loaded with a small but significant burden.

An alternative is to use human porters, both men and women, who hire themselves out to whoever needs goods transported. For the most part, local traders do not use these porters, since it is cheaper to use their animals, but porters are useful for special high-value loads, such as the hydroelectric generators and cables being taken up into the high Himalayas, beyond the reach of access roads, as part of modernisation schemes. In the past, teams of porters using litters carried in objects as bulky as grand pianos and motor cars, for the use of the affluent rulers of Lhasa, the capital of Tibet, and Kathmandu, capital of Nepal.

A good porter can, surprisingly, carry as much as an average mule. He or she moves faster and is far less likely to slip and lose the precious cargo. The loads are slung down the back, supported by a band of fabric across the forehead, or over the top of the head. This is almost exactly the same design as used by the New Guinea highlanders for their *bilum* bags: both groups of mountain people have hit upon a design that is the most efficient, and the least stressful to carry, when ascending steep slopes. The only major drawback is that the band can wear away the hair on the front of the head, repeatedly breaking it off at the roots. A bald patch above the forehead is the mark of a traditional porter in the Himalayas.

THE FLOW OF HUMANITY

The trade routes that have long carried goods across the Himalayas have also frequently carried populations, pilgrims and missionaries, so that the complex patchwork of ethnic groups, languages and religions is the outcome of thousands of years of successive migrations, local conflicts, displacement, resettlement, integration and religious conversion. No one knows when the first people moved into these mountains and took up residence here, but the Himalayas and the Hindu Kush were probably the earliest mountains on Earth to have permanent inhabitants. Since that time many different peoples have been swept up into these mountain peaks in response to local conflicts, or to wars, persecution, famine or epidemics elsewhere.

Kathmandu is set in a deep valley that lies between the Himalayan and Mahabharat Ranges. The valley's main ethnic group, the Newars, have a faith that combines elements of Buddhism, Hinduism and a more ancient animist religion, the

three principal religious traditions in this region. During the festival of Dasain in October they sacrifice ducks, chickens and goats. It is only a century since human sacrifices were also performed.

The dead are cremated as in Hindu practice, but a special Newar ritual has long been practised when a king dies. A priest must eat a piece of the charred skull of the monarch, then ride away to India on an elephant and never return. This rite is intended to take away the sins of the king and ensure his salvation.

Other Himalayan peoples also combine Hinduism with Buddhism and animism, people such as the Gurung of Nepal, who are mountain farmers and hunters of wild game. Many more tribes and ethnic groups combine Hinduism with animism, or Buddhism with animism. Because of the influence of Tibet, Buddhism is most prevalent in the highest parts of these mountain ranges. The influx of Tibetan refugees has also brought a vibrant Buddhist tradition into the heart of Kathmandu, where an ancient Buddhist stupa, or monument, has been restored and augmented.

Meanwhile, within India, the mountain region of Ladakh – once an independent kingdom – still has a formal, structured Buddhist 'government', with substantial powers over the lay population vested in the lamas (head monks). This is moral government of the kind that has been systematically destroyed by the Chinese authorities in Tibet since 1950. Ladakh is often called 'Little Tibet' – its people are of Tibetan stock – and this small region maintains traditions that are thousands of years old.

Older religions, which worshipped spirits of mountains and streams amid a pantheon of other gods, run through both the Buddhist and the Hindu communities of the Himalayas, not as a distant echo of old folk-beliefs but as a powerful strand in the religious tradition. A few tribes, such as the Adi and other hill tribes of the Arunachal Pradesh region in the far north-east of India, still hold exclusively to their ancient beliefs. The Adi are farmers, but much of their livelihood comes from hunting wild animals, such as boar, deer, monkeys, squirrels and rats, in the upland forests. Because this area is claimed by China, the Indian government keeps it closed to outsiders, helping the Adi to survive with much of their ancient culture intact.

HOLY MOUNTAINS *A mass of stupas, or Buddhist shrines, a typical sight in the Himalayas. The stupas are solid structures with no interior.*

PEOPLE OF THE ANDES

The ancient cultures of the Andes, culminating in the Inca Empire, evolved finely balanced ways of life that enabled them to survive and even thrive in their rugged mountain homelands. Many of their traditions have lasted to this day.

In the high Andes, among a jumble of crags and precipices, the traveller comes across flights of neat stone steps cut into the mountainside, often followed by a stretch of well-made roadway paved with carefully cut stone. The road may continue to a point where the stone paving is overgrown with soft grass, or where the way vanishes over a sheer drop, or deteriorates into an unpaved path that becomes lost in a scree slope or a tangle of vegetation. This ghostly highway is 500 years old, built by the imperial Incas to carry their armies along the spine of the Andes, extending both north and south from Cuzco, their capital, in what is now Peru.

In its time the Inca road was a masterpiece of engineering, with tunnels boring through impassable rocks and raised causeways over marshland. The road triumphed over the great altitude, impossibly chaotic terrain and shortage of raw materials. Where ravines and gorges had to be crossed, the Incas, often lacking wood,

HELD BY A THREAD *Made of rope fashioned from twisted plant stems, this bridge in the Peruvian Andes follows an ingenious design from the time of the Incas and before.*

built rope bridges. They needed only grass to make the rope, and twigs to give a more secure footing. Suspended over dark echoing spaces, with foaming water or murderous rocks far below, these bridges looked too flimsy to support a child. Yet the Spanish conquistador Francisco Pizarro found to his amazement that horses and even cast-iron cannons could be taken across them.

The Incas' road system covered some 25 000 miles (40 000 km). It spanned almost the full length of this elongated empire, which, at its height, dominated a 2200 mile (3500 km) stretch of the Andes and the adjoining coastal region, including most of modern Peru, Bolivia and Ecuador, the southern tip of Colombia, northern Chile and the north-western corner of Argentina. Two main highways ran north-south, one along the spine of the Andes, the other at the western edge of the mountains largely through the coastal deserts. More than 20 east-west routes connected the two highways at different points, and there were also minor roadways pushing eastwards. The central parts of this network were as much as 52 ft (16 m) wide, so that columns of troops could march through at maximum speed. More distant branches were narrower, but never less than 3 ft (1 m) wide, so that a llama, loaded with goods, could pass comfortably along.

ROYAL ROAD *Part of the ancient Inca Highway passes through the Andes at an altitude of 13 000 ft (4000 m).*

EMPIRE BUILDERS

Llamas were essential to the success of the Incas, and of earlier Andean cultures such as the Chavín and the Huari. Sure-footedness is instinctive to them, and in a landscape where a small slip can lead to a dizzying, bone-crushing fall, this is an overriding asset. Llamas are also hardy creatures which can tolerate the rain and sleet freezing solid in their thick coats, and are virtually immune to the effects of thin air at high altitudes.

But llamas are not fast-moving, and the Incas, who ran a highly centralised regime, needed rapid communications to retain their grip on this region. Again, the terrain, the altitude and the elongated shape of their empire posed huge obstacles, but they overcame them with typical organisation and discipline. Couriers were trained to sprint 1 to 2 miles (2 to 3 km) along the mountain roadways, and relays of them could carry a message 155 miles (250 km) in a day. A message from Cuzco could reach either end of the Inca Empire within seven days. The messages were not written down, for the Incas had no system of writing, but were recorded on knotted strings known as *quipu*.

Inca rule achieved a level of prosperity in the high Andes that modern civilisation cannot match. It did this despite a far higher population: about 6 million at the empire's height. The eastern Andean peaks intercept rain from the east that would otherwise fall on the valleys and the *puna* – the high, dry, windswept plateaulands of the central Andes – creating arid conditions that make agriculture a precarious enterprise. But the people of the Andes knew how to control the water supply to irrigate the fields.

Today descendants of the Incas and their subject peoples can still be found in the puna, or cultivating tiny terraced fields

WOOLLY WEALTH *A herd of alpacas is driven to market in a distant valley. Alpacas are the source of a rich warm wool.*

Patches of Plenty *Tiny irregular fields, nestling into the contours of the mountains, allow Andean farmers to grow enough food for their families when the rainfall is adequate.*

on the steep slopes. Very few are pure-blooded Indians: there has been too much intermarriage with the Spanish colonists or with their descendants, the part-Indian part-Spanish people called mestizos. But many still regard themselves as Indian, wear a colourful semitraditional form of dress based on handwoven fabrics, speak an Indian language such as Quechua or Aymara, and keep to the old beliefs and customs. These beliefs are intermingled with the teachings and rituals of Catholicism, but there is little doubt that the ancient patterns of thought and behaviour are the stronger, giving the people of the high peaks a sense of identity as solid as the mountains themselves, a continuity with the past, and a powerful attachment to the landscape.

Although they may think of the Inca era as the Golden Age of the Andes – 'We are Incas' they say with pride – in truth, the traditions and rituals of these people reach farther back in time, to the cultures that preceded the Incas, and to the local village-based culture of the tribes which the Incas conquered. A central part of that culture was the concept of *ayllu*, meaning the community, and two forms of communal labour: *ayni* and *mink'a.*

Foot Plough *Using a simple type of foot plough known as the Inca plough, a husband and wife plant potatoes on the cold, windswept puna.*

The first, ayni, is a system of give-and-take, whereby neighbours and kinsmen help each other with tasks such as ploughing a field, sowing potatoes, irrigation work, rethatching a house, or building one from scratch. People who give their labour under the ayni system are social equals who expect the favour to be returned at a future date. The obligations are remembered by both sides and duly honoured when the need for help arises. In addition, the host provides food and drink during the day for all those working for him.

The mink'a system operates in unequal relationships such as that between father and son-in-law, where the father can expect help without offering his own labour in return. Recompense is made solely in food and drink for the day, and some small payment in kind such as a handful of coca leaves to take home.

The ayni and the mink'a are sociable traditions that allow the mobilisation of work-parties, in which four, five or more people join forces to carry out a task. The involvement of so many people, who sing, joke and talk as they work, alleviates the boredom and solitude of subsistence farming at high altitudes, and makes each task a significant event that confirms the cohesion of the ayllu and the survival of its values. In a land without maps and with scattered landholdings, the communal working of one man's fields also reinforces his claim to those fields.

The work parties embark upon the day's task with a sense of ceremony. Having trudged up the mountainside to the field that must be ploughed, planted or harvested, its members then sit down while the owner of the field distributes coca leaves to each participant. In a gesture of dedication, each person selects the three best coca leaves and carefully arranges them, one on top of the other, in the traditional manner. Holding the three leaves aloft, they each blow gently on the leaves while intoning the name of nearby mountain spirits and other deities. By this ritual act, the essential energy of the coca leaves is offered up to

Ancient Ways *Quechua women of Peru wear time-honoured costumes and drink the traditional home-brewed maize beer called* chicha.

the spirits of the mountain and other sacred places, who will, it is hoped, ensure the prosperity of the crop. The coca leaves are then chewed, in combination with a little ash from the hearth, brought along for the purpose. The chewing is slow and meditative, focusing the minds of the participants on the work ahead of them, in a ritual that takes about half an hour. By the time the day's toil begins, the workers are rested, revived and full of energy.

The effect of chewing coca leaves is to give a mild stimulus to the heart, similar to that from a cup of coffee or tea. The leaves also have a gentle painkilling action, roughly equal to that from two aspirin tablets, and they take the edge off the worker's hunger. But that is all. There is no comparison between chewing coca leaves and the dramatic effects of taking the purified narcotic cocaine, which drug traffickers, operating in the forest regions far away, produce from the leaves by a long chemical process. Coca leaves contain about a dozen other alkaloid substances besides cocaine itself, and the addition of the pinch of ash helps to release these. It is the combined action of all these different alkaloids which is thought to contribute to the overall effect of chewing coca leaves. (Something similar occurs with coffee, which contains more than 200 alkaloids; tea and chocolate likewise rely on a cocktail of chemicals for their stimulating effects, caffeine being only one ingredient in this cocktail.)

Coca also supplies some calories and nutrients such as vitamin C, beta-carotene from which vitamin A can be made, vitamin B_1, vitamin K, calcium, magnesium, iron and phosphorus. Such vitamins and minerals are greatly needed in the high Andes where green vegetables and fruit are scarce.

Pots for Chicha and Maize

A mild alcoholic beverage called *chicha* is also a crucial ingredient in organising work parties. It is a form of beer brewed using maize (corn), although barley and oatmeal can also be used, as can an indigenous Andean seed-crop called *quinoa*. Plentiful supplies of chicha are available to the workers. By tradition women alone can brew chicha, so they have a vital role in making the work party happen even though it may be men doing the heavy work. A widow or other single woman who is responsible for growing crops can still call on the help of the community because she can make chicha and therefore recruit a work party.

BREWING VESSELS *Giant pots for brewing chicha are made by itinerant potters. They alone can make such a pot without it collapsing while wet, or cracking when fired.*

THE SALT PANS OF THE ALTIPLANO

Some parts of the high Andean plateau known as the Altiplano (literally, high plain) have no rivers draining them – they are like enormous saucers in the sky. In eras of high rainfall, lakes built up in these regions, followed by a slow evaporation of the water. This is what happened in south-western Bolivia, where a vast expanse of the Altiplano was covered by water between about 40 000 and 25 000 years ago. Geologists call this vanished expanse of water Lake Minchin. After it had evaporated about 25 000 years ago, the land lay dry for 14 000 years. Then rainfall began to increase once more, and another lake, called Lake Tauca, appeared. This had a lifespan of only 1000 years, although it has never vanished altogether: two expanses of shallow water, nothing more than vast puddles, have survived. They are called Lake Poopó and Lake Uru Uru.

The ancient shorelines of Lake Minchin and Lake Tauca can still be seen. The receding waters have left behind a dazzling but sterile vista of white salt and minerals leached from the Andean peaks by the rainfall. Here and there among the salt deposits fossils of coral formations that grew up in the lake can also be seen. At its margins, the salt gives way to a desert landscape of rust-red rocks and brown cacti. Across it in winter blows a vicious wind, cold and relentless, that can produce hypothermia in minutes in someone not warmly dressed.

Following a storm, the salt flats are for a while covered by a thin film of water, which perfectly reflects the deep blue of the sky above. This creates a landscape illuminated by an extraordinary rippling blue light and dancing gleams of sunlight, a scene of immense and awesome beauty.

Since people first reached the Altiplano, this area has been used to provide salt. It is estimated that there are some 2000 million tons of salt here. Small traders can still collect salt by hand and load it onto their llamas, or carry it on their backs to the railway station at nearby settlements such as Colchani. A commercial salt-processing plant also operates, producing about 20 000 tons of salt each year.

NATURAL SALT *An Aymara Indian worker (right) shovels salt in the Salar de Uyumi, a huge salt flat covering 3500 sq miles (9100 km²) in south-western Bolivia. Mountain peaks rise above Laguna Colorada (left), a salt lake in the same region. In the Andes, as in Tibet, salt is a valuable commodity which traders from the Altiplano can exchange for crops from lower altitudes.*

Chicha is brewed in huge ceramic pots, some large enough for an adult to climb inside, crouch down and be entirely hidden. These pots are made by local potters skilled in a technique known as coiling, whereby the pot is built up from rope-like lengths of clay set one on top of the other, and worked together with rubbing and smearing actions to form the wall of the pot.

As well as making pots for his own village, a potter usually supplies other villages as well, and is repaid in kind. When a potter gets word that a village needs a new chicha pot, or other domestic pot, he loads up a llama with baskets of dry powdered clay from his storeroom. This prepared clay was dug from the ground some months before, allowed to dry out, pulverised and then sieved to remove stones and roots. By taking dry clay on his journey, he is keeping the weight of the raw material down, so that the maximum amount can be transported. After walking along mountain trails for a day or more, the potter reaches his destination and is formally greeted by those who have ordered the pots. Having asked for the blessing of the local mountain spirits, with rituals involving coca leaves and chicha, the potter sets to work. First, he wets the powdered clay and works it into the required consistency, then rolls out a flat slab of clay for the base of the pot and begins to build up the sides of the pot.

It is a long process to make such large pots, and then to fire them, requiring a stay of many days. The potter is fed by the villagers, and supplied with liberal amounts of chicha; his llama is given alfalfa or hay. When all the pots are made, the potter is paid in time-honoured fashion: the pots are filled to the brim with maize. A pot, in other words, is worth all the maize it can hold.

Potters often come from highland villages, above about 11 000 ft (3300 m), where maize is difficult to grow, or above 12 000 ft

(3600 m), where its cultivation is impossible. By mastering the art of pot-making, the people of the Andean puna have a useful item that can be bartered in villages at lower altitudes for the golden grains of maize, a highly valued food.

CONNECTING THE ANDES

The exchange of pots for maize forms just one small part of the great network of trading links that crisscross the Andean range. The people of the high puna also have the wool, meat and fat of llamas to offer to those in the lower regions, as well as *chuño* (dried potatoes), fava beans, woven fabrics and medicinal plants. In exchange, they seek crops that they cannot grow and other goods which their high, inhospitable puna does not provide, such as hot chilli peppers, wood, honey and coca leaves.

When the llama caravans linked the highlands with the coast, shellfish, dried seaweed, starfish and other products were also among the goods exchanged. During the 20th century, roads and lorries have usurped the role of the llama and mule trains on the coast and in the Andean foothills, yet there is still plenty of scope for such traditional forms of trade in the many areas not reached by roads.

It is the immensity of the Andean landscape and its great diversity that fosters this trade. To the west are deep fertile valleys with rich agricultural produce, including wheat, olives and grapes. In the north are the cold misty moorland regions known as *páramos*, similar to the puna in vegetation and agricultural possibilities but not so dry; here animal herding is practised and barley or potatoes grown. The high cold Altiplano de Bolivia is the principal puna region, cut by a few warmer valleys and forming a gigantic basin between two cordilleras. To the east, there is a sharp descent into the densely forested slopes called *ceja de la montaña*, 'eyebrow of the mountain region', where coca bushes grow wild and are cultivated. Below this is the mountain region itself, a high-altitude zone of dense tropical forest. Here coca, tea, coffee, cocoa and tropical fruit can be grown.

TEAM WORK *On the shores of Lake Titicaca, a small work party tills a field in preparation for planting potatoes.*

Today there is often an overlap between the traditional barter of the ancient trade routes and the modern economy. Peasant women from the valley of Yucay in Peru, near the former Inca capital of Cuzco, take part of their maize crop up into the puna each year and exchange it for the fresh meat of llamas and alpacas. On reaching their homes again, they salt the meat and dry it in the sun. Once it has been preserved in this way the women set off again, this time descending to the town of Quillabamba in the subtropical valley of La Convención.

For this part of the journey they hire a lorry rather than rely on pack animals. The meat is sold for money which the women use to buy consumer goods such as soap, candles, kerosene, radios, cassette players and aluminium pots.

All these trading exchanges across the mountains help to integrate the different ecological zones of the Andes into a common production area, where the deficiencies of one part are alleviated by the products of another, making life possible in regions such as the puna which suffer the most inhospitable climate, the shortest growing season and the poorest soils.

This 'vertical integration' can also be achieved in other ways, such as having a variety of different agricultural areas, grazing areas and foraging zones for each village, ranging from the valleys up to the puna. The people of the Ecuadorian páramo make up for the shortage of fuel on their moorlands by descending into the wild cloud forest below their villages to collect firewood.

In some areas a single ayllu, or community, may include two villages that are more than a day's walk apart and in different environmental zones. The lower village concentrates on growing maize while the upper one produces potatoes, but both crops are distributed among villagers at the other level according to kinship ties and the system of mutual obligation. This system protects against vagaries of climate that can produce a serious crop failure. If one level is affected by such a disaster – a hailstorm that devastates the young potato plants, or a drought that shrivels the maize before it can ripen – there is a good chance that the other area will escape and provide food to fill the gap.

Chuño, Charqui and Cuy

The ability to endure times of scarcity is a prerequisite for survival in the Andes. Two forms of preserved food then become enormously valuable. The first is chuño, a freeze-dried potato that was invented in prehistoric times on the frosty Altiplano where the potato was first domesticated from wild tuberous plants. The method of making chuño was recorded by the Spanish chroniclers of the 16th century, and the same techniques are still in use.

After harvesting and washing, the potatoes are spread out on the ground and left overnight to freeze. This breaks down the walls of the plant cells within the potato, so that the water is no longer held inside each cell. When they thaw in the sun the following morning the potatoes are, consequently, less firm than before. When squeezed, they 'give' like rubber, and a little water oozes out. The next stage in making chuño involves trampling the potatoes underfoot to expel as much water as possible. Men, women and children are all enlisted for this task, which is performed barefoot despite the cold.

The extracted water then evaporates in the dry air. When night falls, the potatoes freeze once again, to thaw again the next day and be trampled for a second time. The whole process is repeated for four or five days in succession, at the end of which a completely desiccated product, though still recognisably potato-shaped, is obtained. Chuño can be used much like bread, being dipped into a stew or soup and eaten as the starchy 'filler' to accompany such a meal.

A second form of preserved food is charqui or dried llama meat. The addition of salt and hot peppers adds flavour to this product, which is the inspiration for similar dried meat products now made in other parts of the world using meat such as beef or pork. The common name used for such dried meat – 'jerky' – is derived from the Quechua word *charqui.*

Although invaluable, charqui is not the only source of protein for the inhabitants of the Andean puna in hard times. Equally useful is the meat of the guinea pig, known as a *cuy* in Quechua. These rodents are the smallest domesticated mammals in the world, reared in a system that is finely adapted to the needs of the Andean villagers. Guinea pigs are shy creatures that, in traditional practice, inhabit the floors and dark recesses of people's houses, feeding on scraps from the kitchen and on forage plants or weeds brought home for them from the fields.

The scuttling and squeaking of guinea pigs is part of everyday life for the Indian people of the Andes. When describing portentous dreams, the speaker often sets the scene with the guinea pigs: 'It was in the

WINTER FARE *Farmers freeze-dry potatoes by leaving them out for several nights in succession. Trampling them under foot by day, when they thaw, removes the water.*

Easy Meat *In a traditional Andean home, the guinea pigs live with the family, eating kitchen scraps and being treated almost as pets.*

darkest part of the night and even the cuys had fallen silent . . .' or 'All the cuys suddenly began calling out at once . . .' Children may be given guinea pigs as presents by their godfather or godmother when they are old enough to care for one, and often take a major part in looking after all the guinea pigs, which are immensely easy to care for. A contemptuous Quechua dismissal of someone incompetent is: 'He'd be no use even for looking after cuys.'

There is little meat on a single guinea pig but it is highly regarded as food and plays an important part in many ceremonies. If a man seeks a young woman as his wife, the proper approach, in many parts of the Andes, is first to go and help her parents while they are working on their fields. The young man is not invited to help, nor does he make a verbal offer – he simply arrives and sets to work. This indicates his willingness to be a useful member of their family. The next step is for the young man and his parents to go to the girl's house with a cooked meal that includes guinea-pig meat, and offer it to the girl's parents. If they accept and eat the guinea pig, this is taken to mean 'yes' and the couple can then be married.

Nutritionally, guinea pigs add a useful amount of protein to the diet, although they are not part of people's everyday meals, being eaten mainly at festivals or cooked for guests. Guinea pigs can be fed on almost anything: alfalfa, potato peelings, grass, maize cobs, grains or carrots, for example, and because they are kept indoors in the family room, they remain largely unaffected by periods of bad weather.

Myths and Reality

According to the beliefs of the Quechua-speaking Indians, the souls of the dead must make a long journey westwards across the puna, over the high sierras and down into the western slopes of the Andes to reach the Mountain of the Dead, Qoropuna. On the way the soul passes through Qowillat, or 'Guinea-pig Town' – a region where the guinea pigs are all-powerful and human souls are helpless: anyone who has mistreated guinea pigs in their lifetime will be severely punished. The soul must also pass through Dog Town, Cat Town and Chicken Town, where again, revenge is taken against humans who mistreated these animals.

Among the many other evocative legends of the Quechua is one that describes the origin of the Indian people of the Andes. Before we came, say the old people as they retell this story to their grandchildren, the mountains were populated by the Nawpa Machukuna or 'Old Ones', a race of giants who lived by moonlight and for whom the moon was like our sun. Finally the sun came up, and the Nawpa Machukuna fled into the forests to the east of the mountains, or to other hiding places. Those who did not escape were dried up by the sun, but on nights with a bright moon they come alive again saying, 'It's day now', and go out to work their fields as they did long ago.

One version of this myth, told by Quechua people in southern Peru, illustrates the Andean talent for absorbing outside influences. In this story, the Nawpa Machukuna offend the supreme god, who sends his son Jesus Christ down to their moonlit world. They kill Christ who goes back to his father. After further unsuccessful efforts to make the Machukuna obey him, God sends down a rain of fire which kills many of them. Then he decides to repopulate the Earth with human beings and begins by making the Sun, whose appearance kills the last of the Machukuna.

The clothing worn by the Andeans shows the same genius for the safe assimilation of alien, and potentially hostile, influences. Two centuries ago, all Indian women were commanded by the Spanish authorities to wear narrow-brimmed felt hats and voluminous knee-length skirts, rather than the long straight ankle-length tunic of the Incas. It was part of the Spanish colonisers' long-running campaign to destroy Indian identity and customs. Both these imposed items of clothing have been absorbed and adapted so thoroughly that they are now taken for traditional Indian dress by both the Indians themselves and most outsiders. The heavy woollen skirts are usually layered one on top of the other, with up to five being worn in the coldest weather, or for festive occasions.

Ancient beliefs have survived despite a relentless persecution of 'idolatry' – any traditional religious practice – by the early Spanish missionaries, and the continuing denigration of all things 'Indian' by city-dwellers and the rest of the population. Even today, the prejudice against the traditional Indian people in their own countries is deep-rooted. When they descend from their mountain homes, the Andean Indians face an utterly different world, where they are despised and humiliated. Many abandon their traditional dress on the days they go into the local town, and hope to pass as mestizos.

If an Indian peasant brings food, such as guinea-pig meat, into a town to sell to a restaurant owner, he or she dares not approach the restaurant for Indians are not allowed into such places. The food must be sold to traders in small street markets on the edge of town, and the traders aim to buy as cheaply as possible so that they can sell at a substantial profit.

The traders are mestizos, but since the Indians themselves are not pure-blooded, the distinction is really about dress, language and custom. However, the mestizos generally do have more Spanish and less Indian blood. Mestizos speak Spanish even at home, wear more westernised clothes and share few Indian customs and beliefs. In most of the Andean countries, other than Bolivia, the mestizos outnumber Indians in all regions except the high puna and the cold, damp páramos. Mestizos generally get the upper hand in business dealings, land disputes and local politics, even in the predominantly Indian areas, because the odds are stacked against the Indians, legally and socially.

The Indian people of the mountains, although sociable, humorous and lively in their villages among those they know, are often reserved and even suspicious with strangers. Many maintain a typical mountain tradition of generosity to travellers, especially in the more remote regions, providing shelter, food and coffee, but usually express no curiosity at all about the origins or destination of their guests, and communicate little about themselves. Hospitality is often provided in an outbuilding or on a rough earthen verandah, not in the warm family rooms. To people from the more gregarious lowlands, there often seems to be an impenetrable mystery about these mountain dwellers, who truly inhabit a 'world apart'.

QUECHUA INDIANS *On market day Andeans display their finest costumes. Although seen as traditional, many elements of these costumes were introduced by the Spanish.*

Survival at High Altitudes

In settling among the world's mountain ranges, people have been forced to change and adapt. Many generations later, the result is a plethora of cultures and traditions that allow people to survive in harsh but often beautiful surroundings.

The sun has long since slipped behind the line of mountains and dusk is approaching. Nuristani women are descending the narrow rocky mountain paths, having spent all day working on their fields high above. To come home empty-handed would be to waste the journey, and each woman carries a bundle of firewood or a basketful of fodder for the animals. On their way down they pass other women, trooping up the same path to spend the night at work. On their backs these women carry bundles of split pinewood to use as torches when darkness falls. All through the night, small flickering points of light will be visible, moving here and there on the mountain slope as the women go about their work.

The reason for the 'night shift' lies in the irrigation system that keeps these mountain slopes of Nuristan green and fertile. Because it relies on mountain streams, there is a fairly steady supply of water, and this is allocated to the different fields in turn: an hour here, an hour there. By working during the night, the women ensure that they make full use of their water allocation during the growing season. Throughout the summer, the nights are alive with the sound of their singing and the glow of their firebrands.

The importance of making the maximum use of all resources is obvious. Both in

Life-giving Water *Irrigation is an essential part of farming in the arid valleys of Tibet. Here brilliant fields contrast with the dry mountain slopes.*

Nuristan and in other mountainous regions of the world, growing enough food at high altitude is never easy.

The Thirsty Slopes

Irrigation of crops is essential in many mountain areas, for the peaks themselves tend to block rainfall. In Nuristan, as in other parts of the Hindu Kush and the Karakoram Mountains, the rainfall is inadequate in most areas. There are rivers at lower levels which flow strong and fast, but the valleys run in such deep canyons – a feature of young mountain ranges – that the water is inaccessible. So the farmers in these dry mountain areas must bring water down to their fields from the high peaks over long distances.

The water from glaciers and mountain torrents is diverted into channels which lead it to the fields. Many of the channels are made from hollowed-out tree trunks, and where they cross gullies they may be supported on tall struts. Constant maintenance work is necessary because mud slides regularly block the ditches and demolish the makeshift wooden channels. Whenever a glacier moves substantially, the head of the irrigation system – the source of the water – is likely to be destroyed by the shifting ice, and a new one must be created.

LIQUID DIVERSION *Skillfully built into the face of a steep cliff, an irrigation canal in the Karakoram Mountains carries water to distant fields.*

The situation is much the same in the drier parts of the Himalayas. Here, the farmers pray not for rain but for sun when the fields are parched: rain is rare; the sun is more dependable. A few hours of sunshine will melt the glaciers a little, sending streams of chilly meltwater rushing down the mountainside.

Where there are dry valleys above barren slopes, it is even possible to create a small glacier that will, in time, provide enough water for irrigation. This is done by cutting a large block of ice from an active glacier elsewhere, and hauling it to the head of the dry valley. 'Planted' in the dry gravel, this block of ice grows year by year as the snows of winter accummulate around it, pile up, melt and refreeze. The planted block is like a seed crystal, causing more ice to form by preventing the snows from melting and evaporating in the sun, as they would if falling on bare gravel. After many years, a small glacier will have built up in the once empty valley – a dwarf compared to naturally occurring glaciers but with enough permanent ice to provide a stream of meltwater on summer days, so that the newly made fields below can be cultivated.

On the Nepalese section of the Tibetan plateau, it is often underground springs that supply the water for irrigation. Here the water is distributed by the throw of dice in a timeless ritual of chance. Two large dice made of compacted barley flour, with the dots neatly impressed on the faces, are used. The villagers sit in a circle, with stones set before them symbolising each household. The village chief solemnly calls out the name of a household and throws the dice. After each throw, a scribe records the number thrown. It is also recorded by placing the appropriate number of small stones beside the large stone symbolising the household. When all the households have been called, the villagers establish the order in which each one will receive water from the irrigation system. Those with the lowest numbers will be the first to get water each day; those with the highest numbers will be last. The ones who are last will probably have a smaller harvest, since water is the limiting factor, but they accept that chance is chance, and hope they may be

GIANT BURDEN *Dwarfed by an immense load of hay, a Nepali woman crosses a stream. Hay provides food for livestock during the cold winter months.*

first next time: ultimately, over the years, the system is fair enough to everyone.

There are mountainsides in Nepal that seem, at first glance, to be made of corrugated cardboard, their surface a series of neat parallel lines. A closer look reveals that these are terraced fields, hundreds of them stacked one on top of the other, ascending to the very limit of cultivation. These terraces are the labour of millions of pairs of hands over innumerable generations. Their lines have been etched on this hillside with sweat and toil, as farming people collected stones, built them into retaining walls, then shovelled soil in behind them to create each terrace. Where irrigation has long been practised – terracing and irrigation often go hand-in-hand – the irrigation water itself has added sediment to the terraces.

PLACE OF PARADOXES

Paradoxes abound in the Himalayas. Places such as Ladakh have less rainfall each year than the Sahara. Nevertheless, by using glacial meltwater for irrigation, crops can be grown. Elsewhere in the high Himalayas it is possible to suffer from both frostbite and sunstroke at the same time – if sitting with one's head in the sun and one's feet in the shade.

AGRICULTURE IN THE MOUNTAINS

Terracing is a solution to the problem of cultivating steep slopes, turning them into a series of small flat fields. It is a solution that was devised independently in many different parts of the world. The Andeans before the Spanish conquest in the 16th century were masters of the art of both terracing and irrigation, as are the farming people of the Himalayas and those of the Hindu Kush.

In parts of the Himalayas, the ground is so barren and stony that the soil has had to be created almost from scratch. Once the retaining walls of the terraces have been built, manure and straw are added, layer upon layer in the little pools of level space created by the terracing work. The droppings of goats and sheep are piled into large baskets on the high pastures where they graze, and carried down to the crop-growing altitudes to be added to the nascent terraces. Human manure or 'night soil' collected from the latrines in the villages is also added. Over the years, a bed of fine rich crumbly soil is gradually built up by this patient labour.

Constant repair work is needed to maintain the terraces, which regularly succumb to the forces of gravity and erosion. Landslides and mud slides can produce more dramatic large-scale destruction, taking only minutes to return hundreds of feet of ancient terracing to its natural form – a rough boulder-strewn slope. With each season, walls must be rebuilt and soil shovelled anew, more manure applied to fertilise the fields, and weeds removed.

Where land is especially scarce, or population pressures are high, even the most awkward slope may be terraced, and every scrap of available land used. This may produce tiny, oddly shaped fields, often triangular, perched alone on a steep slope. In the Japanese mountains they call such fields 'the cat's forehead'. While they yield precious little individually, these fragments of land, multiplied many times, add up to a worthwhile harvest. But the labour of cultivation is increased hugely by the effort of simply getting to them. In parts of Nepal, a farmer's holding may be less than 1 acre (0.4 ha) but made up of 30 or 40 separate plots, some as distant as two days' journey on foot.

Good flat land is at a premium in such regions. For this reason, the houses in the Himalayas and the Hindu Kush are built with flat roofs, and the roof used as a work platform for threshing, drying grass for winter fodder, rope-making, spinning wool and other activities. This saves agricultural land from being squandered on such activities. Many other patches of land have dual roles. An area may be fenced with thorny branches for use as an animal pen during the winter,

FLIGHT OF TERRACES *Like steps in a staircase, terraces create valuable farmland on a Nepali hillside. Terrace maintenance is an essential part of daily life.*

GRAIN DRYING *Grain is spread out to dry after the harvest in Nepal. The process is helped by strong sunshine and by thin air, which accelerates evaporation.*

but when spring comes the fences are removed. The temporary animal shelter built of turves and dung is removed, and the land broken up with a plough or hoes for use as a vegetable garden. Villages in the Karakoram Mountains are traditionally sited on barren land, such as the bleak rubble-stone moraines deposited by glaciers. This again saves agricultural land from being wasted.

Hot Beds for Cold Spots

Many examples of agricultural skill are found in the New Guinea highlands. In the Laiagam Valley of the Engan highlands, crops are grown at 7200 ft (2200 m), the highest agricultural enterprise in New Guinea. Frosts are a regular occurrence here, and the lush but delicate crops of the highlanders such as sweet potatoes, yams and dasheens – all root crops which originate from hot humid zones – are not adapted to withstand the ravages of ice crystals forming inside their leaves. So the highlanders grow them on 'hotbeds' – coincidentally, a system used to grow pineapples and melons in northern Europe in the 17th and 18th centuries. Huge mounds of compost and manure are built up, each standing about 3 ft (1 m) high and 8 ft (2.4 m) long. The earth around the mounds is stamped down hard to resist the rain and to form paths from which the crops can be tended and weeds removed. Sweet potatoes (called *kaukau* by the highlanders) are planted along with other crops in the top of the mound, where they flourish on the rich soil. As well as being extremely fertile, the mound generates heat as its damp interior rots away. In effect, the mound is like a heated greenhouse without glass, the fuel being the energy stored in leaves and roots that grew the previous season, now released as heat by the action of bacteria.

In the Himalayas hardier crops have long been available, and this allows cultivation to penetrate farther into the high peaks, sending tentative fingers of delicate green up the harsh grey-brown mountain slopes. At the highest levels, buckwheat is a reliable standby, a tough almost weedy plant with tiny brown triangular seeds. Its strong, earthy flavour is an acquired taste, and it is rarely grown or eaten in large amounts. In the highest fields, potatoes, too, may be grown. They are a true mountain crop, imported to the Himalayas from the Andes. They travelled first to Europe, then from Europe to India, and so reached the Himalayas by a roundabout route. On the way, the potato was bred for survival in a cool, damp northern climate. It lost some of the adaptations to mountain climates, tropical day lengths and a short growing season it had inherited from its Andean forebears.

HIGHLAND HOTBEDS *These compost heaps in the highlands of New Guinea have been planted with sweet potatoes. Warmth from the compost will protect the plants from frost.*

PLOUGHING A PLOT *Small terraces create problems when ploughing time arrives. This Nepali farmer has to manoeuvre his animals in a space just a few yards across.*

The potato that arrived in the Himalayas was not the same high-altitude subtropical crop that had left the Andes centuries before. Nevertheless, it has served the peasant farmers of the Himalayas well.

In the Hindu Kush, onions, tomatoes, chillies, aubergines, sunflowers, potatoes and carrots are the main crops. In the wetter villages, where there are forests of evergreen oak, goats are reared on their leathery but nutritious leaves – fodder which only they could relish. Where the climate is not so harsh, wheat, barley, maize and millet can be raised, and in the mildest and best-watered villages rice is cultivated. Orchards and single much-cherished fruit trees supply small sweet apricots, cherries, almonds, peaches and pomegranates.

BEATING TIME

The growing season is short in mountain regions, because the spring sun has to melt the snow and ice of winter before it can begin to warm the soil and the newly sown grain. Various stratagems have been devised by mountain people to overcome this problem. In northern Nepal, rice is grown on high mountain fields by germinating the seed before it is planted. At the end of March, one room in each home is set aside for this purpose, and the floor covered with mats made from the bark of birch trees. A fire is started in the hearth, then the rice is scattered over the floor and sprinkled with water by the women. All the while, prayers and invocations are recited. Pine needles are spread over the rice to keep out the light, and more water is applied to dampen the pine needles and prevent them from soaking up the moisture from the rice.

The fire is stoked regularly, and more water sprinkled over the floor each morning and evening. The room, dark except for the flames flickering in the hearth, becomes hot, humid and richly scented with the damp pine needles and the germinating rice. After four days, the rice grain has swollen and grown soft. The first hint of a small white root can be seen emerging from some of the grains. The women remove the pine needles, gather up the grain and, while the seeds are still damp, scatter them on the prepared fields, amid more prayers and rituals. By germinating the grain indoors, they give it a head start. Each seed begins putting down roots as soon as it enters the soil – soil that is still too cold to allow seed to germinate naturally. By this technique Nepalese farmers manage to grow rice, a tropical and subtropical crop, at altitudes of between 7500 and 9000 ft (2300 and 2700 m), higher than anywhere else on Earth.

BLACK AND WHITE

A solid mass of fallen snow takes a long time to melt in the spring because its white crystalline surface reflects the sun's rays, turning away the warmth that could otherwise melt

HITTING THE HIGH NOTES

The acoustics of mountains produce many strange and intriguing effects. The thinness and dryness of the air allow sound to travel farther, and the unearthly silence of the remote peaks augments this effect. The voices of people who are visible only as distant specks on a far-off slope may carry across the intervening space with surprising clarity.

Even in the New Guinea highlands, where the air is often quite damp, this sound effect is evident, and in times of peace there is a traditional call known as *singaut* – calling amicably, with high-pitched musical notes, to anyone on the surrounding slopes who might be listening. If someone hears it, they return the call. The coming of helicopters, roads, jeeps and motorboats to certain areas is lamented by some highlanders, who can no longer singaut most of the time because of the insistent noise of engines.

Certain types of sound carry more readily in mountains than elsewhere, and the fact that yodelling was invented in both the Swiss Alps and the New Guinea highlands is a matter of common acoustics, not coincidence. Yodelling is used for a variety of communication purposes in New Guinea, but some of the early exploration parties in the 1930s became convinced that the yodel was a 'kill-cry', and reacted with panic and aggression whenever they heard it, sometimes shooting highlanders whose intentions were peaceable. Whistles also carry well at altitude, and mountain villagers in the Canary Islands have a traditional whistle language, used to communicate with those working on distant fields, or herding flocks on a far-off slope.

The silence of the peaks gives way to a deafening roar alongside mountain torrents. Ordinary speech is futile if people on one bank wish to communicate with those on the other side, as they frequently do when herding goats across rope bridges, for example. In Nuristan, a local sign language was devised for use in these circumstances.

the ice crystals within. Farmers in parts of Ladakh and the Zanskar Valley, both Himalayan regions now within India, solve this problem in a simple but ingenious way. Each autumn, after the harvest, they plough the soil, add manure, and pile some of the soil and manure up in a conical mound in the centre of the field. The mound must be high enough to project through the thick snows of winter. In spring, before the snow has melted, the farmers shovel this soil over the crust of snow, spreading it out to cover the snow entirely and turning the field from white to black. The change in colour causes far more of the sun's rays to be absorbed. Within a few days the snow has melted and the soil is ready for planting.

At lower altitudes agriculture becomes easier, and the crops that can be grown are more varied. Even maize, which requires 60 days without frost to ripen, may be cultivated in some areas. The drawback of the lower slopes is that far more animal pests hover about each field ready to plunder the crop before it is harvested. In Nepal, monkeys are among the most serious pests, descending on the fields in troops 20 to 30 strong and quickly stripping ears of barley, wheat, millet and other crops. Less brazen, but almost as voracious, are wild boar, porcupines and Himalayan blue bears. Up to a quarter of each crop may be destroyed by animals, despite constant vigilance.

In some areas, *bharals* or Himalayan blue sheep may ravage the crops. The traveller and writer Eric Valli describes watching a Buddhist lama burning incense in a field of barley in northern Nepal, while reciting prayers to protect the crop from insects. Concentrating intently on his prayers, the monk did not hear the group of bharals immediately behind him eating the young barley shoots. Eventually a woman of the village noticed the bharals and drove them off with shouts and stone-throwing.

Domesticated animals can also damage crops, and a system of redress exists in parts of Nepal. If a yak, goat or horse simply crosses a field, each footprint the animal makes is charged to its owner at one measure (a bowlful) of barley. Extra fines are

Blue Sheep ***Himalayan bharals (left) normally live on scant mountain grass, but verdant fields sometimes prove an irresistible attraction. In Nepal, a Manang house (opposite) accommodates people, animals, stored crops and firewood. Ladders provide access from one roof to the next.***

payable if the animal stops to eat, based on the proportion of the crop destroyed. These fines act as an incentive to the villagers to keep their animals well tethered or fenced in.

Above the tree line in any mountain region, fuel for fires and cooking is scarce. Yak dung is burned in the high Himalayas as llama dung is in the Andes – mountain people in widely separated parts of the world hitting on the same solution to a common problem. Villagers in the Hindu Kush even burn the pellet-like droppings of sheep and goats, which children collect from the mountain slopes where flocks have grazed. The drawback of using dung for fuel is that it denies the land fertilising manure.

FUEL AND COOKING

On the lower slopes of mountains, below the tree line, wood may be used. The Karnali people of Nepal burn pine wood, and in their chimney-less houses the black oily smoke coats walls, possessions and people alike. A local saying describes the change of the seasons: 'When the snows of winter turn the mountainside white, then the people turn black.' In Nuristan, oak is put on the fire when an honoured guest is being entertained rather than pine or cedar because it makes less smoke.

One readily available source of warmth is the body heat of domestic animals. By corralling the animals beneath the family's living quarters, it is possible to benefit from the rising warmth during the night. Not all the Himalayan peoples do this, but in parts of Nepal villages are built in tiers, like ramshackle tenement blocks, propped against a sheer cliff-face. Home-hewn wooden ladders, or simple notched timbers that can be climbed like stairs, link one storey with the next. Four or even five storeys high, they house many families, with each family occupying a vertical 'slice' of the building.

DAILY GRIND *Using technology that has changed little in centuries, a woman grinds wheat in Bhutan. Meanwhile, her chillies dry in the sun.*

Precious fuel must be conserved as much as possible. In parts of Afghanistan, broad, low tables known as *sandals* are covered with eiderdowns while a small stove, glowing with red-hot coals, is installed beneath. When snow-laden winds howl down from the peaks of the Hindu Kush, whole families can sit together around such a table, their legs stretched out in the blissful warmth beneath.

The natural volcanic heat that boils deep in the heart of mountain ranges is also a potential source of warmth in some regions. Where it bursts up into hot springs and thermal pools, the luxurious penetrating comfort of a hot bath may be available to mountain dwellers, as long as the waters are safe to use – at just the right temperature, and free from the caustic chemicals that can leach into the water from some volcanic rocks. At Cajamarca in the Peruvian Andes, the Incas turned natural hot springs into luxurious royal baths.

The shortage of fuel in many mountain regions puts certain restrictions on traditional cooking. So too do the crops grown, and the physical effects of altitude. Because the atmospheric pressure is so much lower than at sea level, water boils at a lower temperature, which means that things take longer to cook. In the high Andean puna, it can take as long as an hour to boil potatoes. Freeze-dried potatoes, or chuño, are popular not just because they can be stored for a long time: the freezing and drying also breaks down the starch and cellulose in the potatoes, so that they need little or no cooking as long as there is some warm liquid, such as soup, to moisten them with.

In those parts of the Andes where barley is a dietary staple, such as the páramo region of Ecuador, special cooking methods are required. Barley contains too little protein to be turned into bread, and boiling it to an edible state takes a full hour, which would consume too much fuel. The answer is to roast the barley, then grind it. The resultant coarse powder, called *machica*, requires no further cooking. It is mixed with hot water or coffee to provide an instant meal.

Coincidentally, the Tibetans long ago devised the same technique for cooking barley. The Tibetan method – also used in the high zones of Nepal wherever there are Bhotias (people of Tibetan origin) – is to roast the barley grains on a bed of hot sand over the fire. The sand prevents the barley from burning and sticking to the metal roasting pan. Once roasted, the barley grains are ground using a flat circular stone, set onto a larger stone and turned by hand. The grain is fed into a hole at the centre of the grinding stone with the free hand, and the brownish powder, known as *tsampa*, flows out from the edges of the stone.

Tsampa can be mixed with yak milk, goat milk or the salted yak-butter tea that is the national drink of Tibet, or simply moistened with water, to provide an instant meal.

OUTDOOR KITCHEN *In Tibet roasted barley meal, or* tsampa, *is a staple food. Here the preparation process is well under way.*

It is kneaded with the fingers to yield an edible consistency, and although the tsampa sticks unpleasantly to the inside of the mouth, the flavour is good. Tibetan travellers rely on tsampa during their journeys, and it is the staple ingredient of most home-cooked meals as well. It is filling and nourishing, the more so if mixed with milk to increase the protein content.

Like yak-butter tea, tsampa features in many Tibetan Buddhist rituals: for example, the traditional rite for disposal of the dead, still practised in parts of Tibet. The corpse is taken to a high deserted peak and fed to vultures that gather there knowing a meal is in store. This custom serves a practical purpose in a land where the soil is often frozen or covered by a thick layer of snow, but the Tibetans who practise the rite believe that it is a spiritual necessity as well: every trace of the body must be gone before the soul can escape its earthly form and re-enter the cycle of reincarnation. To dispose of the bones completely and promptly once all the flesh has been picked off them, the Tibetans grind them to powder, mix them with moistened tsampa, and feed this mixture also to the vultures.

MANAGING THE LAND

In some mountain regions, the difficulties of growing crops or rearing animals at high altitudes have long been moderated by a system of land management which aimed to give each family fair access to the best lands, while keeping the pressure on the land within sustainable limits. The age-old system on the Tibetan plateau, or Chang Tang, depended on keeping a pasture book, where the number of goats, sheep or yaks that could be supported by the different tracts of grazing land were recorded. A census of the livestock was taken every three years to establish which pastures were overpopulated. A family whose herds had increased in number could be allocated more land, while those whose animals had declined would have their pasture reduced since they no longer needed as much. This system kept the level of grazing over the whole plateau evenly spread. Sometimes, an entire family and its herd would be re-allocated to another area to prevent overgrazing.

Although taking land rights away from those with a dwindling herd might seem harsh, it helped to maintain the overall level of productivity, and since poor nomads could always seek to work as hired hands for families with larger herds, being paid with yak milk, butter, grain and other food, the system ensured that no one went hungry. This system was abolished by the Chinese authorities in the 1970s, but with the return of traditional herding methods, some of the old rules have become established again.

Re-allocation of land was also once a feature of the southern slopes and valleys of the Hindu Kush. Under the so-called '*wesh*' system, land was redistributed once every five to ten years to ensure that different clans each had a fair chance to farm the best land. The clan members, along with their servants and craftsmen, would migrate to a new village, taking all their possessions with them, and moving into the houses and farm buildings just vacated by the departing clan. Instituted in 1530, it survived until the 19th century in many areas. By preventing the sale of land, the wesh system helped to protect mountainous lands from over-exploitation. The survival of the ancient forests of oak and pine in much of the Hindu Kush may in part be due to this system.

Health and Sickness in the Mountains

A Chinese official returning from Tibet 2000 years ago renamed the high Tibetan plateau 'The Headache Mountains'. He had almost certainly been suffering from altitude sickness, which frequently sets in at heights above 7900 to 9900 ft (2400 to 3000 m). Another early traveller to high altitudes wrote of 'a strange effect which the air or wind which blows has . . . namely that men get seasick with it no less, yea even more than at sea'. Human beings are lowland creatures, whose origins lie on the plains of Africa. Mountains are not their natural home, although those born and bred on the mountains do far better than newly arrived lowlanders such as the Chinese official.

Altitude sickness begins with a sense of utter exhaustion, often accompanied by tingling of the hands and feet, a deep depression, nausea, headaches and dizziness. Children and teenagers are more often affected than adults. There is an overwhelming urge to lie down, although the best cure is to turn back and descend into the valleys where more oxygen is available.

More severe attacks of altitude sickness produce hallucinations and disorientation, which can be very dangerous for the lone traveller. Most hazardous of all is pulmonary edema, in which fluid accumulates in the lungs causing coughing and the production of a frothy phlegm. Pulmonary edema is life-threatening because it interferes with breathing. Sometimes this is accompanied by cerebral edema, a build-up of fluid in the brain. Hallucinations, confusion and unsteadiness are the first signs of cerebral edema. Vomiting and seizures are also indicative of water collecting in the brain, and if these signs are not heeded, the victim may go into a coma. Recovery from cerebral edema may require several weeks' stay in hospital. If left untreated it can result in death.

Tending the Herd *In a landscape that seems devoid of vegetation, a Dropka nomad from Tibet brings back a pail of goat's milk. The milk is a valuable food.*

HOT-BLOODED HIGHLANDERS

Although adaptations to altitude are probably not inherited traits, the remarkable tolerance of low temperatures among both Andean Indians and Tibetans may be a genetically determined characteristic. The nomads of Tibet, although they have warm clothes, will happily go bare-chested in an icy wind. Their body temperature seems to be naturally higher, as does that of Andeans. A Spanish chronicler, Father Cobo, described this ability: 'The Indians are red-blooded to an extreme degree, from whence they derive their excessive heat . . . if in the time of greatest cold and ice one touches their hand, one will always find heat in it, amazingly . . . When they are on a journey, they sleep, even though it be on very cold high plateaus, wherever night overtakes them under the open sky, and if a span's depth of snow falls on them, they go on sleeping under it as restfully as if they were in soft and downy beds.'

SANDALS IN SNOW *A raised metabolic rate – the rate at which the body uses energy – may help to explain why mountain people seem impervious to the cold.*

All these effects were graphically described by a Spanish priest, Father Acosta, travelling in the Andes in the late 16th century: 'I was suddenly seized with such a mortal anguish that I was of a mind to throw myself off the horse onto the ground . . . and thereupon I was seized with such retchings and vomitings that I thought I should give up my soul, for after the food and phlegm came bile and more bile, this one yellow and the other green, until I came to spit up blood, from the violence which was being done to my stomach. Finally I declare that if it had gone on, I believe I would most assuredly have died, but it only lasted a matter of three or four hours until we got down a good long way and came to a more healthy air-temper.'

All these effects are due to a lack of oxygen in the air at high altitudes. At 17 000 ft (5200 m) the number of oxygen molecules entering the lungs is only half the number entering at sea level. Exactly how this produces the symptoms of mountain sickness is not understood, but the reduced level of oxygen in the blood has direct effects, as well as some indirect ones through alterations in the chemistry of the blood. These direct and indirect effects combine, and act on the muscles, nervous system, heart and lungs. In an attempt to compensate for the shortage of oxygen, blood supply to the lungs and the brain is stepped up – in the hope of acquiring more oxygen from the lungs, and delivering more oxygen to the highly sensitive oxygen-hungry brain. Unfortunately there is also an increase in the permeability (the 'leakiness') of the blood vessels, for reasons that are not fully understood, and when combined with the increased blood flow can push fluid into the brain and lungs, causing edema.

Altitude sickness can be avoided by making a slow ascent. After reaching 7900 ft (2400 m) it is wise to take the subsequent climb gradually, in stages of about 2000 to 3000 ft (600 to 900 m), with a day or two of rest between each stage. During the rest days it is safe to make a short excursion to a higher altitude, as long as the night is spent at the lower level. It is also important to drink plenty of fluids. This staged ascent allows the body to manufacture more red blood cells, the tiny disc-shaped particles in the blood that are responsible for carrying oxygen around the body. Seen under the microscope, red blood cells look like coins, and they are indeed a type of currency, circulating around the body with a wealth of precious oxygen. In the poor air of the high mountains, human blood needs to be richer in this currency.

A lowlander going up into the high mountains takes about a month to build up the number of red blood cells to the minimum level. Those who ascend gradually and avoid altitude sickness still experience a racing pulse (as the heart tries to compensate for low oxygen levels) and extreme fatigue when they first reach high altitudes. The smallest physical task exhausts them in a very short time. This initial reaction usually abates within a week or so, and the pulse rate returns to normal.

But even when acclimatised, lowlanders are still feeble creatures compared to the

natives of the high mountains. Western travellers are invariably left gasping and astonished by the ability of Andean peasants or Himalayan porters to ascend dizzying slopes at a sharp trot, even when heavily laden. Tibetan nomads, who live at heights of about 17 000 ft (5200 m) have 22 per cent more haemoglobin in their blood. Haemoglobin is the pigment that gives red blood cells their colour, and which does the work of picking up and transporting oxygen molecules. Curiously, native Andean Indians living at lower levels in the Andes have more haemoglobin than this, although they show no greater adaptations to altitude than the hardy and agile Tibetans. This may indicate that the Andeans and Tibetans have followed different evolutionary routes in their adaptation to altitude.

Andeans, especially pure bred Indians, also seem to have a larger lung capacity – they are conspicuously barrel chested. It has long been assumed that they were genetically endowed with some of these high altitude adaptations, inheriting an intrinsic ability to deal with heights that no incoming lowlander could hope to match. Recent research in South America has cast doubt on this idea. It seems that when native highlanders go to live at lower levels (as is more common now, with migration in search of

Approach to Everest
For people accustomed to life at low altitude, trekking can be exhilarating but exhausting. Altitude sickness is usually quick to pass, but each step is still hard work in the thin air.

work to the shanty towns around Lima and other coastal cities in Peru) they lose their adaptations to high altitude. Conversely, a lowlander who stays for many years in the highlands can become increasingly well adapted, and if children of lowland parents are raised at high altitude they can breathe as freely as the natives.

The tale of Heinrich Harrer, author of the classic *Seven Years in Tibet*, bears this out. Harrer escaped from a prisoner-of-war camp in British-held India during the Second World War, and walked up into the Himalayas with a view to reaching Tibet. Exhausted and dizzy with the altitude at first, Harrer gradually adjusted to the lower levels of oxygen. An Italian prisoner who escaped with him, despite his apparent fitness, was soon forced to admit defeat as he tried to grapple with the rarefied air, the difficult paths and the lack of food. Harrer reached the Tibetan border, but was recaptured before he could get across and taken back to India. He escaped again, and once more hiked up into the mountains, travelling mostly at night and hiding up by day. By the time he reached Lhasa, the capital of Tibet, in January 1946, almost two years after his escape, Harrer was as fit as the Tibetan pilgrims following the same road to Lhasa, who gasped for breath as they ascended to 20 000 ft (6000 m) to cross the Guring La Pass. Harrer noted that the Tibetans believed the symptoms experienced when climbing to this height were due to poison gas in the air around the pass, and that they chanted Buddhist mantras to ward off its evil effects.

Not every immigrant to the world's high places thrives as well as Heinrich Harrer. For reasons that are not yet understood, some succumb to a disease called Chronic Altitude Sickness. This usually affects people who have lived at heights of over 13 000 ft (4000 m) for several years. Their blood becomes enriched with haemoglobin, as it should, but the level is excessive, and the rate of blood flow to the brain declines. As a result, the part of the brain that senses the amount of oxygen in the blood and regulates breathing stops functioning properly. The sufferer no longer breathes faster when the body is short of oxygen, and begins to experience symptoms such as coughing, giddiness and headaches. No treatment has been found for this disease except a return to lower altitudes.

Blinded by the Light

Altitude sickness is only one of the sufferings that mountains can inflict on the human body. Another hazard is snow-blindness caused by the high levels of ultraviolet light at high altitudes. The thin atmosphere of mountain heights filters out less of the ultraviolet light coming from the sun. In addition, the snowfields and glaciers, ice falls and mountain lakes all reflect the ultraviolet light from their glittering surfaces in a breathtaking splendour that enchants the eye of the traveller, while doing untold harm to the eye's outer layer, the cornea. The surface of the cornea can become so badly damaged that it peels away like sunburned

FIRST AID *Wrapped in a pressurised bag, a climber (below) is given oxygen to treat altitude sickness. With extra oxygen, the symptoms are usually quick to disappear. At 18 000 ft (5500 m), a base camp below the Kumbu Icefall (bottom) gives mountaineers a chance to acclimatise before an attempt on Everest.*

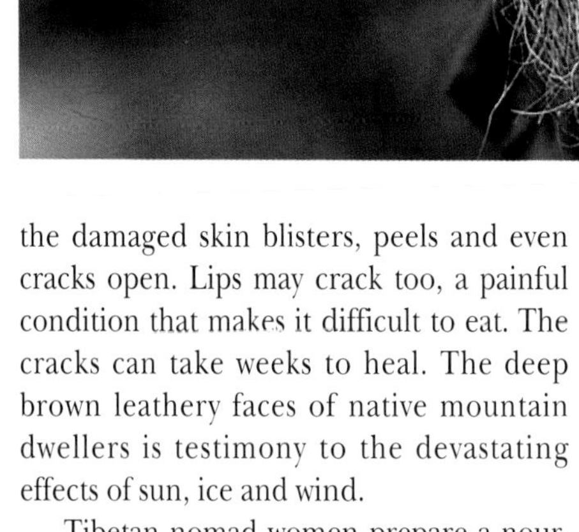

CHILD OF THE MOUNTAINS
At birth, the children (above) of mountain dwellers already have some of the adaptations for life high up. The rigours and rewards of mountain life are reflected in the face of this Himalayan man (right).

skin, exposing sensitive nerve endings in the eye that are normally covered. The pain of snow blindness is excruciating. It feels as if the eyeballs are on fire, yet the world is in utter darkness. An attack usually clears up within two days as the cornea regrows, the pain subsiding and vision slowly returning.

The intense ultraviolet radiation of the mountains also takes its toll on the skin, especially that of the face. It can become badly sunburned, frozen during blizzards, and chapped by searing winds as well, until the damaged skin blisters, peels and even cracks open. Lips may crack too, a painful condition that makes it difficult to eat. The cracks can take weeks to heal. The deep brown leathery faces of native mountain dwellers is testimony to the devastating effects of sun, ice and wind.

Tibetan nomad women prepare a nourishing skin treatment by boiling down the whey of yak milk to give a brown paste that is spread on the cheeks like a face pack. Despite such efforts, their skin ages prematurely. In the Andes it is the same story: it is commonplace to see a child with an apparently elderly woman who looks as if she must be the child's grandmother – until she puts the child to her breast, and it becomes clear that she is the mother.

HANGING ON

Newborn babies have a grasping reflex which makes them grip tightly onto anything placed in the palm of the hand. In the West, this reflex disappears after about four months, but in the remote parts of Nepal, where babies are often carried along narrow and perilous mountain paths by children as young as six, babies seem to retain this reflex, and to hang onto the clothing of the child carrying them. This allows the child to carry a small load in addition to the infant.

INFERTILE PEAKS

At the beginning of the 17th century, every Spanish boy in the Andean mining town of Potosí was called Nicolas. Potosí had been founded in 1545 next to a mountain in which silver had been discovered by an Indian llama herder. (Legend has it that the herder lit a campfire that melted the earth beneath it and produced a shining stream of silver.) The new town grew in what one contemporary observer called 'a pandemonium of greed', attracting some 20 000 Spanish inhabitants. Yet for 53 years, not one Spanish child survived beyond infancy. Most of the Spanish in Potosí did not even succeed in having babies, while the 100 000 Indians, forced to live there and work in the silver mines under appalling conditions, were as fertile as ever. Finally, 53 years after the founding of Potosí, a baby boy was born and survived. His parents had dedicated him to St Nicolas, and other anxious parents called their children Nicolas as well, in the hope of their survival. Gradually, more children survived – probably as a result of acclimatisation by their parents – and belief in the protective powers of St Nicolas increased. Only the most reckless of parents would call their boy anything else.

Potosí stands 13 000 ft (4000 m) above sea level, and such high altitude undoubtedly affects fertility, both human and animal. Cows, horses, dogs, rats, rabbits, cats, geese and chickens are among the lowland animals that fail to breed when first taken to high altitudes. When a British explorer, Suydan Cutting, reached Lhasa in 1935, he showed a great interest in the unusual breeds of Tibetan dog, such as the Tibetan apso. The Dalai Lama later sent Cutting three Tibetan apsos, which bred well in Calcutta, but the dachshunds and dalmatians sent by Cutting as a gift never produced puppies in Lhasa. It seems that the testicles of male animals stop producing sperm, probably as a result of the increased level of ultraviolet radiation, or the low level of oxygen, or a combination of both. In time, sperm production may begin again.

UPS AND DOWNS

Mountain dwellers have no notion of moving from A to B in a straight line. Mountain travel is often an exhausting series of ups and downs that produce only an insignificant forward movement in the course of a day. A mistake in navigation can lead to an entirely wasted journey, along a pathway that has been destroyed by an earthquake or a rockfall, or a ridge that leads to a sheer drop. It is nothing for an inhabitant of the Andes or Himalayas to clear away a fall of earth or rocks from a path, edging forward slowly on a dangerous slope, to shovel the debris over the edge, so that the journey may continue.

While travelling up a steep slope is exhausting, coming down can be just as taxing because of the constant muscular effort needed to counteract the pull of gravity: with each footfall, the body must be braced to prevent a fall. At the end of a long descent, this can leave the legs trembling and shaking: Japanese mountaineers call this phenomenon 'laughing knees'.

On snow-covered slopes sledges or skis can be used to exploit the force of gravity. Skis have been used in Scandinavia for at least 4000 years, although nothing equivalent exists among traditional mountain peoples elsewhere. Sledges were invented in the Arctic for easy travel across level ice and snow; nothing similar was devised in mountain zones. When Heinrich Harrer and another German prisoner of war, lodging in a Nepali village during their escape to Tibet, decided to make some skis from local wood and to ski on the nearby slopes, they met with angry opposition from the local people, particularly the Buddhist monks, who regarded this as a sacrilegious act likely to offend the mountain spirits.

Some traditional mountain dwellers do use long handheld poles as a means of descending more easily. In the mountainous Canary Islands, villagers in the more remote areas skim down steep slopes at astonishing speed by using the pole to brace themselves and leaping from tussock to tussock.

Crossing mountain streams, which often flow fast and furious, is a challenge that has produced many ingenious solutions among the inhabitants of high altitudes. Suspension bridges, often made of nothing more than twigs and home-made rope, are a common solution. They are valuable for crossing ravines and gorges, although their swaying motion and apparent instability, strike terror

HIGH VISIBILITY *Brilliant Himalayan peaks rise above the haze-covered foothills. At extreme altitudes, thin dust-free air leaves the sunlight dangerously intense.*

into the hearts of inexperienced travellers. Another device for crossing chasms is a simple chair or box, suspended from a rope, and pulled across on a pulley system from one side to the other. Such crossings are found in both the Andes and the Himalayas, and are useful where people alone, without any pack animals, wish to cross.

Where a stream is not buried deep in a gorge, it may be possible to cross on a raft. An age-old system for making rafts, used in both the Himalayas and the Hindu Kush, uses inflated animal skins. To make a large raft of this kind, ten or eleven goats are killed, and the skins removed carefully from the meat and bones, leaving only a neat slit along the belly, and holes at the neck and at the end of each of the four limbs. The belly slit is sewn up tightly and daubed with animal grease to make the seam airtight. The neck and three of the limb openings are tied tightly with twine made from wool. Finally, the skin is inflated by strenuous blowing into the opening of the fourth leg. When the skin is as round and tight as a balloon, this leg too is tied with twine. Next comes the process of checking for leaks: listening carefully for the hiss of escaping air, hunting for the source of the sound, then sewing up the hole with twine and daubing it with grease.

A rectangular frame made of wood is constructed, and the inflated goat skins are lashed to its underside. The largest skins are positioned along the side that forms the front of the raft. Launching the raft is done with considerable caution, and half an hour or more is spent checking that it will stay afloat. Only then is the raft loaded.

A raft of this size will take several large sacks of barley and a huge load of wood, as well as the two men who sit at the corners of the front edge and navigate using wooden shovel-like paddles. A herd of goats can be taken across six at a time, amid vociferous bleating, by tying their legs together to immobilise them and then laying them on the raft on their sides. After each crossing, the raft has to be hauled out of the water, turned upside down, and the skins reinflated. Not surprisingly, rubber inflatable dinghies are now preferred by those mountain dwellers who can afford to buy them.

Cautious Progress *Bathed in dazzling sunshine, a man urges his beast of burden onwards over a precarious bridge in Chitral, Pakistan.*

Inflatable *Pilgrims cross a Tibetan lake on a raft made of inflated skins.*

4 Spirit of the Mountains

Reaching for the Top *A climber pits his skill against a wall of ice in the Himalayas.*

Inspired by the shape of Mount Olympus, the ancient Greeks believed it to be the home of their gods. To the ancient Chinese, a mountain was a sacred pillar that linked the material and spiritual worlds. From Tibet to the Andes, local people have believed that mountains are inhabited by spirits. And many individual mountains have provided society with religious and cultural inspiration. In many of the world's religions, the ascent of a mountain has represented a route to higher knowledge or a path to salvation. And in more recent times people have been drawn by the sheer physical challenge of conquering the world's highest peaks.

Celebrations *Lama musicians at a religious ceremony in Tibet.*

IN HIGH PLACES

Throughout the ages, mountains have inspired feelings of awe, reverence and fear. In the traditions of many mountain peoples, individual peaks are places of sanctity and pilgrimage – a belief that still retains its power today.

Chinese characters are essentially pictures conveying ideas, not letters that denote sounds as in the Western alphabet. It is significant that the character for 'an immortal' is a combination of the character for 'a human being' and that for 'a mountain': in effect, a person who lives alone on a mountain. In the Chinese Daoist religion, to retire to a mountain cave, rejecting human company and the pleasures of the material world, is to pursue the quest for spiritual understanding and, so it is said, to achieve immortality.

In classical Chinese belief, the mountain is thought of as a cosmic pillar that links the material with the spiritual world, supposedly allowing communication between them, and progress from one to the other. Simply to climb a holy mountain such as Hua Shan, in the Shaanxi Province of central China, is to aspire to higher knowledge and communicate with the gods.

But it is more complex than that. The business of walking the winding path, passing the shrines to local earth gods and the deities of the mountain along the way, encountering rocks and caves each with their own legend, and reading the inscriptions of other pilgrims – all this signifies the idea of the path of the Dao. The walk up the mountain is endlessly punctuated by stops to honour the shrines, to remember the legends associated with each twist and turn of the path, to consider the inscriptions. It symbolises the adventure of human existence: to climb the mountain you must permit 'the Path' – which is what 'the Dao' means – to take you where it will, and the same is true of life itself. What matters to Daoists is not trying to control life and assert one's own powers, but being in tune with the flow of nature, of letting go and being in harmony with life, whatever it brings. 'The willow branch that bends in the wind survives unbroken, but a stiff unbending branch which fights the wind will be snapped,' say the Daoists.

This is not an invitation to passivity, however. One of the legends told on the path up Hua Shan is that of the Hairy Girl Rock, a craggy outcrop encountered in the early stages of the pilgrimage. According to the legend, in the time of Qin Shi Huang Ti, who was Emperor of China from 221 to 210 BC, a girl named Yu Jiang was among those chosen to be buried in the emperor's tomb at his death. Yu Jiang was only 14, and she preferred life to death. With six other girls she escaped from the palace and found refuge on Hua Shan, where there were berries to eat and clear mountain streams from which to drink.

THE GREAT STELE OF TAI SHAN *The gold inscription on China's holiest mountain was composed by the Emperor Xuan Zong in AD 726.*

INTO THE SNOWS *Shrouded in smoke, pilgrims prepare for their ascent to the Andean shrine of Qoyllur Rit'i.*

For the rest of her life, which was a happy and serene one, Yu Jiang lived on the mountain. Lacking scissors, she never cut her hair, and in the damp air of the cave where she lived, it turned green and grew upwards like plant stems seeking the light. Finally, the great mass of green hair turned into the craggy rock that stands by the path on Hua Shan and is contemplated by thousands of pilgrims every year.

Hua Shan is just one of the nine sacred mountains of China, five of which are Daoist and four Buddhist. Under the influence of Daoism, Chinese Buddhists have established pathways of pilgrimage up their mountains. Whereas the emphasis of the Buddhist mountains is on moving from one monastery to the next and on spectacular views along the path, on the Daoist mountains the pilgrim is caught up in nature, rather than contemplating it from afar, and is embroiled in the adventure of the path.

On Tai Shan, in Shandong Province, a vast massif that rises from the plains of eastern China and divides the waters of the Yellow River, the path is said to be surrounded by gods who cheerfully greet the pilgrim at every bend and every shrine, rising to their feet and journeying with the pilgrim to the summit. In Daoist legends, Tai Shan is the holiest mountain of all, the original Mountain of Creation, where life was spilled onto the Earth. It is also the place to which the souls of the dead return. Throughout China, and in much of Japan as well, there are shrines to Tai Shan. A stone collected on the mountain is supposed to bring good luck and to guard against evil.

STAR OF THE SNOW

Pebbles from the mountain of Sinakara, over 10 000 miles (16 000 km)away in the Peruvian Andes, are believed to have the same magical properties, while ice from a glacier on the same mountain is said to cure any illness. Huge blocks of the ice are hacked out by pilgrims returning from the annual Qoyllur Rit'i pilgrimage and carried down to their home villages strapped to their backs, soaking their clothes and adding to their cold and exhaustion. What remains of the ice is carefully melted by the pilgrims on their return, and the resultant water is given to the sick to heal them, and to the healthy to keep them well.

Qoyllur Rit'i means 'Star of the Snow', and it is the focus for the largest and most colourful mass pilgrimage in the Andes, an event that continues for several days. A huge crucifix is carried and various shrines are visited during the pilgrimage, including the shrine of Qoyllur Rit'i itself, which stands at almost 16 000 ft (4900 m). Among the pilgrims, some wear headdresses of long, brightly coloured feathers; they represent the people of the old time, before the existence of the sun, who fled into the forest when the sun rose. Others, in white knitted masks with dark rings for the eyes, are thought to symbolise bears or possibly guanacos. All trek up the mountain in a long, snaking line.

Sleeping for a few hours in freezing conditions, they are awoken at 2 am by blasts on whistles from the men in the bear masks, who act as the stewards of the pilgrimage. This is the moment to begin the final ascent of the glacier, a desperately cold and treacherous climb that is made by starlight. If anyone falls into a crevice, they are not helped to climb out: if they die, according to local belief, this indicates that they were meant to be sacrificed, and so become the spiritual seed for the year ahead.

This perilous night-time ascent is the climax of the pilgrimage, when they reach the shrine of Qoyllur Rit'i itself. Some pilgrims make hollows in the snow and place lighted candles inside. Prayers are said to the Christ child, who is believed to have appeared here in 1780.

Despite this Christian element of the pilgrimage, its origins lie much farther back in time, and are rooted in the worship of mountain spirits and the ordering of the Andean Indians' year by the movements of the stars across the sky. The Andean year begins in June, when a cluster of bright stars known as the Pleiades, which have been absent from the sky for a month, reappear. In the month when they are missing, the normal order of the world is thought to dissolve, and their reappearance is a time for rejoicing. The last stage of the pilgrimage coincides with this moment, and it takes place at night: the pilgrims can witness the exact moment when the Pleiades reappear over the sacred glacier. Shortly afterwards, the first light of the morning sun begins to reflect on the ice, and at the same moment Venus ascends over the snowy peaks. It is the brilliant light of Venus, sparkling above the celestial whiteness of the Andes, which led to the name Qoyllur Rit'i, 'Star of the Snow'.

The pilgrimage to Qoyllur Rit'i is just one small part of the intense spiritual life of the Andes, a system of beliefs and rituals that is dominated by reverence for mountain spirits. To the native people of the Andes the whole landscape seems alive and conscious. In some senses it is thought of as a single living being, whose flesh is the rocks and soil, and whose vital fluids bubble up as streams and springs. Known as 'Pacha-mama', this spirit of the earth is a female deity, whose energies cause the grass and crops to grow. The people of the high *puna*, who rely heavily on potatoes for food, say that Pacha-mama 'nurses the potatoes lying on her breast'. Whenever beer is drunk a few drops are poured onto the ground for Pacha-mama, and the same is true of other food and drink. On reaching the summit of any hill or mountain, the wad of spent coca leaves in the mouth is ritually deposited on the ground as an offering to Pacha-mama.

Complementary to this belief in Pacha-mama, individual mountains are given a spiritual identity of their own. Tall snow-covered peaks that overlook huge areas and are widely visible are linked to *apu*, or powerful mountain spirits. The word *apu* means 'lord', and the collective name for these spirits is *Fayatakuna*, meaning 'the Fathers'. Some are so sacred that it is dangerous to look directly at the mountain concerned.

Less lofty mountains without snowy crests, along with the lower hills immediately around a settlement, are seen as embodying more intimate and approachable spirits, who have special links with the local community. Some have particular roles in the natural order, such as summoning rain or clearing the sky of clouds. On some peaks there are said to be fierce wild bulls that are never seen, but which can mate with the cattle of the Andean Indians, if the spirit of the mountain favours the owner of those cattle. The offspring of such a union are believed to be unusually vigorous and fertile creatures.

Many Andean Indians look back to the Inca Empire as their Golden Age: the Incas, they say, could talk directly to the mountain spirits or apu. Today these spirits can only be contacted indirectly, and their moods and intentions must be guessed at through dreams and divinations, or by the interpretation of unusual events, illness or bad luck. The mountain spirits must be placated with offerings of food or, symbolically, of girls, whom the mountain spirit is said to take as lovers.

Mountain passes in the Andes are also believed to have their own protective spirits. It is customary on reaching the highest point of a pass to pull out an eyelash or an eyebrow hair and blow it into the air, as an offering of thanks to the resident spirit for help in the ascent. Next, a stone, a stick or a handful of earth is added to the *apachita*, or cairn, beside the path. The Indians believe that they leave their troubles behind with the stone that they place on the apachita, and can therefore continue on the mountain trail with new optimism.

The practice of making cairns on summits, or at the highest points of mountain passes, with each passing traveller adding a stone, occurs throughout much of Europe, Asia and the Himalayas, as well as in the Andes. Each mountain region adds its own special touch to this ancient practice. In the Himalayas and Tibet, for example, strings of Buddhist prayer flags are often attached to long rods stuck into the cairns. In Mongolia, ribbons, tassels of horse hair, and the skulls of favourite horses are added to the larger cairns, here called *oboo*, which double as altars.

The Hub of the World

Ascending a mountain is one way of honouring it, but to the Buddhist and Hindu pilgrims who reverently approach Mount Kailas, such an idea would seem strange and rather shocking. This most holy of mountains, set deep in the Himalayan chain and regarded as the centre of

Prayers on the Wind *Prayer flags – seen here on the lower slopes of Mount Everest – invoke good fortune for travellers in the Himalayas.*

THE NEVER-DYING MOUNTAIN

The name Fuji-yama, or Mount Fuji, means 'Never-dying Mountain'. Legend has it that this conical mountain came into being in a single night. It is held in awe by the Shinto religion of Japan, and Shinto pilgrims ascend the sacred slopes wearing white clothes, ringing bells and chanting, 'May our six senses be pure, and the weather on the honourable mountain be fair'.

One tale about Mount Fuji tells how its fame reached an Emperor of China who, on hearing that the mountain was formed in a night, concluded that it must produce the elixir of eternal life. He sailed to Japan in a fleet of golden boats, and climbed the slopes with a retinue of servants. On reaching the snowy summit the emperor, who was old, ran forward to be the first to drink the elixir of life. When the others caught up with him they found him lying on his back, smiling at the sky, his eyes closed for ever. He had found eternal life, but through the gates of death.

THE PERFECT PEAK ***Mount Fuji's symmetry has always inspired devotion and artistic appreciation.***

Mount Kailas – also known as Mount Meru or Sumeru in Sanskrit, and as Kangrinboqe Feng in Tibetan – is a mountain of a most unusual shape, not a craggy peak as most summits are in this ice-scoured part of the world but a stately rounded dome of immense height, standing alone in the midst of the Himalayas. It looms up, vast, snow-covered and magnificent, from the surrounding plateau. Two lakes lie at its base: Lake Manasarovar, which is round like the sun and represents the forces of light to the Buddhists; and Lake Rakastal, which is shaped like the crescent moon and symbolises the hidden forces of the night, forces that can erupt as demonic powers if not respected and channelled correctly. Lake Manasarovar is surrounded by many monasteries while Rakastal is devoid of human habitation, and is said to be haunted by a strange and unsettling atmosphere that seems to hang heavily over the waters of the lake.

The journey around Mount Kailas is an arduous one, involving an ascent to a mountain pass called Dolmo La, which stands at almost 19 000 ft (5800 m) above sea level. Blizzards here can freeze the pilgrim within a few minutes, and many have been killed, either by their exertions or by the extreme cold. But death is not feared by the devout pilgrims because to die on the journey around Mount Kailas would be to die at the most exalted moment of their lives.

Indeed, the Buddhist pilgrims – for whom reincarnation is a central point of their faith – believe that if the circuit of the mountain is made with a perfectly devoted and concentrated mind, the pilgrim goes through a full circle of death and rebirth. This is desirable because it hastens their release into nirvana, or eternal bliss, which

creation by Buddhists and Hindus alike, is worshipped by walking around it in a complete circle, an arduous journey of about 30 miles (50 km) that takes two or three days. Some make this pilgrimage on their knees, using leather pads to protect their hands.

As the Buddhist Lama Anagarika Govinda explains, there is a profound difference between the pilgrimage around Mount Kailas and the mountaineering feats of those who climb nearby Everest or K2: 'While the modern man is driven by ambition . . . to climb an outstanding mountain and to be the first on top of it, the devotee is more interested in his spiritual uplift than in the physical feat of climbing. To him the mountain is a divine symbol, and as little as he would put his foot upon a sacred image, so little would he dare to put his foot on the summit of a sacred mountain. To see the greatness of a mountain, one must keep one's distance; to understand its form, one must move around it; to experience its moods, one must see it at sunrise and sunset, at noon and at midnight, in sun and in rain, in snow and in storm, in summer and in winter and in all the other seasons. He who can see the mountain like this comes near to the life of the mountain.'

Rampart of Rock
The forbidding north wall of Mount Kailas in Tibet looks down on pilgrims circling its base (above). Each of the discarded garments (right) signifies the completion of a physical and spiritual journey around the mountain.

eventually replaces the painful cycle of reincarnation.

The crossing of the high pass of Dolmo La symbolises the death of the pilgrim walking around Mount Kailas. After this point, pilgrims descend from the pass joyfully, passing a small lake of an exquisite emerald colour set among snowfields, then down into a gentle green valley with silver streams, symbolising a happy rebirth.

At the end of the pilgrimage, devout Buddhists often leave behind some of their clothes, or their shoes, to show that they have entered a new life. Consequently, on an area of bare rock not far from Mount Kailas there is what looks like the world's largest jumble sale: a huge mound of discarded shoes and clothing.

Racing the Magician to the Top

Although no devout Buddhist would today think of climbing Mount Kailas, there is a legend about a Buddhist monk called Milarepa who aroused resentment in a magician or shaman of the old Bon religion, Tibet's ancient animist faith (the belief that natural phenomena and animate and inanimate things have souls). The story illustrates the 1000-year rivalry between Buddhism and Bon, the subject of many colourful pageants in the Buddhist countries of the Himalayas. The magician challenged Milarepa to race him to the top of Mount Kailas as a test of their magical powers. Milarepa agreed and then sat down to wait while the magician set off. It was very early, before the dawn, and the magician struggled upwards in the grey light. When he neared the top, he looked down and taunted Milarepa with his imminent success. Just

continued on page 138

then the Sun rose, and its first rays struck the summit of Kailas. Focusing all his powers of concentration, Milarepa became one with the sunbeam and so arrived on the summit in an instant. The magician was so disconcerted by this that he dropped his magic drum, which bounced down the side of the mountain, booming loudly each time it hit the rock, and leaving a large dent with each strike. This perpendicular line of star-like impressions can still be seen on one flank of Mount Kailas.

The implication of the story is that the Bon religion was defeated by Buddhism. In truth, it was merely absorbed, and much of Tibetan Buddhism – the reverence for mountain spirits and other 'spirits of place', the demons and superstitions, the shamanistic rituals, divinations and exorcisms – are directly inherited from Bon. The struggle between the two continues in a subtle way within Tibetan Buddhism today, played out by the muted rivalry between the two different orders of Buddhist monks in the Himalayas. These are identified by the colour of their pointed hats, red or yellow. The red-hatted order incorporate far more elements from Bon into their Buddhist faith and practice, while the yellow-hatted order tend more towards pure Buddhism, although they too have many Bon-derived rituals and legends.

Stately Progress *A symbolic umbrella is held above the* Rimpoche *(abbot) of Thyangboche monastery during a ceremony in Nepal. Previous pages: Buddhist monks summon the faithful at a monastery in Ladakh. On important occasions, visitors deposit prayer stones as they approach the shrine.*

Whipping the Mountain

The animist influence of Bon inspires the great reverence for mountains found in Tibetan Buddhism. Farther north, in Mongolia, where Buddhism and animism have merged only a little and have a more open rivalry, the ancient worship of mountains survives in a much more robust form. People feel they have an individual relationship with particular mountains. If a man or woman has to travel away from home, far from their special mountain, they become concerned at being unable to make daily offerings to the mountain, but send prayers to it from afar. The prayers assure the mountain that it has not been forgotten, and ask it not to become angry at the temporary neglect but to continue giving help and protection.

Mongolian Buddhists believe that it is dangerous to speak the name of a mountain carelessly, within 'hearing distance' of the mountain – the same sort of deference that they show to elders in Mongolian society. In their presence, mountains are referred to as *xairxan,* which means 'dear one'. People make offerings of animals – not sacrificed, but raised and cherished as if the animal belonged to the mountain spirit and had simply been left in the care of a human family.

Sacred Hermit *The Buddhist poet-saint, Milarepa, lived from 1038 to 1122 AD. This bronze and gold statue portrays his eight-year period of meditation.*

Such close personal relationships can go sour. An 18th-century governor of Ulaan-Bator rode out to Bogdo Uul Mountain one spring to worship the mountain, but during his journey a heavy storm began. The governor, who was easily angered, held the mountain responsible for the bad weather and sentenced it, as if it were a prisoner, to be whipped and wear fetters. It is not recorded if the whipping was carried out, but the fetters were left on the mountain altar where sacrifices were normally made. When summer came the weather grew worse, and the governor thought that Bogdo Uul must again be responsible. He decided that the mountain should be heavily fined, and, rounding up all the horses on the mountain, he drove them away.

Mongols traditionally live in tents, and their view of the world is shaped by this experience: the sky is the fabric of the great azure tent of the Universe, while a mountain is like a tent-pole holding up the sky. They also draw a parallel with the column of smoke ascending from a fire in the hearth: like the tent-pole and the mountain, it symbolises the central pillar that upholds the structure of the world and around which life revolves.

In November or December every year, hundreds of thousands of people come to Mount Arunachala in southern India, a natural pyramid of stone that rears up out of the arid plains and dominates the landscape. Mount Arunachala, so legend has it, was once a column of pure light that extended indefinitely into the sky, and deep down into the depths of the Earth. This light was the embodiment of the creator God, Shiva, and was so bright that no one could look at it without losing their sight. Only at the request of another god, Brahma, was the radiance of the column extinguished so that mortals could come and worship Shiva.

During the annual festival at Arunachala, a great procession of chariots makes its way slowly around the mountain, each bearing the image of one of the Hindu gods. This procession takes place every morning and evening for ten days. On the tenth day, a huge cauldron of ghee (clarified butter) is hauled up to the top of the mountain. At the base of the mountain, the chariot bearing the image of the goddess Parvati is rocked from side to side signifying her desire for marriage to Shiva. In the midst of a crowd of pilgrims on the mountaintop, a wick made of cloth is pushed into the butter and set alight, re-enacting the great column of light that was once Arunachala. At the moment when the flame soars upwards into the night sky, the pilgrims below let out a roar and stop rocking Parvati's chariot, for she is now united in marriage with Shiva.

Mount Arunachala is also believed by Hindus to be the hill that survives the catastrophic floods that periodically devastate the world. On its summit, the plants and animals survive to populate the Earth anew. Every day, hundreds of local people worship Arunachala by walking around it barefoot in a clockwise direction, a walk of 15 miles (25 km). The worshippers keep to the left side of the path, for it is believed that the souls of the dead walk around the mountain in the opposite direction, keeping to the right-hand side.

The Christian Tradition

The story of Creation told in Genesis, the first book of the Bible, makes no mention of mountains. This omission has caused great concern to Christian theologians over the centuries. Were the mountains not created by God at all? Did this make them the work of the Devil, and places to be avoided? This uncertain and cautious view of mountains has coloured the Western approach to the high peaks.

An ingenious explanation for the omission of mountains in Genesis was proposed in 1681 by a theologian, Thomas Burnet. He suggested that mountains had not been created 'in the beginning', but that the early Earth (where the Garden of Eden was located) was as smooth as an egg, with 'not a scar or fracture in all its body, no rock, mountain nor hollow cavern'. The great change in the Earth's surface had come about during the Flood, which was necessary to cleanse the world of humanity's wickedness.

Burnet argued that all the waters of the Flood could not have come from rainfall alone, so water must have welled up from the interior of the Earth. He imagined the surface of the Earth to be like the shell of an egg, but thicker. It had cracked open under the heat of heavenly rage, releasing turbulent tides of water from within. As these welled up and later drained away, their mighty force carved out river gorges, mountain ranges, ocean basins and lakes on the surface. In contrast to the smoothness of the original egg-like Earth, a scarred and ravaged globe remained, with the mountain ranges representing the worst of the chaos: 'wild, vast and indigested heaps

Uplifting Journey *Dressed in their finest clothes, Buddhist pilgrims press onwards towards Mount Kailas.*

of stone – the ruins of a broken world' in Burnet's poetic description.

The association of mountains with the punishment and ruination of the world was already familiar in Christian countries. For centuries, mountains had been regarded as the realm of dragons, flying demons who embodied evil and destruction. A tale was told of Pedro III of Aragon who, in 1280, set out to climb the Mont Canigou, a spire of rock 9000 ft (2743 m) high that stands between Aragon and Provence. No one had ever attempted this feat before.

Part way up the mountain, the king and his knights were terrified by deafening thunder, great flashes of lightning and a bombardment of hail: they threw themselves on the ground 'and lay there, as it were, lifeless in their fear and apprehension of the calamities that had overtaken them'. The knights would go no farther, and the king pressed on alone. According to the legend: 'Pedro with great labour made the ascent alone and when he was on top of the mountain he found a lake there; and when he threw a stone into the lake a horrible dragon of enormous size came out of it and began to fly about in the air and to darken the air with its breath.' Although he did not manage to slay the dragon, Pedro escaped with his life, an achievement that was seen as a spiritual victory over the forces of darkness.

So great was the fear of mountain dragons and ghosts that in the 14th century a local law laid down the death penalty for anyone who threw rocks into the lake on Mons Pilatus, a mountain close to Lucerne in Switzerland. The mountain was originally called Mons Pileatus, meaning 'capped', a reference to its perpetual cap of clouds, but the name had become corrupted to Pilatus, and a legend had then grown up about the name, claiming that Pontius Pilate's grave was at the bottom of the lake. He was said to rise only on Good Friday, dressed in blood-red robes.

The malevolent ghost of Pilate was believed to have given rise to a terrifying dragon. In 1649, the sheriff of Lucerne confirmed the existence of the dragon and provided a detailed description: its head 'terminated in the serrated jaw of a serpent' and 'when flying . . . it threw out sparks like a red-hot horseshoe, hammered by the blacksmith'. The dragon was supposed to be the cause of many evil happenings, and of the unpredictable local weather.

Ideas of this kind survived well into the 18th century. In 1702 a professor of physics at Zurich University assembled records of dragon sightings in the Swiss Alps into a comprehensive guide. He noted the existence of fiery and non-fiery dragons, snake-like dragons, flying and non-flying kinds, cat-faced dragons, bat-like and bird-like species, those with scales, those with feathers and even one with a diamond-studded tail.

Alongside the view of mountains as alien and terrifying places was another: that of mountains as places of potential salvation. Writers such as the poet Petrarch described how the ascent of a particular mountain – in his case, Mont Ventoux – turned into a spiritual journey, leading to penitence and renewed religious fervour. These two traditions, however, were not so very different, as the idea of the mountain as a source of salvation relied heavily on the awe and terror that mountaintops evoked, and on the painful exertion needed to reach them.

There was rarely any sense of the mountain itself being sacred, as in Asia and other parts of the world, except in the case of a few 'sacred mountains', which were usually little more than hills. They were carefully set with chapels, statues and tableaux representing the Christian story, culminating in three large crosses on the summit. The most popular of these was Mont Valerien near Paris, where, beginning in 1633, three crosses, five chapels and various tableaux were erected, and where the aristocrats of Paris regularly congregated. On these 'sacred mountains' it was only the man-made chapels

MOUNT OLYMPUS, HOME OF THE GODS

Mount Olympus stands on the shores of the Aegean Sea, its precipitous south face rising sharply from the shore. From a massive base, the mountain soars to 9570 ft (2917 m) in a continuous sweep of rock, and is often cloaked with clouds about the summit, giving it a mysterious air. Down the sheer slopes, mantled with dark woods, flow rapid mountain torrents that have gouged out deep furrows, like the folds of a huge cloth. The rocks at the summit are heaped up into piles that distantly resemble gigantic seats. It was this aspect that the ancient Greeks saw from their homeland, and which inspired them to call Mount Olympus the home of the gods. Homer wrote of the mountain: 'Never is it swept by the winds nor touched by snow; a purer air surrounds it, a white clarity envelops it and the gods there taste of a happiness which lasts as long as their eternal lives.'

MOUNT OF MYSTERY *In Greek legends, Mount Olympus was the home of twelve gods who ruled the Earth and the underworld.*

Seat of Dragons *Frequent 'sightings' of dragons ensured that Switzerland's Mons Pilatus inspired deep and tenacious fears.*

and other artifacts that mattered, not the natural forms of the rock, nor the hill itself.

Only in the 19th century did a feeling of reverence for the mountains themselves begin to emerge in Europe, growing partly out of the Romantic movement, particularly the influence of Romantic poets such as William Wordsworth; and partly out of the new sport of 'Alpinism', or mountaineering, with a few climbers experiencing a profound sense of awe at the extraordinary sights, the clear air and utter stillness of the summits. Such climbers often claimed that no one else could understand the mountains as they did: that it required the physical exertion of climbing truly to know a mountain and appreciate its spiritual qualities.

The New World

When an earthquake struck the Sierra Nevada range of California in 1872, one man ran out into the moonlit meadows to see the spectacle. High on the south wall of the valley, a great mass of stone known as Eagle Rock was tumbling down. The explorer and writer John Muir bounded towards the mass of falling rock, shouting with joy and leaping about among the tumbling fragments before they had found their resting places. Muir was not a lunatic, but a profoundly religious man who, following in the footsteps of European Romantics of the previous generation, delighted in every aspect of the mountains, from the tiniest alpine flower to the wildest storm, avalanche or earthquake.

The early colonists of North America had brought with them their age-old European dread of wilderness in general, and mountains in particular. But the vast landscape of the New World, both physical and psychological, produced mystics such as Muir who found beauty, serenity and meaning in the Earth's wild places.

Muir called the Sierra Nevada 'the Range of Light' and these great basalt crags were his spiritual home, although he also walked – months-long rambling walks, sleeping out under the stars – in the Rockies, the Appalachians and many other North American mountain ranges.

He would sometimes climb as well as walk, wearing spiked boots to improve his grip on ice and smooth rock, but he was in no sense a mountaineer. Muir paced the mountains not to attain summits nor to set

continued on page 144

Roosevelt and Muir *Seen here in California's Yosemite Valley, Theodore Roosevelt and John Muir shared a love of the American wilderness.*

Ghost in the Clouds
Extreme altitude can make light behave in unfamiliar ways. A projected shadow, or 'Brocken Spectre', floats on a bank of cloud in the Himalayas.
Previous pages: The peaks of Mount Everest and Mount Nuptse lit by the setting sun.

himself challenges, but to be at one with nature and God. 'There is no upness comparable to the mountains . . .' Muir wrote. 'Climb the mountains and get their good tidings. Nature's peace will flow into you as sunshine flows into trees. The winds will blow their own freshness into you, and the storms their energy, while cares will drop off like autumn leaves.'

During a wild storm he would often climb a tall fir tree, clinging onto its swaying trunk like a bird on a tossing reed stem, revelling in the gusts of wind bringing the scent of wildflower meadows, or the salty aroma of the sea.

He took nothing more than dry bread to eat at noon, and wrote: 'To dine with a glacier on a sunny day is a glorious thing and makes common feasts of meat and wine ridiculous. The glacier eats hills and sunbeams.' Muir's impassioned writing awakened the American people to an appreciation of their extraordinary mountain ranges, and led to the formation of Yosemite National Park in 1864. This has protected a large area of the Sierra Nevada from development and damage.

Mysterious Lights

Just after sunset in a mountain range, something strange occurs. The sun has vanished below the horizon, the world and the peaks themselves are shrouded in dusk. Then, a moment later, a magical glow, sometimes golden, sometimes rosy pink, illuminates the peaks. It lasts for a short while, then fades. This is alpenglow, an effect that has dazzled mountain dwellers, travellers and climbers for centuries, and which may have contributed to the sense of mystery surrounding the mountains.

Today, the phenomenon of alpenglow can be explained scientifically, though it remains just as beautiful and awe-inspiring. After the sun has set, its rays can still travel around the curve of the Earth by means of reflection from the boundaries of the atmosphere. The light rays follow a zigzagging path, 'trapped' in a layer of air around the Earth, and reflected successively from the upper and lower boundaries of that layer. At a crucial moment just after the sun slips below the horizon, the path of the light is such that it strikes horizontally onto the mountain peaks. The same effect also occurs just before sunrise.

Mountains can generate other, more mysterious light effects. Mountaineers

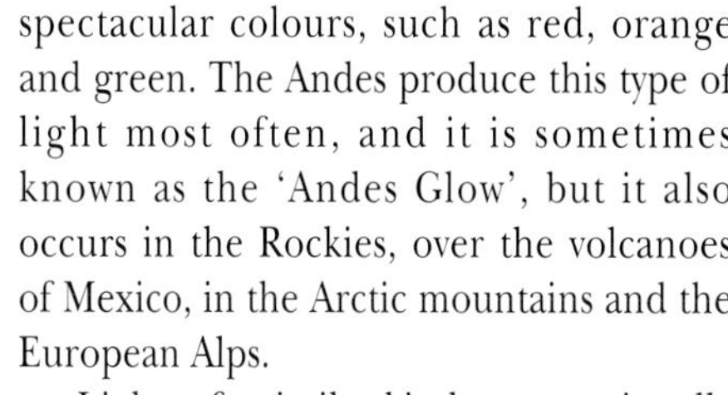

sometimes see gigantic ghost-like shadows looking down on them. This phenomenon is particularly common on the Brocken, the highest peak of the Harz Mountains in Germany. The 'Brocken Spectre' is a monstrous shadowy figure seen in the mists of early morning or late afternoon. Such spectres are actually the shadow of the observer cast upwards by a low sun onto a bank of mist or cloud. The millions of tiny drops of moisture in the cloud near the observer act as magnifying lenses, while the more distant cloud is like a cinema screen on which the shadow is projected. If the droplets also split the light like prisms, a halo of white or coloured light may be cast about the shadow. Such a figure can easily be interpreted as a saint, or a monster. The illusion is immediately revealed as such by raising an arm – the giant shadow does the same – but many people are too terrified or awestruck to move.

In 1865, Edward Whymper, the first person to climb the Matterhorn, described seeing a circle of light in the foggy sky above the Matterhorn, with three crosses within the circle. To a Christian, the religious implications were obvious, especially as four of the mountaineers in Whymper's party had been killed earlier in the day in a fall from a precipice. Whymper was overcome by 'the ghostly apparitions of light . . . a strange and awesome sight, unique to me and indescribably imposing at such a moment'. This effect, known as a parahelia, or sun dog, has been observed several times since 1865, and is now known to be created by ice crystals in high-altitude clouds, reflecting and splitting the sunlight in a process not unlike that which creates a rainbow.

Static electricity in the atmosphere – similar to that discharged during thunderstorms but occurring in dry weather and not delivered in dramatic flashes – can also create mysterious mountain lights. The mountains act as giant conductors for the electric discharge, producing rays of light, streamers, halos, flashes or steady glows that last for hours. One name for this type of light is 'St Elmo's Fire'. While it can occur anywhere on Earth, it is especially dramatic in mountain ranges, and develops spectacular colours, such as red, orange and green. The Andes produce this type of light most often, and it is sometimes known as the 'Andes Glow', but it also occurs in the Rockies, over the volcanoes of Mexico, in the Arctic mountains and the European Alps.

Lights of a similar kind are occasionally seen during earthquakes, over the tops of young mountains that are still in the process of forming. They are especially common in Chile and Japan. Sometimes, huge balls of light seem to sit poised on top of a mountain summit. Such lights are probably generated by the gigantic forces compressing the rock deep within the mountain. Such squeezing of some rocks can generate a stream of subatomic particles called electrons, which are forced out of the rock like water out of a squeezed sponge. The electrons form an electric current that in turn generates a static electric field above the mountain, ionising the air and so creating light.

This type of effect, in which mechanical pressure generates electrons, is called piezo-electricity. It is the same phenomenon that, on a tiny scale, converts pressure on the needle of a record-player into electrical impulses that activate loudspeakers.

Spectres and Sundogs *On the slopes of the Matterhorn, Edward Whymper (top) saw spectral crosses in the sky. Parahelia (right), or sundogs, are a common optical phenomenon in mountains.*

THE MOUNTAINEERS

The world holds few greater challenges than those posed by its highest mountains. After tentative beginnings, mountaineering has become an immensely popular sport, and climbers have conquered peaks that were once thought beyond human reach.

In 1492, the year that Christopher Columbus discovered America, Charles VIII of France happened to pass by Mont Aiguille, 25 miles (40 km) south of Grenoble. It was known then as 'Mont Inaccessible'.

The limestone ramparts of the mountain rise almost perpendicular from a sloping plinth of shale, and stretch upwards for 1000 ft (300 m). Charles ordered his entourage to stop, so impressed was he by the strange appearance of the mountain. Intrigued to know what was on the apparently flat summit, irked by the name 'Inaccessible', and determined that no part of his kingdom should be beyond his power, the king ordered his chamberlain, Dompjulian de Beaupré, to climb the mountain. Royal whims could not be ignored, but the chamberlain did succeed in delegating the task to a younger man, Antoine de Ville, the captain of Montelimar. A military man, de Ville was far more suited for the seemingly impossible task than the rather portly chamberlain.

MONT AIGUILLE *Scene of the world's first known alpine climb, the summit of this French mountain can now be reached by cable car.*

De Ville selected six other men to help him: a master carpenter, a stonemason, a maker of siege-breaking ladders, a theologian and two priests. They attacked the mountain as if it had been a well-fortified castle, spending several weeks building military-style ladders and other 'subtle means and engines', as de Ville later described them.

It was a successful campaign, and the seven men not only ascended to the summit but carried enough provisions to spend several days there. De Ville reported that the little plateau atop the mountain, 'about a French league in circumference, a quarter of a league in length, and a crossbow shot in width', was covered by a lovely meadow full of fragrant flowers with sparrows and other small birds, and 'a beautiful herd of chamois which will never be able to get away'. De Ville had his men erect three wooden crosses and build a simple chapel so that the priests could perform Masses on the summit. Since it was no longer inaccessible, they renamed the peak Mont Aiguille, meaning 'Needle Mountain'. The king had long since ridden away, but a clerk was sent from Grenoble to verify that they were standing on the summit.

So difficult was the climb that it was 342 years before anyone reached the top again. By the time of this second ascent, in 1834, the chamois had mysteriously disappeared – perhaps, on their high-altitude 'island', they had succumbed to an outbreak of disease. Only 44 years later, in 1878, the world's first cable car was installed to take sightseers to the top.

The ascent of Mont Inaccessible in 1492 was probably the first exercise in true mountaineering: an ascent made for no practical purpose, nor motivated by any spiritual quest, but purely as a response to the existence of the mountain – 'because it was there'.

Battling with Altitude

For all the technical difficulties of climbing Mont Aiguille, it is not particularly high: the summit stands only 6844 ft (2086 m) above sea level. As the enthusiasm for conquering higher peaks grew – something that only

ALPINE EXCURSION *Early devotees of the new sport of 'Alpinism' cross the ice near Grindelwald, Switzerland, in 1900.*

WOMEN AT THE TOP

In the early days of mountaineering, or 'Alpinism', women played a controversial role. When Henriette d'Angeville reached the summit of Mont Blanc in 1838, she carved the words, *'Vouloir, c'est pouvoir'* ('To wish to do it is to be able to do it') into a glacier. She had been opposed by most of the inhabitants of Geneva and Chamonix, and her decision to wear a costume that incorporated voluminous trousers further scandalised public opinion. She had designed the outfit herself: it included a large, loose skirt that mostly covered the outrage of the trousers, puff sleeves, a wide-brimmed bonnet and a feather boa.

Henriette was not the first woman to conquer Mont Blanc, for she had been preceded by an illiterate peasant, Marie Paradis. Marie accompanied a group of male friends, not out of any great ambition to reach the top, but egged on by her companions, who had laid a bet with others in their village that they could take her to the top.

With Henriette, a fiery French aristocrat, it was a matter of burning ambition. Her pride was such that she forbade her guides to carry her under any circumstances – unless she died, in which case they were to take her body to the summit so that she should not be cheated of her goal. In the event, she did not die – though she felt close to death when afflicted by altitude sickness. Nevertheless, the guides disobeyed her when they reached the top, lifting Henriette up into the air and shouting, 'You are higher than the top of Mont Blanc!'

TYROLEAN CLIMB *In the early days women 'Alpinists' were hampered by constricting clothes and ankle-length skirts, as in this illustration of 1885.*

APPROACHING THE LIMIT
Climbing Everest in 1922, Edward Norton and George Mallory reached 27 000 ft (8230 m) without extra oxygen.

began in the 18th century – the aspiring mountaineers, or 'Alpinists' as they were then called, found that they had to battle with other factors besides the problems of ascent itself.

Apart from the cold, ice, and the unpredictable and violent winds, they found themselves up against the unnerving effects of altitude, especially the drop in the quantity of oxygen in the air. When, after 27 years of obsessive planning for the scaling of Mont Blanc, Horace de Saussure finally reached the summit in August 1787, he was bitterly disappointed. Altitude sickness had afflicted him with a tide of dreadful nausea, a burning and unquenchable thirst, laboured and painful breathing, a racing heartbeat, depression and a throbbing headache. His skin was cracked and burned by the harsh sun and the dryness of the air: 'I was like a gourmet invited to a superb banquet whose utter revulsion prevented him from enjoying it.' In frustration, he angrily stamped his foot on the summit of his longed-for mountain.

In time, mountaineers learned how to cope with altitude sickness by making gradual ascents that allowed their bodies time to acclimatise. Climbing techniques also improved, and specialised equipment was introduced, such as crampons for the feet – metal spikes that give a secure grip in ice. Ropes and pegs allowed more difficult precipices to be tackled with some safety, although accidents remained a hazard as mountaineers relentlessly pushed themselves and their equipment to the limit.

Eventually, however, modern mountaineers came up against an apparently insurmountable barrier: at altitudes of about 26 250 ft (8000 m) and above, climbers seemed to be at their physiological limit. In 1924 an attempt was made on the summit of Everest – the world's highest mountain at 29 022 ft (8846 m) – by two British mountaineers, Lt Col. E. F. Norton and Howard Somervell. At 28 000 ft (8535 m), Somervell became too ill to continue, and Norton pressed on alone to a point known as the Great Couloir, at 28 100 ft (8565 m).

In terms of the physical effort required, that last 100 ft (30 m) was equivalent to a journey of thousands of miles. Norton later wrote: 'Our pace was wretched. My ambition was to do 20 consecutive paces uphill without a pause to rest and pant, elbow on bended knee; yet I never remember achieving it – 13 was nearer the mark.' No one could get past this point in the 1920s and 1930s.

SO NEAR *The 1924 British Everest Expedition included Norton (standing, centre) and Somervell (seated, second from right), who came within 1000 ft (300 m) of the top.*

Between 1921 and 1938, eight people reached 28 000 ft (8535 m) and another 17 people reached 27 000 ft (8230 m). But the effects were frightening. Some had suffered hallucinations, others were killed by the cold, there was severe dehydration and one porter had suffered a stroke. Muscle wasting was also a problem at such altitudes: one climber even claimed that he could almost encircle his thigh with the fingers of one hand. These debilitating effects occurred even if the climbers rested: above 26 250 ft (8000 m) there is no such thing as recuperation. Just beyond 28 000 ft (8535 m), there seemed to be a 'glass ceiling', and the last 1000 ft (300 m) of Everest remained out of reach.

With the ending of the Second World War, people began to believe that anything was possible, including the conquest of Everest. A keen sense of competition grew among mountaineering nations to be the first to stand on the roof of the world: among the contenders were the Swiss, the French, the Americans and the British. It was clear that mountaineers could benefit from knowledge about the effects of high altitude that medical scientists had gained from assisting flying missions during wartime. In 1946 a landmark experiment, 'Operation Everest I', took place at Pensacola Air Base in Florida. Four volunteers lived in a decompression chamber for five weeks while the atmospheric pressure around them was gradually decreased, until it was at a level equivalent to the summit of Everest. The experimenters even took the pressure below that point, to the equivalent of 30 000 ft (9100 m). Two of the four subjects were still able to sustain physical effort – 20 minutes on a cycle machine – at this 'altitude'.

The experiment was heartening for those who dreamed of conquering Everest, but there was still no certainty that the climb could be made without artificial oxygen. Some pointed to the Florida experiment as evidence that it could. Others, citing the experience of Norton, Somervell and other prewar climbers, had doubts. Pedalling bicycles in a decompression chamber is one thing; hauling your own weight upwards against the pull of gravity in extreme cold, while contending with jet-stream winds and blinding sunlight, is another.

The problem, as it seemed then, was that no mountaineer could climb fast enough at this altitude to reach the summit of Everest and then return safely to below 28 000 ft (8535 m) in a day. (It was – and

UNEASY BREATHING *Portable oxygen systems designed for climbers – like this set tested in the 1920s – often proved as much of a hindrance as a help.*

HIGH-FLYERS

In 1875, three Frenchmen ascended to 28 000 ft (8535 m) in a hot-air balloon. Two died from the effects of the altitude, while the third only just survived. This tragedy influenced medical experts up until the 1920s: they firmly believed that mountaineers could not ascend to these heights without the aid of oxygen. However, they had underestimated what can be achieved through gradual acclimatisation.

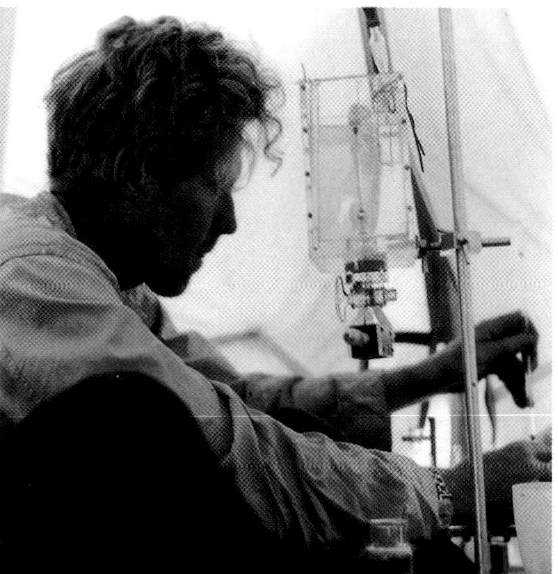

SCIENTIFIC SUPPORT *Griffith Pugh, accompanying the 1953 British-New Zealand Everest Expedition, working in his 'laboratory' on the mountain.*

still is – thought impossible to survive a night above 28 000 ft.) In the end, most people decided that extra oxygen would be necessary. However, equipment tried out in the 1920s and 1930s was so heavy that some climbers went faster without it.

By the late 1940s, two types of oxygen system were available: open-circuit and closed-circuit. The open-circuit system added oxygen to the air inhaled by the climber. It could be set to deliver small extra amounts at low altitudes, and larger amounts at high altitude. It was a simple and robust piece of apparatus, but a large number of oxygen cylinders were needed because the oxygen was being used up continuously.

The newer, closed-circuit system used a chemical process to absorb the carbon dioxide in the climber's exhaled breath and convert it back to oxygen, recycling the air breathed by the climber and cutting him off from the mountain air around him. The oxygen concentration was set to the equivalent of that found at sea level.

The closed-circuit system represented a more ambitious approach to solving the problem of lack of oxygen, and fewer oxygen cylinders were needed. But because the apparatus was more complex it was also heavier and more liable to break down. If it did malfunction, the consequences were terrifying: a mountaineer could, in effect, be whisked from sea level to 28 000 ft (8535 m) in a matter of moments, without any chance to acclimatise to the decrease in oxygen, with potentially lethal effects.

Two British climbers using closed-circuit oxygen, Tom Bourdillon and Charles Evans, made an attempt on the Everest summit in 1953, and were able to climb at a stunning speed until one set malfunctioned at 28 250 ft (8610 m). The fault was mended in moments, but after this alarming accident they had no choice but to turn back. In the end, it was the open-circuit system that enabled two other members of the same expedition, the young New Zealander Edmund Hillary and the Nepali Sherpa Tenzing Norgay, to reach the summit three days later, on May 29, 1953. The success of the British-New Zealand team was radioed to London, and the news arrived just in time for the celebrations that surrounded the coronation of Elizabeth II.

Although the courage of the two who reached the summit and the teamwork of the other British and New Zealand mountaineers and Nepali Sherpas were crucial, scientists undoubtedly played the major

THE VALIANT SHERPAS

In the history of Himalayan climbing, a remarkable role has been played by one of Nepal's ethnic groups, known as the Sherpas. Despite their renown for mountaineering, they took to climbing less than a century ago. In the early 1900s Sherpas began to be recruited by European 'Alpinists' to assist with the first expeditions into the Himalayan peaks. In a matter of decades, a tradition of assistance with mountaineering expeditions grew up among the Sherpas, many of whom became expert guides. Many more Sherpas and Sherpanis (female Sherpas) have acted as porters for expeditions.

The Sherpas are a Buddhist people who traditionally regard the mountains as sacred, and they once considered that the mountain gods would be angered by anyone climbing the peaks. Although they remain very religious, this particular belief has been relaxed in view of the enormous economic advantages that mountaineering has brought to the Sherpa people: over half now live either by mountaineering or tourism. Since Tenzing Norgay's ascent of Everest in 1953, over 80 Sherpas have reached the summit, and one man, Ang Rita, has been to the top seven times. In 1991, the first all-Sherpa team climbed to the summit.

TEAM EFFORT *Sherpa porters at the foot of North Col, Everest, photographed by Howard Somervell during a British expedition in 1922.*

role in this first successful ascent of Mount Everest. One scientist, Griffith Pugh, accompanied the expedition and set up a physiological 'laboratory' on the high slopes of Everest, measuring factors such as breathing rates (which increased from 210 pints/120 litres per minute to as much as 400 pints/230 litres per minute), loss of water from the lungs and blood pressure, as well as taking blood and urine samples for analysis.

SUCCESS AT LAST *His face hidden by an oxygen mask, Tenzing Norgay plants a foot on the summit of Mount Everest – the 'roof of the world' – in 1953. Bourdillon and Evans (below), members of the same expedition, used a different oxygen supply system and did not reach the summit.*

The 1953 expedition took 350 000 pints (198 000 litres) of oxygen to Everest. Pugh advised the climbers to use oxygen even when sleeping, although at a lower rate, and this helped to maintain the physical and mental condition of the team. There were no accidents and only two minor cases of frostbite on the whole expedition – a tribute to the well-being and alertness achieved by these measures: shortage of

oxygen leads to mental slowness and an impaired ability to respond to potentially dangerous situations. In the decade that followed, each of the world's ten highest peaks was climbed using the scientific methods established on Everest in 1953.

ALONE, WITHOUT OXYGEN

The next great milestone in mountaineering history was passed in 1978: the ascent of Everest without the use of supplementary oxygen. The ascent was made by the South Tyrolean Reinhold Messner and the Austrian Peter Habeler. They were backed up by the usual large support team of Austrian climbers and Sherpa porters, who established a series of camps on the ascent and brought up food, tents and other supplies, so that the two mountaineers who ascended the summit were relatively fresh.

Two years later, Messner ascended alone by a different route, without oxygen or even a radio, perhaps the most courageous feat in mountaineering history. This, the smallest-ever expedition to the roof of the world, included only one other member: the Canadian mountaineer and journalist Nena Holguin, who accompanied Messner to 21 325 ft (6500 m), where they established base camp. Yaks were used to transport supplies up the lower slopes of the mountain. Once at base camp, Messner pressed on alone while Holguin waited four days, not knowing if Messner had achieved his goal, nor even if he was still alive. Badly affected by the lack of oxygen, Messner was hallucinating long before he reached the summit, talking to his rucksack and his ice axe as if they were human companions. Summoning his last few ounces of energy, he managed to take photographs of himself posed against an aluminium tripod set up on the very highest point of Everest by the Chinese in 1975. When he reached base camp again he was on the point of collapse.

This achievement, like the original climbing of Everest in 1953, stimulated worldwide interest in mountaineering and led to the conquest of many more unclimbed summits. Everest itself has now been climbed hundreds of times, and with each expedition abandoning its surplus gear, parts of the mountain are huge rubbish tips. Elsewhere in the world, rock faces on popular climbing routes are disfigured by metal bolts, hammered in to take ropes and harnesses for a safe ascent. Mountaineers are realising that the wildness and remoteness, the very qualities that they cherish in the high peaks, are in danger of being destroyed by their own activities.

OPEN-AIR CLIMB *Reinhold Messner and Peter Habeler climbed Everest without oxygen in 1978.*
Opposite: With most of the world's tallest peaks now conquered, climbers test their skills on ever more demanding routes, such as the Hornli Ridge on the Matterhorn.

RIVALS AT THE TOP

Everest is the highest mountain on Earth as measured above sea level, but not as measured from the centre of our planet. Because the Earth is not a perfect sphere, but bulges outwards at the Equator, tropical mountains are farther from the centre. Chimborazo, a volcanic peak in Ecuador, stands 20 700 ft (6310 m) above sea level, compared with Everest's 29 022 ft (8846 m), but its summit is 7050 ft (2150 m) farther from the Earth's centre than the summit of Mount Everest. Until the 1800s, when the Himalayas were surveyed, Chimborazo was thought to be the highest mountain in the world.

MOUNT CHIMBORAZO *Although less dangerous than Everest, Chimborazo confronts climbers with hazardous mud slides and unstable scree.*

MOUNTAINEERING FIRSTS

Mont Blanc (*France/Italy*) 15 771 ft (4807 m)
Climbed by Jacques Balmat and Michel-Gabriel Paccard in 1786

Matterhorn (*Switzerland/Italy*) 14 688 ft (4477 m)
Climbed by Edward Whymper, Lord Frances Douglas and others in 1865
North face first climbed in 1931

Piz Bernina (*Switzerland*) 13 284 ft (4049 m)
Climbed by Johann Coaz and the brothers Jon and Lorenz Tscharner in 1850

Traverse of Bezingi Wall (*Caucasus Mountains*)
Traverse completed by Josef Schintlmeister, Karl Moldan and Karl Poppinger in 1931

Mount Everest (*Himalayas*) 29 022 ft (8846 m)
Summit reached by two members of a British/Nepali/New Zealand expedition, Edmund Hillary (now Sir Edmund Hillary) and Tenzing Norgay, in 1953

K2 (*Himalayas*) 28 250 ft (8611m)
Summit reached by two members of an Italian expedition, Achille Compagnoni and Lino Lacedelli, in 1954

Broad Peak (*Himalayas*) 26 400 ft (8047 m)
First peak over 26 000 ft (8000 m) to be climbed in the 'Alpine style', without oxygen or high-altitude porters: climbed by Hermann Buhl and Ernst Sondheimer in 1957

Panch Chuli V (*Himalayas*) 21 118 ft (6437 m)
Summit reached by four members of an Indian/British expedition, Dick Renshaw, Stephen Sustad, Victor Saunders and Stephen Venables, in 1992

CROWDED AT THE TOP
A group of climbers who made the ascent of Everest in 1985, using an additional oxygen supply, celebrate standing on top of the world.

INDEX

Picture Credits

Abbreviations:
T = Top; B = Bottom; C = Centre;
R = Right; L = Left
AUS = Auscape International
BCL = Bruce Coleman Ltd
DRK = DRK Photo
HUT = The Hutchison Library
NHPA = Natural History Photographic Library
OSF = Oxford Scientific Films
PEP = Planet Earth Pictures
RGS = Royal Geographic Society
SA = Siena Artworks Ltd, London
SPL = Science Photo Library
TSA = Tom Stack & Associates
WWI = Woodfall Wild Images

3 BCL/John Shaw. **6** NHPA/N. Callow. **7** WWI/Peter Moore. **8** BCL/Jorg & Petra Wegner. **9** Wild Images Bristol/Martin Dohrn. **10** Ardea/Eric Dragesco, TL; Ardea/Joanna Van Gruises, BR. **11** OSF/Dr H. Baseman. **12** Wild Images/Andy Lane. **13** Tony Waltham, TL; HUT, TR. **14** NHPA/Eric Soder. **15** SA/Pavel Kostal. **16** SPL/Geospace, CR; SA/Leslie Smith, TC. **17** Colin Woodman/Toucan Books Ltd. **18** AUS/Tom Till, TL; SA/Leslie Smith, BR. **19** Bryan & Cherry Alexander, CL; SA/Leslie Smith, TR. **20** DRK/Larry Ulrich. **21** SA/Leslie Smith. **22-23** PEP/Adam Jones. **23** Ardea/Ferrero-Labat, TR; SA/Leslie Smith, BR. **24** AUS/Jean-Paul Ferrero, TL; BCL/Orion Press, BR; SA/Leslie Smith, TR. **25** Mountain Camera/John Cleare, TC; SA/Leslie Smith, TR. **26** SA/Leslie Smith. **27** PEP/Franz Camenzind, TR; PEP/Martin King, BR. **28** PEP/Alberto & Marco Majrani, TL; AUS/Colin Monteath, BR. **29** WWI/David Woodfall. **30** Ardea/Jean-Paul Ferrero, TR; SA/Leslie Smith, BL. **31** RGS/Chris Bradley, BR; SA/Lorraine Harrison, TR. **32** DRK/Tom Bean, TR; SA/Leslie Smith, BL. **33** WWI/N. Hicks, BR; SA/Lorraine Harrison, TL. **34** Telegraph Colour Library. **35** Tony Stone Images, T; SA/Lorraine Harrison, BL. **36** SPL. **37** BCL, BR; SA/Eugene Fleury. **38** AUS/S. Wilby & C. Ciantar, TL; NHPA/A.N.T, BR. **39** AUS/P. Leroux/Explorer, BR; Panos Pictures/Zed Nelson, CR. **40** OSF/Doug Allan. **41** Chris Bonington Picture Library/Alan Hinkes, TL; Mountain Camera/John Cleare, TR. **42** Wild Images/Michael McKinnon, TL; SPL/Geospace, TR. **43** Ardea/François Gohier, TL; TSA/Rod Planck, BR. **44** OSF/Breck Kent. **45** Hedgehog House/Grant Dixon. **46** PEP/Dave Lyons. **47** BCL/Geoff Doré, TC; Ardea/John Mason, BR. **48-49** DRK/Jeff Foott. **50** WWI/David Woodfall, BL; Hedgehog House/Grant Dixion, TR. **51** BCL/John Shaw. **52** OSF/Tom Leach. **53** WWI/David Woodfall, BL, BR; Colorific/Brian Harris, TR. **54** Ellis Nature Photography/Alan Kearney. **55** WWI/David Woodfall, BL; BCL/ Dr S. Schmidt, TR. **56** Ardea/Eric Dragesco. **57** Ardea/Jean-Paul Ferrero. **58** Ardea/Eric Dragesco. **59** PEP/Jonathan Scott. **60-61** DRK/Tom & Pat Leeson. **62** WWI/David Woodfall, TL; Ardea/Hans Dossenbach, BL. **63** Ardea/Eric Dragesco. **64** PEP/Frank Krahmer. **65** OSF/Tom Ulrich. **66** NHPA/Laurie Campbell. **67** TSA/Wendy Shattil/Bob Rozinski, TL; BCL/Keith Gunnar, BR. **68** BCL/Luiz Claudio Marigo. **69** NHPA/Kevin Schafer, TL; BCL/Luiz Claudio Marigo, TC; PEP, BR. **70** Ellis Nature Photography, BL; Ardea/Adrian Warren, BR. **71** Hedgehog House/Colin Monteath, TL; OSF/Richard Packwood, TR; NHPA/Nigel Dennis, BR. **72** NHPA/Manfred Danegger, BL; Ardea, TR. **73** Ellis Nature Photography/Terry Whitaker. **74** BCL/Uwe Walz, TL; Ardea/Eric Dragesco, BR. **75** Gerald Cubitt, TL; Chris Bonington Picture Library, BR. **76** Ellis Nature Photography. **77** BCL/Brian Coates, TL; PEP, BR. **78** Ellis Nature Photography. **79** PEP/John Downer, TC; HUT, BR. **80** Colorific/Bryan & Cherry Alexander, BL; Ellis Nature Photography, TR. **81** HUT, TR; Gerald Cubitt, BC. **82** Hedgehog House/Colin Monteath. **83** DRK Photo/Barbara Cushman Rowell, TL; RGS, CR; Hedgehog House/Colin Monteath, BR. **84** Hedgehog House/Colin Monteath. **85** Mountain Camera/John Cleare. **86** Ardea/Richard Waller, BL; Ardea/K. Fink, TC. **87** Hedgehog House/Bob McKerrow, TR; HUT/Sarah Murray, BL. **88** HUT, CL; Mountain Camera/Colin Monteath, BL. **89** Tony Waltham. **90** HUT/Sarah Murray, BL, BR. **91** HUT. **92** DRK Photo/Barbara Powell. **93** Magnum Photos/Marc Riboud. **94** Mountain Camera/John English, TL; Mountain Camera/Colin Monteath, BR. **95** DRK Photo/Barbara Cushman Rowell. **96** HUT/Jon Burbank. **97** HUT/E. Lawrie. **98** OSF/R.K. Paul, TC; Panos Pictures, BR. **99** Chris Bonington Picture Library. **100** BCL/Jules Cowan, BL; Panos Pictures, TR. **101** Mountain Camera/John Cleare. **102** NHPA/G. I. Bernard. **103** HUT/ H. Dörig, TL; HUT, BR. **104** BCL/Keith Gunnar. **105** HUT/Eric Lawrie, TR; South American Pictures/Tony Morrison, BL. **106** Wild Images/John Bulmer, TR; RGS/Eric Lawrie, BL. **107** RGS/Eric Lawrie, CL; South American Pictures/Tony Morrison, CR. **108** HUT/Eric Lawrie. **109** South American Pictures/Tony Morrison, TR; Wild Images/John Bulmer, BL. **110** South American Pictures/Tony Morrison. **111** South American Pictures/Tony Morrison. **112** Hedgehog House/Grant Dixon. **113** Hedgehog House/Ian Whitehouse, BL; Mountain Camera, John English, TR. **114-15** RGS/John R. Jones. **116** AUS/S. Wilby & C. Ciantar, TL; HUT, BR. **117** Mountain Camera/John Cleare. **118** AUS/Colin Monteath. **119** Hedgehog House. **120** Hedgehog House/Colin Monteath. **121** Robert Harding Picture Library/Nigel Blythe. **122** DRK/Barbara Rowell. **123** Tony Waltham. **124** TSA. **125** Hedgehog House/Hall & Ball Archive, CR; Mountain Camera/John Cleare, BR. **126** Wilderness Photographic Library/John Noble, TL; Chris Bonington Picture Library, TR. **127** DRK/Barbara Rowell. **128** RGS/Steve Razzetti, T; RGS/Chris Bradley, BC. **129** Chris Bonington Picture Library, TL; Colorific, BR. **130** Werner Forman Archive. **131** Robert Harding Picture Library. **133** Wilderness Photographic Library/John Noble. **134** Bridgeman Art Library/Private Collection. **135** RGS/Bruce Herrod, TL; DRK/Galen Rowell, R. **136-137** BCL/Jaroslav Poncar. **138** Mountain Camera/Bill O'Connor , TR; Werner Forman Archive/Philip Goldman Collection, London, BL. **139** RGS/Norma Joseph. **140** Ardea. **141** NHPA/Eric Soder, T; Corbis-Bettman, BR. **142-3** NHPA/Grant Dixon. **144** Mountain Camera/John Cleare. **145** Mary Evans Picture Library, C; Hedgehog House/Mike Darran, BR. **146** Mary Evans Picture Library. **147** Mountain Camera/John Cleare, TL; Mary Evans Picture Library, BR. **148** Mountain Camera. **149** RGS, BL, TR. **150** RGS, BL, TR. **151** RGS/Edmund Hillary, TL; Wilderness Photographic Library, B. **152** Wilderness Photographic Library/John Noble. **153** Robert Harding Picture Library, BC; Chris Bonington Picture Library/Leo Dickinson, TR. **154-5** Chris Bonington Picture Library.

Front Cover: Tony Stone Images/Keren Su; WWI/David Woodfall, C.

The editors are grateful to the following publishers for their permission to quote passages from the books below:
Hutchinson, *The Way of the White Cloud* by Lama Anagarika Govinda, 1966.
British Museum (Natural Hisory), *The Early History of Palaentology* by W.N. Edwards, 1976
Hart-Davis, *Seven Years in Tibet* by Heinrich Harrer, 1953 (Now published by Flamingo)